Like All the Nations?

Like All the Nations?

The Life and Legacy of Judah L. Magnes

Edited by
William M. Brinner
and
Moses Rischin

State University of New York Press

Cover photo: Magnes (Courtesy of the Central Archives for
the History of the Jewish People and the Jewish National and
University Library)

Published by
State University of New York Press, Albany

© 1987   State University of New York

For information, address State University of New York Press,
State University Plaza, Albany, N.Y., 12246

Library of Congress Cataloging in Publication Data

Like all the nations?

   Includes index.
   1. Magnes, Judah Leon, 1877–1948. 2. Universitah
ha- Ivrit bi-Yerushalayim — Presidents — Biography.
3. College presidents — Israel — Biography. 4. Rabbis —
United States — Biography. 5. Zionists — Biography.
6. Zionism — United States. 7. Jewish-Arab relations —
1917–1949. I. Brinner, William M. II. Rischin, Moses.
LG341.J45M365   1987   296.6'1 [B]   86-29992
ISBN 0-88706-507-4
ISBN 0-88706-508-2 (pbk.)

For
Seymour Fromer
and
Arthur A. Goren

Contents

Illustrations

Acknowledgments

Like All the Nations? *The Life and Legacy of Judah L. Magnes* is the product of an international symposium held at the University of California-Berkeley on October 12–14, 1982 to commemorate the twentieth anniversary of the Judah L. Magnes Memorial Museum. We are grateful to the National Endowment for the Humanities and the San Francisco Jewish Community Endowment Fund for their assistance; to the University of California for its cooperation; and to the Magnes Museum's staff and many friends for their dedicated support.

We are most indebted, of course, to the distinguished scholars whose papers, commissioned for the symposium by the editors, lend individual grace and distinction to this collective enterprise. In addition, we should like to express our appreciation to the University of California-Berkeley faculty — Paula Fass, Samuel Haber, James D. Hart, Daniel Koshland, Jr., Ralph Kramer, the late Philip Lilienthal, and Sheldon Rothblatt — who enlivened the occasion by their participation. Others who played important roles are: David Dalin, Abba Eban, Ron H. Feldman, Lynn Fonfa, Rabbi Gary Greenebaum, Jane Levy, Deborah Lipstadt, Rabbi Brian Lurie, Eleanor Mandelson, Anita Navon, Ruth K. Rafael, and the late Sidney Vincent. Ruth Aubrey painstakingly prepared the manuscript for publication; Yehudit Goldfarb compiled the index; and Miriam Aroner, photographic archivist of the Magnes Museum, aided by Hadassah Assouline, Margot Cohen, Hayim Goldgraber, Rosemary Krensky, Rabbi Morton Berman, and above all, by Hava Magnes, assembled the splendid illustrations that bring a photographic verisimilitude and immediacy to the text.

Finally, we reserve our deepest gratitude for Seymour Fromer, founder and, for the past twenty-five years, director of the Judah L. Magnes Museum and for Arthur A. Goren, foremost Magnes scholar and biographer, whose lives and works bear witness to the weight of the Magnes legacy and whose selfless efforts over the years have made this volume possible.

William M. Brinner
Berkeley

Moses Rischin
San Francisco

Contributors

ARNOLD BAND, Professor of Hebrew and Comparative Literature at the University of California, Los Angeles and a past president of the Association for Jewish Studies, is the author of *Nostalgia and Nightmare: A Study in the Fiction of S. Y. Agnon, The Tales of Nahman of Bratslav,* and a forthcoming monograph on Franz Kafka.

DAVID BIALE, Koret Associate Professor and Director of the Center for Judaic Studies at the Graduate Theological Union, Berkeley, California, is the author of *Gershom Scholem: Kabbalah and Counter-History* and *Power and Powerlessness in Jewish History.*

WILLIAM M. BRINNER is Professor of Near Eastern Studies at the University of California, Berkeley. Currently editor of *Middle East Review,* his research and publications deal with Arabic literature, Islamic History and religion, and Muslim-Jewish relations. His most recent publication is a translation from the Arabic of Volume 2 of the *History* of al-Tabari titled *Prophets and Patriarchs.*

JOAN DASH, a graduate of Barnard College and a resident of Seattle, Washington, is the author of *Summoned to Jerusalem: The Life of Henrietta Szold* and other works.

EVYATAR FRIESEL, Professor of Modern Jewish History at the Hebrew University of Jerusalem, is the author of *American Zionism 1897–1914, Zionist Policy after the Balfour Declaration,* and *Atlas of Modern Jewish History.*

SHELOMO DOV GOITEIN (1901–1985) was Director of the School of Oriental Studies at the Hebrew University of Jerusalem until 1956;

Professor of Arabic at the University of Pennsylvania, 1957–1970; and a member of the Institute for Advanced Study, Princeton, 1971–1985. His numerous publications range from studies on Yemenite Jews, and Jewish and Islamic religion and civilization, to the economic life of the medieval Middle East. The fifth volume of his monumental work, *A Mediterranean Society*, was published posthumously in 1986.

ARTHUR A. GOREN, a member of the Department of American Studies and the Institute of Contemporary Jewry at the Hebrew University of Jerusalem, is the editor of *Dissenter in Zion: From the Writings of Judah L. Magnes* and the author of *New York Jews and the Quest for Community* and other works.

PAUL MENDES-FLOHR, is a member of the Department of Religious Thought at the Hebrew University of Jerusalem. His works include *A Land of Two Peoples: Martin Buber on Jews and Arabs* and *Contemporary Jewish Religious Thought*, edited with Arthur A. Cohen.

DEBORAH DASH MOORE chairs the Department of Religion at Vassar College where she teaches Jewish Studies and American Culture. She is the author of *At Home in America: Second Generation New York Jews* and *B'nai B'rith and the Challenge of Ethnic Leadership*.

MARC LEE RAPHAEL is Professor of History and Director of the Melton Center for Jewish Studies at Ohio State University. He is the author of *Profiles in American Judaism* and other works, as well as a forthcoming biography of Abba Hillel Silver.

MOSES RISCHIN, Professor of History at San Francisco State University, Director of the Western Jewish History Center of the Judah L. Magnes Museum in Berkeley, and a past president of the Immigration History Society, is the author of *The Promised City: New York's Jews 1870–1914* and othe works. His latest book is *Grandma Never Lived in America: The New Journalism of Abraham Cahan*.

FRED ROSENBAUM, the Director of Lehrhaus Judaica, the school for adult Jewish education in Berkeley, San Francisco, and Stanford, is the author of *Free to Choose: The Making of a Jewish Community in the American West* and *Architects of Reform: Congregational and Community Leadership, Emanu-El of San Francisco, 1849–1880*.

GABRIEL STERN (1913–1983) was a distinguished Jerusalem journalist and for thirty-five years the political correspondent for *Al Hamishmar*. A leading member of Ihud, he dedicated his life to bringing Jews, Christians, and Moslems together for which he was honored, most notably with the Human Rights Award in 1981 of the Association for Civil Rights in Israel. His selected essays and sketches, *Al ha-mirpeset shel Musa ha-Gingi* (*At the Coffee House of The Red-Musa*) was published posthumously in 1986.

MARIE SYRKIN, Professor Emerita, Brandeis University, is the author of *Golda Meir, Golda Meir Speaks Out,* and *The State of the Jews*.

MELVIN I. UROFSKY, Professor of History at Virginia Commonwealth University in Richmond and a past chairman of the Academic Council of the American Jewish Historical Society, is the author of *American Zionism: From Herzl to the Holocaust, A Voice That Spoke for Justice: The Life and Times of Stephen S. Wise,* and other works.

BERNARD WASSERSTEIN, Professor of History at Brandeis University, is the author of *The British in Palestine* and *Britain and the Jews of Europe 1939–1945*.

Figure 1. Magnes in his study atop Mount Scopus, c. 1946. (*Courtesy of Hava Magnes*)

Introduction:
Like All the Nations?

MOSES RISCHIN

For the Jewish people, no high end will ever justify low means. We have been nurtured too long in the rabbinic tradition for that.

> Judah L. Magnes

In his last twenty years, the most enigmatic, original, and controversial figure in American Jewish life in the first half of the twentieth century spent his best energies confronting the Arab-Jewish dilemma. In April 1948, desperate to defuse a seemingly endless civil war between the Arab and Jewish Palestines proclaimed in the United Nations partition proposal, the ailing President of the Hebrew University flew from Jerusalem to New York on what proved to be his last peace mission. He failed, of course. Five months later, while preparing a design for a United States of Palestine, an Arab-Jewish confederation of two independent nations, one of California's, America's, and Israel's most distinguished sons died in near oblivion.

No one had labored more ardently and more selflessly in the cause of peace in the Middle East than had "the loneliest voice among the Jews."[1] Ignored by Arabs, barely recognized by the British mandatory power, and grimly tolerated by his beleagured fellow Jews, Judah Magnes had been sustained in his efforts by a small circle of dedicated idealists represented most notably by Martin Buber, the universally renowned Jewish philosopher and theologian.[2] In the wake of World War II and the Holocaust, when six million of their number were expendable, Jews, of all peoples, had no reason to be trusting. A Jewish state had become an unequivocal necessity. Even Magnes, for whom survival was never enough, after calling upon Chaim Weizmann on May 15, 1948, to congratulate the president-designate on the proclamation of the State of Israel, confided to one

1

of his sons who accompanied him, "Do you think that in my heart I am not glad too that there is a state? I just did not think that it was to be."[3] Neither did Weizmann, in quite the way it came about. A year earlier, Weizmann had insisted that it was not a matter of right and wrong, but a matter of the greater or lesser injustice — that "moral force" alone must prevail if Zion is to be "redeemed in justice." Better than anyone, the dying Magnes knew that "The Arab Question" would continue to be, as Arthur Goren has phrased it, "the touchstone of the moral integrity of Zionism."[4]

More than three decades later, in the summer of 1982 when "the moral integrity of Zionism" was put to the test, as it never quite had been before, Magnes would not have found it wanting. Israel's "sixth war," precipitated an unprecedented moral crisis and debate over Jewish values and ideology and divided the Jews of Israel and the Jews of the United States as they had never been divided during Israel's five earlier wars for survival. "The world expects more of Israel," announced Magnes's unknowing disciples in public forum and newspaper proclamation. "The very criticism of Israel demonstrates international faith in Israel's high moral standing,"[5] added his latter-day surrogates. In the midst of a war that went beyond the legitimation of "Peace for Galilee," tens of thousands of Israelis on the streets and plazas of Tel Aviv demonstrated their displeasure with their government. Their government listened and, in a spirit of civil courage, rare at any time in all but a few nations of the world, responded in no uncertain terms.

By coincidence, a few months earlier, Harvard University Press published a landmark collection of 140 brilliantly selected documents, primarily drawn from the vast Judah Magnes archive in Jerusalem, and masterfully edited and introduced by Arthur Goren of the Hebrew University. Reclaiming "a virtual nonperson to modern Zionist scholarship,"[6] *Dissenter in Zion: From the Writings of Judah L. Magnes* at last made public the private record of the mind and soul of a pioneer figure in the development of Jewish religious life and thought in the twentieth century, a record studded with the provocative and intimate reflections of one to whom the life of the spirit expressed in words was as sacred almost as life itself. Clearly Magnes's journal entries, notes, letters, and speeches testify to the transcendent power of an historic voice that speaks for our time, as it did for his, with undiminished vitality and urgency. ". . . [h]e had exceptional powers of analyzing his own mind and formulating his thoughts," wrote his good friend Norman Bentwich, "and a signal industry in recording his actions and his talks, his reading and his reflections on problems which he had to face. He had a belief in the written word: his right hand was never at rest, and he was everywhere, 'a chiel among ye takin' notes.'"[7]

The concatenation of these two events in 1982, the one military and political, the other cultural and intellectual, lent uncommon resonance and currency to the international symposium held in Berkeley, just a few miles from Magnes's birthplace in San Francisco and the scenes of his childhood and youth in Oakland.

At a time when events in the Middle East, notably in Lebanon, eclipsed all other aspects of the Magnes legacy, the major speaker at the Magnes symposium responded to the occasion with the pithy eloquence that had become his hallmark. Without demur, Abba Eban, who knew Magnes in his last years "as a remote and eminent figure" of "frigid temperament" whose views he did not share, paid tribute to Magnes's prescience, integrity, and dedication to bringing Arabs and Jews together in the spirit of Camp David and saluted him as "The Great Dissenter." His was

> . . . an intuitive understanding, perhaps above and beyond that which endowed anybody else in the establishment of those days, that the fundamental predicament of our people would lie in its relationship with the neighboring world and that without it the concept of harmony and reconciliation was not built into the very texture of our national life.

Israel's distinguished elder statesman continued:

> We would go on our way unthinking, perhaps oblivious to the dangers before us . . . [yet] sooner or later the problem of Arab-Jewish harmony would present itself as the second theme of our national adventure. He certainly pursued this task with obstinacy and tenacity, not caring very much about the obstacles which he had to overcome, arousing just as many antagonisms as he did feelings of admiration, but leaving behind a legacy of rectitude and, above all, the possibiity that those who would look back would understand him perhaps better than his contemporaries ever did. Because this ensued, the relationship of Israel with the neighboring world is the central moral and political predicament of our age.[8]

The life and legacy of Judah Magnes, the subject of this book, focuses the best historical scholarship and intelligence upon an American Jew, who more effectively than all but a few of his contemporaries, exemplified a profound and unwavering commitment to the moral life — as an American, as a Jew, and as a man. If one accepts Isaiah Berlin's characterization of Chaim Weizmann as "the first totally free Jew of the modern world," then Judah Magnes certainly was the first "totally free" American Jew. On his seventieth birthday in 1947, the illustrious Jewish historian Gershom Scholem called him simply, "*adam-hofshi* — A Free Man."[9]

Like All the Nations? is organized chronologically around a series of themes central to Magnes's life and world. Implicit in the book is the assumption that Magnes was one of the founding fathers of American Jewish life in the twentieth century, and a distinguished American and world figure, and that it is imperative that his life in all its historical ramifications be understood and made known. Before the publication of Goren's authoritative collection of documents, only the memoir by his close friend, Norman Bentwich, published three decades earlier, had even hinted at the richness, breadth, and importance of Magnes's life.[10] Goren's seminal work, of course, has confirmed all expectations, leaving no doubt that Magnes was a pivotal figure in the twentieth century, whose life and thought has only begun to gain the exposure and the scrutiny that it merits. *Like All the Nations?* is an initial effort to open the way to a greater understanding of what it has meant to be an "*adam-hofshi*."

The five parts of this book focus respectively on Magnes's youth and education, his New York years, his place among the leaders of American Zionism, his role as first chancellor and president of the Hebrew University, and his efforts to bring Arabs and Jews together. These themes in no way comprehend the vast range of Magnes's activities. They appear, however, to be the central themes.

Magnes's California birth and upbringing long have been assumed to be critical to the making of a new American Jewish identity, one so distinctive in its aspect and outlook as to decisively distinguish him from all of his associates. Born in 1877 in San Francisco, the nation's ninth ranking city, and raised across the Bay in Oakland, then California's booming new second city, young Magnes was the son of a new world-centered Western America, barely a generation old. Looking westward to Asia and the Pacific, and eastward to an older America, Europe, and the Atlantic, these Bay-area cities were intended, if they so willed, to link, not to isolate, the American subcontinental republic to the continents overseas with their ancient pasts and peoples, and to condition a young man's sense of himself in ways that are barely beginning to be explored.

At the American rim of the Pacific, at the western edge of the last frontier, and in the midst of a rising new cosmopolis, the boy was destined to meet the earth's diverse peoples, the old and the new, as they were to be encountered nowhere else — as individuals, face-to-face. On the street and at school, on playing field, ferry boat, and cable car, the young lad, avid for life, rubbed shoulders with all of humankind, almost as inevitably as he did at home with members of his own family. What is at least equally noteworthy is that the Oakland youngster also responded with special ardor and discernment to the richly diversified and supportive Jewish family, religious, and communal culture of his German-Russian-Polish parents. By the age of seventeen, when the promising youth departed California, he was well on his way to integrating the discrete elements of his rich and varied public and private worlds. Already he revealed the traits of behavior and habits of mind of a special kind of nonconformist that were to be emblematic of "The Great Dissenter," destined to live intensely and alone amidst the great crowds, a long way from his native state. Fred Rosenbaum insightfully demonstrates how thoroughly and profoundly Magnes's California years helped shape a youth whose Americanness and Jewishness were manifestly supportive of one another to a degree not quite equalled elsewhere in the United States.

At the Hebrew Union College and the University of Cincinnati, young Magnes took full advantage of the opportunities for self-development, both inside and outside the classroom. As Marc Raphael carefully demonstrates, the young Californian rebelled against the stale and stodgy late nineteenth century university and seminary, and left with no doubt that he was a free-born American and one with whom to be reckoned. Whether voicing his passion for student rights, academic freedom, or civil liberties, expressing his hatred of war, writing on Palestine and Judaism, or immersing himself in the East European immigrant Jewish ethos nearby, the fledgling American rabbi was laying the foundations for a strenuously original and eventful life. At its core, already, lay a nascent Zionism that was to vitalize his conception of a new American Judaism, that he was to champion during his brief tenure as an instructor at the Hebrew Union College, and that he was to implement two decades later in the association he establshed between the Hebrew University and the Hebrew Union College.

A critical interlude in Magnes's education and growth came in his graduate years in Germany. "Those days of a great Jewish awakening,"[11] as he called them, exposed him to the most vital Jewish intellectual currents in the modern world. As Evyatar Friesel and Arthur Goren make clear, Magnes had come to Berlin at a critical formative time when it was becoming the hub of the new Zionist movement and the crossroads of a new Judaism of the twentieth century. For Magnes,

Berlin became the West European intellectual and ideological halfway house between the East European Jewish heartland and the emergent American Jewish metropolitan frontier, a relationship whose outlines have been sketched by historians but whose full import needs to be established at many different levels, something that neither Goren nor Friesel pretend to do. There, apparently, he was inspired, for the first time, to declare his Zionist *Lebensprogramm*, and as Goren demonstrates, the Zionist credo was indeed to become his lodestar. Upon Magnes's return to America, he was not only Judaized inwardly, but possessed a German Ph.D., the first Hebrew Union College graduate to be so distinguished, and bore a new name to boot: the former Julian Leon or J. Leon, or, mostly simply Leon, had become Judah Leib, with all the twice-born ancestral connotations that the change of name elicited.

The logical next step, after a teaching stint in Cincinnati, for a young rabbi of Magnes's passionate temperament, independence, spirit, and ambition, was, of course, New York, where he was to appear at a critical juncture in American Jewish life. In the course of his brief lifetime, New York had been transformed and had emerged to become the most vibrant Jewish center in history, as the great Jewish migration from Eastern Europe, accelerated by the Kishinev pogrom and succeeding massacres, imploded the city's Jewish population, which grew from 80,000 in 1880 to ten times that number a quarter of a century later — with no limits in sight.

To the inspired young rabbi and to other perfervid Jewish intellectuals, New York's tumultuous Lower East Side and its extensions were to prove as magnetic as they were to the thronging immigrant multitudes. Free to speak, assemble, exhort, and write as it had not been possible for them to do in Tsarist Russia, the volatile newcomers manifested themselves with a vitality, immediacy, and power never experienced before. In an era when all Jewish values were being challenged, immigrant audiences, their numbers continually augmented from abroad, and prospective guides to the perplexed were to meet and respond one to another with near messianic fervor.

Part II focuses on Magnes's years in the great metropolis, at the new center of gravity of American Jewish life where anything and everything seemed possible. Deborah Dash Moore not only deftly analyzes the implications of these changes for Jewish organizational life, but authoritatively demonstrates how creative and vital was the sense of new Jewish beginnings in the consciousness of a generation of sophisticated young American-born and immigrant Jewish intellectuals gathered about Solomon Schechter and the freshly reconstituted

Jewish Theological Seminary. A remarkable group, they were in fact the first and most gifted circle of Jewish intellectuals ever to be concerned seriously with Jewish tradition and its place in the American scheme of things. In many respects, Solomon Schechter, Israel Friedlaender, Henrietta Szold, Mordecai Kaplan, and Magnes comprised the Jewish counterpart to the totally secular progressive intellectuals of their day who played so incisive a role in reappraising American values and institutions. Until World War I cut short their plans and grounded their dreams, they attempted to design and to pilot a new American Judaism into being that would be responsive to Jewish diversity, to Jewish peoplehood, and to a renaissant Jewish civilization that seemed destined to emerge out of the religious, social, and cultural turmoil of the era.

In these watershed years, young Magnes came to occupy an exalted place. He was the only American Zionist of national standing, the rabbi of the nation's cathedral synagogue, Temple Emanu-El, and the founder of the *Kehillah*, the New York Jewish experiment in community organization, and so was singularly positioned and prepared to define and enunciate a new American Judaism based on a fresh conception of American and of Jewish life. Magnes' cultural Zionism, inspired by Ahad Ha-Am, emphasized the mutual interdependence of Jewish culture in the diaspora and in a resurrected old Zion; his multiethnic America celebrated a pluralistic United States where diverse ancestral folkways reinforced every American's instinctive love of his country; and his Judaism, quickened by Zionism and his Zionism in turn deepened by Judaism, anchored his vision in the ancient faith. So tenacious was Magnes's formulation, contends Friesel, that it would remain unchanged for the remainder of his life.

In the exhilarating New York of these years, young Magnes, intoxicated by the plethora of possibilities and eager to implement them, stood forth as the most dynamic Jewish leader on the American scene. Attempting to interject himself at every level of Jewish life, he espoused causes, launched institutions, and spearheaded organizations that came to be viewed as "Magnes's follies" by puzzled and often exasperated contemporaries. Yet, as Goren demonstrates, through it all, Magnes's public Jewish philosophy never lost its clear purpose, direction, and coherence. His commitment to the mission of the classic American reform rabbi as the "bearer and interpreter of prophetic Judaism," with its universal message, propelled him to join the imperatives of American Protestantism's social gospel to Ahad Ha-Am's cautiously prophetic Judaism. Fortified with a Jewish social gospel for the dual role of prophet-priest, the radical conservative builder of a new American Judaism pursued the mission of a new Zion in New York. In its effort to find common ground between uptown and downtown, capital and labor, reform and tradition, Magnes's *Kehillah* came to be regarded by many as the prototype for Jewish community organization in America. If the role of the *Kehillah* as a model for subsequent communal developments has been seriously questioned, the thrust that it gave to a reordering of the parameters of Jewish life in America appears undeniable.[12] Undoubtedly, Mordecai Kaplan's Reconstructionist ethos, which has infused itself at virtually every level of American Jewish institutional life, is in great part indistinguishable from Magnes's germinal conception of what Kaplan later called "Judaism as a Civilization." If in no way aspiring to Kaplan's philosophical rigor, architectonic scale, or naturalistic theology, Magnes, in his clarion call for reconstruction in 1910, by encouraging his younger associate, surely opened the way to the most authentically American Jewish religious movement to emerge in the twentieth century, a theme that has yet to be explored with the imagination and tenacity that it merits.[13]

Historians differ in their judgments about the critical importance which they attribute to successive phases in Magnes's life and their relationship to his subsequent development. His California youth, his sojourn in Cincinnati, his Berlin awakening, and the climactic New York epoch all make claim to a special place in the shaping of the fully realized life. Clearly each of these phases calls for more intense and wide-ranging explorations than even the symposium's incisive papers generated and the literature thus far has allowed. The last decades of the nineteenth century and the first two decades of the twentieth century were the founding years of modern America and of modern Jewish life. In this era, key institutions, ideas, and social and cultural patterns, later taken for granted and regarded as commonplace, began to acquire definition and to assert their claims. The singular fascination that Magnes's life has for students of history, of course, is that it personifies, as does the life of no other American and perhaps no other Jew, the full range and depth of the modern Jewish experience extending into our time and into the foreseeable future. Deeply felt, generously and intensively experienced, and copiously and sensitively recorded, as Goren's work has made evident, Magnes's life bears witness to his unquenchable passion for questioning the status quo.

In Part III, Magnes is juxtaposed with the three outstanding American Zionists of his era and slightly beyond — Stephen Wise, Henrietta Szold, and Golda Meir. If Louis Brandeis was American Zionism's most eminent public figure and Horace Kallen its long unacknowledged ranking social philosopher, in the early years of the twentieth century Stephen Wise and Magnes certainly were its most charismatic leaders. Born three years apart, both young rabbis rebelled against rigid nineteenth century institutions and congregational restraints. In their special ways, first Magnes and then Wise, as Goren has pointed out, attempted to transform the world's greatest and most turbulent Jewish metropolis into a forum and sounding board for an American Zionism attuned to the complex new world of the twentieth century. Their prideful Americanism and Judaism amplified by their superb oratorical gifts singularly equipped them to give voice to an intrinsically American ideal. As Melvin Urofsky makes abundantly clear, Wise was destined to lead the American Zionist movement between the two World Wars, because the nation's most well-known rabbi best mirrored the hopes and fears of America's Jews. In the longer view, however, Magnes's impact would appear to be far more profound and enduring. The centrality and vitality of his Zionist vision in our own time is only beginning to be recognized. "No one made a greater impression" on her, recalls Barbara Tuchman, who knew and admired both Magnes and Wise in her childhood, than did the California-born rabbi. "Magnes was different; there was a quality about him I cannot describe without sounding sentimental; something beautiful in his face, something that inspired a desire to follow, even to love . . . ." What Tuchman was driving at was not Magnes's pleasing appearance and aspect but his transparent integrity and wholeness of mind and soul which greeted all who beheld him. Magnes's commitment to cultural and spiritual Zionism with all that it implied for the energizing of a high Jewish and American civilization was inseparable from his ardor to build a Zion based on Jewish ethics that would be both a light unto the Jews and to the nations. Furthermore, Magnes's obsession with "the Zionist dilemma especially," Urofsky has reminded us, made him rather than Wise "the realist of the highest order," for "he identified the problem" of Arab rights as critical, writes the historian of American Zionism, and "refused to ignore its existence . . . . His role was prophetic in the ancient tradition, in that he spoke truth to power. The Zionist ideal . . . will not be achieved until the issues Magnes raised can be resolved."[14]

One of only two prominent American Zionists to settle in Palestine after World War I, Magnes was preceded by two years by Henrietta Szold, founder in 1912 of Hadassah, the women's Zionist organization, which was to become the largest women's organization in the world. Intimately associated with Magnes in the Schechter circle since their early days in New York, they were to be coworkers, friends, and allies to the last. In sketching their relationship, Joan Dash, Henrietta Szold's biographer, sees them as American Jewish missionaries in Zion, not at all *olim* (immigrants to Palestine/Israel) in the conventional sense, but outsiders to the Yishuv in their every aspect. Whether Dash's mordant profile of the two American Zionists is quite on the mark surely will be spiritedly debated. Clearly, other American Jews dedicated to Jewish self-renewal and the establishment of a Jewish homeland in Palestine might be seen in a similar light and indeed were, as Marie Syrkin makes evident. Like Israel, Palestine was a country of diverse immigrants. The rule-of-thumb consensus that has led scholars to classify *olim* as Americans based on a five-year residence in the United States has not made it easy to acquire a precise notion of the number of Americans who settled in Palestine or of the nature of their composition, motivation, or commitment. During the British Mandate period (1919–1948) of the perhaps 7,000 who did so, however, it is unlikely that more than 1500 were of American birth. Yet it is difficult, in the absence of careful research to judge what effect American birth, citizenship, or length of residence, not to speak of so many other variables, had on the reception of Americans who made *aliyah*. Even for the two contingents of Americans who came to Palestine on the eve of the British Mandate during World War I, we know only a few bare facts. Of the forty-four doctors and nurses who landed in Jaffa in the summer of 1918, calling themselves the American Zionist Medical Unit, twenty-six remained to become members of the Histadrut Sick Fund and the nucleus for the later Medical Faculty of the Hebrew University and the Hadassah network of hospitals and clinics. We also know that of the 1,720 Americans in Vladimir Jabotinsky's Jewish Legion who fought with the British, 530 remained in Palestine. But what became of them, what roles they played, and how they fitted in with the other pioneers, we have no clear notions.[15] We are not likely to know much more until a detailed and comprehensive study of the lives of Americans who made *aliyah* before World War II is undertaken.

Golda Meir, the most renowned American to be associated with both the State of Israel and Palestine during the British Mandate, unlike Wise and Szold, is not easy to compare with Magnes. If Henrietta Szold shared Magnes's worlds and commitments in large part, Israel's first woman prime minister shared little with either. Yet perhaps the contrast with Magnes is all the more edifying. At age twenty-three, after fifteen years of absorbing all that America had to give to a Russian immigrant committed to Socialist Zionism, Golda

Meir made *aliyah*, reaching Palestine a year after Szold and a year before Magnes. A classic Zionist, a generation younger than Magnes, a secularist, and a transmigrant born in Tsarist Russia, she may never even have encountered the chancellor of the Hebrew University, Marie Syrkin conjectures. On the central issue of Arab-Jewish relations to which Syrkin gives major attention, Meir differed radically with Magnes. Like her mentors, David Ben-Gurion and earlier, Berl Katznelson, Golda Meir recognized Arab rights in Palestine as Syrkin emphasizes, but would not in any way sacrifice Jewish rights, compromise Jewish independence, or put off the free immigration of the survivors of the Holocaust for the sake of what appeared to be a utopian solution.

Without doubt, Magnes's most singular and lasting achievement was "his . . . contribution . . . to the creation of the first Jewish university, the Hebrew University of Jerusalem," as David Biale makes apparent in his study of Magnes's spirited role in defining the idea of a modern Jewish university, first proposed by Rousseau in the eighteenth century. "The Jews in dispersion have not the possibility of proclaiming their truth to mankind," wrote the author of *Émile*. "We shall learn what the people have to say to us when they have a free commonwealth, with schools and universities of their own where they can speak out safely."[16] As Biale demonstrates in the opening essay in Part IV, Magnes's monument, the Hebrew University, was to be Palestine's first and only universal Jewish nonpolitical institution, the academy for the discovery of truth, the pulpit for its dissemination, and the single most important agency for developing a Jewishly harmonious life in which Jewish and humanistic traditions would be blended. There, all the ideals and causes that Magnes had espoused earlier were to find expression, a world Hebrew renaissance was to be fuelled, and despite its name, Arabs especially, were to be welcomed.

We have, as yet, no history of the university and no concerted inquiry into Magnes's role. No one has thus far detailed the battles with Chaim Weizmann, Albert Einstein, and countless others that might inform our understanding, illuminate Magnes's ways, and shed light on the divergent cultural, philosophical, and political gusts that swirled around Mount Scopus.[17] We have, however, in Paul Mendes-Flohr's superb study, an intellectual portrait of a circle of brilliant Central Europeans at the Hebrew University who found in Magnes a friend, a colleague, and a leader, one who shared their commitment to radical politics and to Biblical humanism that would prod the way to a dynamic living Judaism. Their intimate association with Magnes led to the establishment of a series of religiously inspired societies pledged to social and political action in the prophetic tradition, culminating in *Mevakshei Panecha* (Those Seeking Thy Face), *Ha-Ol* (The Yoke — of the Coming Kingdom of God), the League for Jewish-Arab Rapprochement and Cooperation, and, finally, in Ihud (Unity), which called for an Arab-Jewish self-governing binational state in a united Palestine. Although recognizing that Magnes was "neither a theologian nor a philosopher," an acutely discerning member of that circle, Shmuel Hugo Bergman, has regarded Magnes as one who "sought God in history"[18] and as one of the six most important modern Jewish religious thinkers. Among them, Flohr reminds us, he was the only American.

By contrast, Arnold Band stresses not only the great gap between Magnes and the yishuv, but "the ideological and temperamental chasm" between Magnes and most of his associates at the Hebrew University. An historian of Hebrew literature, Band assesses the Magnes image in the works of two great Hebrew writers, S. Y. Agnon, the Israeli Nobel laureate, and Uri Z. Greenberg, the twentieth century poet. Band also portrays Magnes through the ideological lenses of Berl Katznelson, cultural oracle of Palestine's labor movement and headmaster of labor's affiliated folk schools and its many other institutions, what Band refers to as Palestine's "alternative post-secondary institution of culture" to the Hebrew University.

The closing essays in Part V are devoted to the efforts that Magnes made, from his initial association with the Hebrew University, to place Arab-Jewish relations — "the touchstone of the moral integrity of Zionism" — at the center of the Zionist agenda. It was our hope to enlist as many of Magnes's key surviving collaborators as possible to analyze this critically important phase of his career. Eliahu Elath, Ernst Simon, and the world-renowned Gershom Scholem, regrettably, were not able to make the great journey. Writing from Berlin, where he was spending what proved to be the final months of his life, Scholem frankly alluded to the exacting demands made upon him.

> The session for which you ask my specific contribution would be, by necessity, the most controversial one and I would have to prepare myself for a long time, which I cannot do this year . . . . The problems arising from Dr. Magnes's activities in this field are so intricate and even delicate that I have some doubts whether they could be discussed seriously before an audience such as you describe in your letter. I have therefore to forego the pleasure [of coming] to Berkeley. . . . Thank you for the honor you do me by this invitation.[19]

Fortunately, however, we were at least able to secure the participation of two of Magnes's close associates, Shelomo Dov Goitein and

Gabriel Stern, to illuminate Magnes's role from two entirely different perspectives. For the first time Goitein's authoritative memoir details Magnes's dedication to developing a great center for Jewish-Arabic and Islamic studies that was to be the keystone of his commitment to building Arab-Jewish cooperation. In delineating the growth of the center, Goitein is especially effective in conveying the tone and spirit of those early formative years when relations between Arabs and Jews, shaped by the recent liberation of the Arabs from the Ottoman Empire, the prevailing liberal Arab ethos, and the Arab admiration for all things Western, sustained Magnes in his commitment to pacifism and to the redemption of the Holy Land in justice.[20]

In Stern's complementary memoir, the editor of Ihud's journal recalls his close association with Magnes during the last decade of his life when their relentless efforts to promote Arab-Jewish cooperation continually teetered on the edge of disaster. Evocatively, Stern depicts the sacred sites of Jerusalem, the eternal and tension-ridden "city of peace," the surrounding country as seen from Magnes's office atop Mount Scopus during his lifetime and as it appeared three decades and more after his death. Stern proves especially effective in portraying the pains that Magnes took in his final efforts to avert disaster, which were mirrored so vividly in the tragic Kfar Etzion episode that in his last year taxed his waning strength to the limit.

Finally, in a hard-headed critique, Bernard Wasserstein points to the ironies and contradictions that dogged Magnes in his elusive quest for Arab-Jewish cooperation. Palestine's Arab statesmen, unable even to comprehend the Western world's premises of discourse, let alone make them intelligible and acceptable to fellow Arabs, threatened by the very idea of a Jewish presence, and lacerated by what Magnes called "the inner Arab terror,"[21] were hardly prepared for Magnes's binational "Holy Land of two equal peoples." Although Wasserstein regards Magnes's thinking and behavior as bordering on the disingenuous, he nevertheless credits him with being the critical figure in establishing "the tradition of vigorous intellectual dissent which is such a crucial ingredient of Israel's political culture." Magnes's concern for the "soul of Judaism," however, leaves no doubt that his perceptions of reality were religious and ought not to be judged by political criteria.

This first collection of essays to critically examine the life and legacy of Judah Magnes is intended to provoke interest in an American Jew who more passionately and more ambitiously than any of his contemporaries personified a modern American Jewish consciousness and identity, rooted above all in a religiously motivated political concern with the vital issues that agitate our world. In striving to incorporate into his own being the diverse strands of emergent twentieth century American, Jewish, Arabic, and other civilizations, Magnes fervently welcomed, courted, and wrestled with the complex fate that in our time confronts all Americans, not Jews alone. Reversing the westward trek of nineteenth century pioneers, the young Californian went east to Cincinnati, Heidelberg, Berlin, New York, the towns and villages of Austrian, German, and Russian Poland, and finally to Jerusalem to assimilate, to reclaim, and to refashion an old heritage and to transform it into a vital twentieth century prophetic force. In retrospect, it seems, Magnes was destined to be the harbinger for what we might become.

Throughout this volume, the themes explored at length and those touched upon only incidentally, reveal Magnes's extraordinary range of involvement. Even contributors least sympathetic to him recognize the extent of his achievement. To the perplexity of his contemporaries, the "radical" and "conservative" in Magnes struggled continually to reconcile the often polar components of our humanity, the old and the new, the scientific, the political, and the religious; the national, the plural, and the universal; America, Israel, the larger diaspora, and the world. He called for individuality and national self-determination, aspired to a coherent Jewish civic presence, and was unreservedly committed to a renaissance of Jewish learning and of the Jewish spirit in an unself-consciously Jewish milieu. He was portentously eager for a new Judaism and unwavering in his efforts to find a middle way in the Middle East. His lifelong quest for integrity mark this native Californian of extraordinary intellectual vitality as one of the unacknowledged great statesmen without portfolio in the first half of the twentieth century, a pivotal and oracular historic figure, surprisingly neglected.

From his youth, he had envisaged the American dream in ecumenically Jewish and American terms. Growing up in the world's most diversely peopled instant international metropolis, he was familiar with both the brutish animality and the perdurable humanity that neighboring Oakland youngsters, Jack London and Gertrude Stein, were to explore and to dramatize in their strikingly contrasting works of the imagination. With uncommon sensitivity, Magnes too, throughout his life, responded creatively to the world about him but his were "religious eyes."[22] Surely, George Santayana might have written of Magnes what he wrote of Josiah Royce, his longtime Harvard colleague. "Although he was born in California, he had never got used to the sunshine; he had never tasted peace."[23]

Like Royce, Magnes's deeply religious nature thirsted for a thicker and fuller civilization than the California of their day could slake. Royce's wise provincialism, his religion of loyalty, his loyalty to the principle of loyalty, and his faith in the Great Community, have their analogues in Magnes's ideals. Like Harvard's Christian philosopher, who recalled just before his death in the midst of World War I, that from earliest childhood, without quite knowing it, "my deepest motives and problems have centered about the Idea of Community,"[24] Magnes, too, yearned for a Great Community that would bond Jews and all mankind as they must be. As this collection of essays demonstrates, Magnes's life and legacy were inseparable from that quest.

I
Youth and Education

Figure 2. The Oakland High School baseball team, 1892. Magnes is in the last row at the right. (*Courtesy of Hava Magnes*)

1

San Francisco-Oakland: The Native Son

FRED ROSENBAUM

Born in San Francisco in 1877, and raised in Oakland until, at age seventeen, he left for college and rabbinical school, Judah Magnes was a native son of the American West. His life's work was a constant struggle on behalf of Jewish humanism fought with a fiercely independent spirit and a courageous personal style which runs like a thread through a tumultous career on two continents and more than half a century. As a seminarian, he led a student strike for freedom of the press; as a young Reform rabbi, he publicly exposed the failings of his own movement; as a community leader, he took on foes who ranged from the New York City Police Commissioner to the Yiddish press; and as Chancellor of the Hebrew University, he did battle with the likes of Chaim Weizmann and Albert Einstein. He embraced Zionism when it was considered unpopular, pacifism when it was viewed as treason, binationalism when it was thought to be a betrayal.[1] Through it all, those who were closest to him attributed this intellectual honesty and fearlessness to his California upbringing. As his biographer and longtime friend and colleague, Norman Bentwich, wrote, Magnes was possessed by "an audacious freedom from the fabulous West."[2]

For the Bay Area in which he lived until 1894 was a notably free and creative environment, supportive of philosophy and the arts as well as commerce and industry. In Northern California, in the generation after the chaos of the Gold Rush, the excitement was still almost uncontrollable. Amidst incomparable physical beauty, vast stretches

of the world's most fertile farmland, as well as a strategic location link-
ing rail and water, Occident and Orient, anything seemed possible. In
the 1880s, the Golden State was poised to make its century-long bid
for domination of the continent. Here, more than anywhere else,
would individualism and innovation be needed and rewarded.

Particularly dynamic was Oakland, the state's second largest city
by 1880, which only two decades earlier had ranked a mere thirty-
eighth. Boasting the western terminus of the first trans-continental
railroad, a fine harbor, a mild climate, and proximity to the new
University of California, Oakland, known then as the "Athens of the
West," felt especially expectant about its future.[3]

This was the Oakland where Jack London spent his youth.
Eighteen months older than Magnes, London was several years
behind him at Oakland High School because he had taken time off to
sail to Japan, march with Coxey's army of unemployed, and ride the
freight trains of Western Canada with a group of hobos.[4] A friend of
Magnes's younger brother Isaac, with whom he explored the colorful
but unsavory life on the East Bay's waterfront, young London
epitomized the sense of adventure which permeated Oakland before
the turn of the century.[5]

Another childhood contemporary who also attained worldwide
fame as a writer lived in East Oakland from her sixth to her eighteenth
year. The child of Bavarian Jewish immigrants, Gertrude Stein was as
bold a nonconformist as any cultural figure of the twentieth century.
Leaving the Bay Area in 1892, she eventually settled in Paris where for
more than four decades she played a significant role in almost every
major literary and artistic avant-garde movement of her time. In
Oakland in the 1880s, like Magnes, she attended the Sabbath school
of the First Hebrew Congregation (today's Temple Sinai) and spent her
leisure hours hiking in the rugged East Bay hills.[6]

Magnes and Stein grew up in an atmosphere almost completely
free of anti-Semitism. Neither one was the sort of Jew who asks the
age-old question, "What will the Goyim think?" Here, unlike in the
older regions of the United States, much less Europe, Jews could not
be viewed as intruders for they had arrived at the same time as other
gold-seekers, as early as 1849, and, as Earl Raab has written, "they
were welded together into a 'frontier brotherhood' community. As the
first families became encrusted, they became encrusted necessarily in
amalgam with the 'first families' of the Jewish community."[7] Other
groups were not so fortunate, however. The American Indians were
virtually exterminated; the Mexicans and Chileans often were driven
from their mining claims; the blacks occasionally were even kept as

slaves. But it was the Chinese who were the most common scapegoat in California, and their plight recalls the ordeal of the Jews in Russia. Persecuted because they clung to a distinct, ancient culture, they banded together for self-protection and were then accused of being "clannish."

Jews were favored because the state's historical experience differed profoundly from that of Europe's. California, obviously, was not scarred by a thousand years of oppression institutionalized by the Catholic Church. Furthermore, the antipathy toward Jewish "influence," so characteristic of Europe with its medieval glorification of peasant and craftsman, was rare in the American West where Jews were generally admired precisely because of their efforts at modernization. A new product like Levi Strauss's jeans, for example, met with admiration rather than resentment; Jewish department store owners, often accused in Central Europe of undermining small shopkeepers, were lauded in California for their contribution to the economy.[8]

While the Jewish community in Oakland numbered less than one thousand in 1885, or about two percent of the population, it enjoyed the tolerance and even the esteem of non-Jews. It also felt free and secure in another important respect. It was far enough removed from the established centers of Judaism in New York and elsewhere in the East, let alone Europe, for radical forms of Jewish expression to evolve without the censure one might expect in an older, larger, and more centrally situated city. Another young Oakland maverick offers an example of bold experimentation within the Jewish religion itself. Rachel Frank, later Ray Frank Litman, who taught Bible and Jewish history in the Sabbath school of the First Hebrew Congregation during the very years it was attended by Magnes and Stein, frequently left Oakland in the 1890s to conduct services and preach in synagogues up and down the coast. Although never ordained, she was known as "the first woman rabbi," and was even asked to mediate the religious disputes of several fledgling Western congregations. A generation before women gained the right to vote, she entered a calling that for millennia had been exclusively male.[9]

Magnes, then, along with London, Stein, and Litman, departed Oakland with a sense of daring, even defiance, which would characterize them in later years. But Magnes's youth also molded him in other important ways, profoundly affecting the content of his ideas as well as the personal style with which he put them forth.

The influence of his parents was crucial. His father, David Magnes, immigrated to San Francisco at age fifteen in 1863, brought by his much older brother, Abraham, who had arrived a decade earlier. They had come from the small Polish town of Przedborg, near Lodz, where their father, Judah Leibush Magnes, was a learned Hasidic community leader. In California David Magnes, who operated a small corset shop, never assimilated to the extent of the majority of his coreligionists, German-speaking Jews, who gravitated toward a Classical Reform position. Although he joined liberal synagogues, and even became an avid baseball fan, he kept a kosher home, sang Hasidic melodies to his five children, and made Judaism the cornerstone of his life.[10]

In 1873 he married Sophie Abrahamson, a native of the town of Filehne in the Prussian province of Posen. If their first-born, Julian Leon, who later adopted his grandfather's name, Judah, would feel strong ties to the *shtetl* through David's side of the family, he would also be connected to German Jewry through his mother. To be sure, the influence of Eastern Europe's Jews was strong even in Posen which had been part of Poland as late as 1772, and again for several years during the Napoleonic period. Sophie's devout father, Jacob, for example, was one of the founders of a small orthodox congregation in Oakland comprised primarily of Polish Jews. But Sophie felt herself a product of German culture, singing German operas at home, and often speaking in that language to her husband and children.[11] She died in 1904 at age fifty-two, and was in very poor health throughout Judah's childhood, especially during the mid-1880s. Yet Sophie, whose three brothers ran a well-known department store in Oakland, was the stronger personality of the two parents, and a major factor in the decision of her first-born to take his doctorate in Germany and later to become a congregational rabbi in New York. But probably the main legacy of his family to Magnes's later philosophy of Judaism was the harmonious blending of German and East European elements. At a time in American Jewish history of great tension between middle- and upper-class German Jews, and poor, Yiddish-speaking immigrants, Judah Magnes, even as a child, learned to appreciate both sides. Early on he thought in terms of the Jewish people as a whole, of *klal Yisrael*.

This was also the notion imparted to the young Magnes by Oakland's first rabbi, the energetic Englishman Myer Solomon Levy. Arriving in the East Bay in 1881 — where the Magnes family had moved a year earlier when Judah was three — Rabbi Levy soon became known for his all-encompassing vision of the Jewish people. Ordained before age twenty, he had served in Melbourne, Australia for two years before coming to the West Coast in 1873 to assume the pulpit of San Jose's Bikkur Cholim, now Temple Emanu-El. A highly observant Jew and, after the turn of the century, a Zionist, Levy faced many disputes over ritual and liturgy during his decade of service in Oakland. To some extent, he accommodated the strident liberal wing of the First Hebrew Congregation by shortening the Sabbath services and facing the worshippers, and not the ark, in prayer. At the same time, he was able to resist their demands for more fundamental reforms such as the adoption of Isaac Mayer Wise's prayerbook, *Minhag America*.[12] By 1891, however, the hard-fought compromise between traditional rabbi and liberal laymen finally came to an end. Levy accepted the pulpit of Beth Israel in San Francisco, where he served essentially as a Conservative rabbi until his death in 1916. At the First Hebrew he was succeeded by Marcus Friedlander, a rabbi who initiated sweeping changes during his long tenure, bringing the congregation by World War I to a Classical Reform posture.[13]

Levy's ten years in Oakland, coinciding with Magnes's boyhood, was marked by less ideological concerns as well. In 1885, the synagogue of the First Hebrew burned down and yeoman efforts at fundraising on the rabbi's part — which took him as far north as Vancouver — were required for the rebuilding of a new house of worship a year later. It was in the new *shul*, at Thirteenth Street and Clay, that Magnes, who later became one of the outstanding public speakers in America, delivered his first "sermons." Beginning at age eight, he preached on Biblical themes at children's services which were attended by many admiring adults, and, like his Bar Mitzvah speech of 1890, they were quoted at length in the *Oakland Tribune*.[14]

In Magnes's teenage years, another local rabbi played an even greater role in his life by becoming his first mentor. Jacob Voorsanger, without doubt the leading rabbi in the American West by the early 1890's, presided over the magnificent Sutter Street Temple of San Francisco's prestigious Congregation Emanu-El. The Dutch-born scholar, still in his thirties when Magnes first encountered him, had mastered thirteen languages and later would found the Semitics Department at the University of California in Berkeley. He was an accomplished orator and an even more effective publicist, establishing in 1895, and editing for the next thirteen years the most influential Jewish periodical on the West Coast, the *Emanu-El*.[15]

But Voorsanger put his unusual skills at the service of ultra-Reform Judaism. Along with other luminaries of the Reform movement's radical second generation, he sang the praises of "progressive, rational Judaism" practiced mainly by Central and Western European Jews and their descendants, and waged war against what he called the "Ghetto Judaism" of the East Europeans. Services at his congregation were so shorn of specific Jewish content — the Shofar was replaced by the cornet — that they resembled the Unitarian worship experience. In 1886, Voorsanger's first year at the Temple, Emanu-El moved its Friday evening services to Sunday morning. Voorsanger despised the Russian Jewish immigrants who began to arrive in California in large numbers in the 1890s, calling their journalists "blackguards," their lay leaders hypocrites, their itinerant rabbis *shnorrers*. Trying to prevent the area South of Market Street where they lived from turning into another Lower East Side, a "reeking pesthole" as he put it, Voorsanger supported the unsuccessful plan of several of his leading congregants to purchase Baja, California from the Mexican government and settle the Yiddish speakers there. Immigration to Palestine, though, he viewed as a great danger, for the talk of settling the "Turk-ridden land," as he termed it, was bound to make it more difficult for Jews to be fully accepted in America.[16]

Informed about young Magnes by Rabbi Levy, Voorsanger quickly came to the conclusion that the brilliant Oakland boy had the ability to become the first California-born rabbi, and took him on as a special student. For years Magnes regularly crossed the Bay by ferry to study the sacred Hebrew texts with Voorsanger.[17] In 1894, the Dutchman's glowing letter of recommendation led to Magnes's acceptance at Hebrew Union College, where Voorsanger was to receive an honorary doctorate in 1903, and on whose Board of Governors he was to serve. They corresponded with one another after Magnes left for Cincinnati, with the rabbi showing an avid interest in the academic progress of his protege whom he invited to preach at Emanu-El following Magnes's ordination in 1900. "Never have I felt so happy or proud as I do in making way for this lad," he told the congregation in turning the pulpit over to the younger man, "whom I sent away with a benediction and who now comes back a rabbi in Israel."[18] Voorsanger also arranged for a stipend for Magnes's doctoral work in Germany, but the two finally had a falling out. In 1906, Magnes had been sent to San Francisco on a fact-finding tour by the National Conference of Jewish Charities to assess the damage done to the Jewish community by the Great Earthquake and Fire. When his estimate of the number of homeless Jews turned out to be far lower than Voorsanger's, he was sharply and publicly rebuked by his former mentor.[19]

In the 1890s, Magnes was apparently deeply affected by his experience with Voorsanger and Emanu-El. On the other hand, he could not have been but impressed with the figure cut by the indefatigable spiritual leader, at once a powerful intellect and communal worker. Yet it may also be that Magnes's incisive critique of American Jewry and the Reform movement in particular, had its roots at Temple Emanu-El as well. To be sure, his first essay on the subject, "Palestine — or Death," was actually written in Cincinnati, in Magnes's sophomore year, about eighteen months after his departure from California.[20] Printed by the fair-minded Voorsanger in the *Emanu-El*, the piece advocates a return to Palestine as the only way to stave off the death of American Judaism. Magnes bewails the growing interest of his coreligionists in various universal religions, a major problem in California around the turn of the century. He laments the loss of religious fervor which structured the lives of his parents' and grandparents' generations. "This earnestness is what we of the present lack," he writes. "Today some who have more wealth than anything else, pay their minister to proclaim them Jews." The teenaged Magnes who left Oakland to study for the rabbinate had a solid grounding in Jewish texts and a deep love for the Jewish people. But he also recognized how rare his own development had been and how attenuated, often sanctimonious was the practice of Judaism which he witnessed, especially at Temple Emanu-El, that threatened the very survival of Judaism in America.

Yet for all of this, Magnes's youth in Oakland was unmistakably American. Endowed with good looks, a naturally curious mind, and self-confidence, he enjoyed everything that his society could offer an adolescent. In addition to concentrating on the classics curriculum at Oakland High School, he was active in the Debating Club, an editor of the well-written student magazine, *The Aegis*, and even a creditable athlete.[21] One summer afternoon he pitched his school's baseball team to victory over St. Mary's College, besting Joe Corbett, who later gained fame in the National League.[22]

From his teachers, in the Lincoln Grammar School as well as at Oakland High, he came away with an ideal image of American democracy, as he remembered a half century later — "no badges, no titles, no special uniforms."[23] This vision of equality often clashed with the reality of California life in the late nineteenth century, perhaps most sharply in the case of the persecution of the Chinese. Young Magnes, according to his brother Isaac, was greatly pained by the bigotry he saw in his own West Oakland neighborhood.[24] It is unlikely, too, that the sensitive, inquisitive lad remained unaffected by the transgressions of the robber barons, the corrupt politicians, and the yellow journalists of his day. Indeed, he admired two influential San Francisco columnists, Ambrose Bierce and Arthur McEwen, who were merciless in their attacks on the state's wealthy few, including the notorious "Big Four" — Crocker, Huntington, Stanford, and Hopkins. In the late 1880s, the sardonic Bierce fought the railroad monopoly in the pages of the *San Francisco Examiner*, and concluded, based on a recent accident in Oakland that the public had a right to a standard of safety, "at least equal to that of a soldier on a battlefield."[25] In February 1894, just when young Magnes had become associate editor of his high school newspaper, another *Examiner* reporter, Arthur McEwen, left that paper to publish and edit his own weekly *Letter*. Attracting enormous attention during its brief life, the trenchant sheet railed against the rapacious clique of millionaires whom McEwen held responsible for the financial panic of the previous year which had brought an untold amount of misery to honest working people.[26] Magnes's brief articles in the *Aegis* do not explore specific social problems, but are essays on human nature, attacking conservatism, sectarianism, and ignorance in general. Yet the high school journalist's choice of the pseudonym, Ambrose Arthur Bierce McEwen, leaves no doubt of his sentiments.[27]

Perhaps the California Magnes had known, as a child, was on his mind when near the end of his life he wrote John Haynes Holmes from Jerusalem, "I know how powerful the forces of greed and hatred can be in America."[29] Yet the "greater and nobler America," to which he referred at the same time, proved much more important to his thinking. And his lifelong hope that people from different backgrounds and different classes could live as equals in a newly created democratic society almost certainly originated with the experience of his own family in Oakland. As a youth he was very much aware of the fact that the Bay Area had been transformed in one generation from a wilderness into a network of cities, and that a medley of people from all over the world somehow coexisted.[29] How could the Zionist dream, even in the nineteenth century, seem quixotic, when so much of the California dream had already been realized?

He also saw in the Far West that the very democracy toward which he and others strove ultimately threatened to break down the precious distinctiveness of each racial, religious, or ethnic group. Cultural pluralism, the antithesis of the melting pot notion of American society, which he eloquently expounded over the course of more than four decades, was perhaps the single most important idea in Magnes's powerful intellectual arsenal. A number of other imaginative thinkers, most notably Horace Kallen, developed and advanced cultural pluralism after the turn of the century.[30] Magnes, however, prescribed cultural pluralism not only for American Jewry but for the Jewish community of Palestine as well. If he rejected the ideal of assimilation for Jews in the United States, he also disapproved of Jewish nationalism in the Holy Land. His vision, like Kallen's, was expressed best in 1909 in the metaphor of a symphony, "written by the various nationalities which keep their individual and characteristic note," he had declared, "and which sound this note in harmony with their sister nationalities."[31]

Again, his youth in Oakland, in all probability, tellingly influenced his thinking. For nowhere were the promises and pitfalls of cultural pluralism clearer than in post-Gold Rush California. Here, in one of the most remote areas of the continent, Magnes's family and his teachers managed to transmit to him a four-thousand-year-old civilization. And here, too, he saw Chinese and Japanese, blacks and Hispanics, Germans, and Irish, along with the Jews, each group clinging to its culture but at the same time in danger, in the long run, of losing it.

Magnes's exuberant Western youth was marked not only by a positive Jewish identity and a thoroughly American sensibility, but, most important, by powerful and vivid first impressions of the relationship between the two. Except for a few visits home, he left California forever in 1894. But California never left him.

Figure 3. Hebrew Union College graduation, 1900. In the group are Magnes, Solomon Lowenstein, Martin Meyer, and Magnes's mother, Sophie Abrahamson Magnes. *(Courtesy of Hava Magnes)*

2

Cincinnati:
The Earlier and Later Years

MARC LEE RAPHAEL

Judah Leon Magnes spent a relatively brief period of his life in Cincinnati, but the academic community as well as Cincinnati Jewry at large contributed much to his thought, values, and interests, and he, in return, gave much to them. Magnes's Cincinnati phase comprises three segments: his student years at the Hebrew Union College, his brief tenure as a member of the Hebrew Union College faculty, and several decades later, his relationship with its leaders and some of its professors.

Magnes attended the University of Cincinnati from 1894 to 1898 while studying simultaneously at the Hebrew Union College (he was ordained in 1900), a joint program common among rabbinic students from the earliest years of the college through the 1960s. In his senior year at the university, he was selected editor-in-chief of the student magazine, and as Arthur Goren notes, "when the faculty insisted on censoring student criticism of professors Magnes led a rebellion that agitated the university for months." That revealing episode, documented in detail in the university's archives, is not only instructive about Magnes at ages nineteen and twenty, but tells us a great deal about the character traits of the future leader.[1]

The trouble began at the "Class Night" or graduation party of the Class of 1897, as Magnes finished his junior year. According to the *Cincinnatian*, the class annual, Magnes would edit the following academic year, "the most talkative man in the class" was Hyman G. Enelow, a brilliant student and record-setting hammer thrower, who

29

would be ordained at the Hebrew Union College in 1898, two years before Magnes, and go on to a distinguished rabbinic and scholarly career. At the party, Enelow, as master of ceremonies, made certain peculiarities of the professors the butt of his humor, and this, coupled with similar remarks in the annual, led the faculty to announce that in the following year — Magnes's last — it would censor the annual and supervise the Class Night.[2]

Magnes, elected editor of the 1898 *Cincinnatian*, understood the faculty's sensitivity and agreed not to publish items ridiculing professors in the annual, while the class agreed to cancel Class Night in order to guarantee that no faculty roast would be staged. But these actions were not enough: the faculty informed Magnes that it intended to read all manuscripts submitted to the *Cincinnatian* for publication to guarantee that nothing objectionable would appear. Magnes vigorously opposed this censorship — with protests and petitions, in letters and meetings, sometimes gently and sometimes much more aggressively — and he succeeded in winning from the faculty, which he labeled "our inferiors," a promise not to read manuscripts submitted to the *Cincinnatian* but to trust the editor. His closest friend, also a senior and a rabbinic student, was said to differ from Magnes in only one way, namely that "Solomon Lowenstein has sometimes treated the faculty with respectful consideration."[3]

Magnes's election as editor was not fortuitous and his vigorous pursuit of academic freedom did not come suddenly; as a sophomore he had argued for private polling booths — previously unheard of — for class elections, and as a junior he had defended Enelow before the English faculty. Enelow, editor of the monthly *McMicken Review* of literature and a Fellow in the Department of English, had written some "scurrilous editorials" regarding the relations between his senior class and the faculty. Having enraged the faculty, Enelow was suspended from the university, removed from the *Review*, and, unless he would "exculpate himself to the satisfaction of the faculty," was to be dropped as a Fellow. Together with his advocate, Magnes, he appeared before the faculty, and after mildly apologizing for his editorials, was reinstated as a student. By then, Magnes had abundant experience with faculty sensitivity to criticism in a student publication, but persisted in arguing for the right to do precisely that in the *Cincinnatian*. When, according to the students, he could no longer "sacrifice his honesty of purpose and personal convictions," and when, according to Magnes, he became disgusted with "men so false," he resigned the editorship. Even after his resignation, however, Magnes "continued to make several trips to the Dean's office by request." Clearly, Magnes's activism and dedication to civil liberties had become an essential feature of his life. As he wrote to his parents during what he called the "rebellion" and would repeat, essentially, many times, "My share in it . . . I don't regret, for after all this is my world, my life, and if we cannot give free expression to our honest convictions, the whole is not worth the worry."[4]

Magnes was not only a skilled writer, but a gifted speaker as well, with "great promise . . . as a preacher." Max Raisin, a contemporary at the college, recalled

> the sermon he [Magnes] delivered one wintry Friday night at the Plum Street Temple. He was well-prepared, his diction was elegant, and there was a special appeal in his voice which captivated his audience. Old Rabbi Isaac Mayer Wise, who was on the pulpit and introduced him to the congregation, praised him highly for his effort and predicted that he would become a shining light in the Jewish ministry.[5]

Magnes, however, chose not to employ his preaching talents immediately, but instead to go to Europe for his doctoral studies, returning in February 1903 to the Hebrew Union College — "a new man," according to Raisin. From February 1903 until June 1903, he served as an instructor in Bible, and during the 1903–1904 academic year, Magnes also served as acting librarian. According to Raisin, "his great interest in the students and their problems made him a very favorite teacher." He was, doubtless, a fine teacher, but he clearly subordinated serious scholarship to his growing passion for Zionism.[6]

If "Zionism . . . was not yet one of Magnes's major interests" in his years as a rabbinic student (1894–1900), Arthur Goren notes the emergence of a receptivity in Magnes to Zionism during these years in the face of the well-known anti-Zionist climate of the Hebrew Union College and the anti-Zionist speeches, letters, and essays of Magnes's mentor and patron, San Francisco's Rabbi Jacob Voorsanger. The first evidence of Magnes's awakening was an article, "Palestine — or Death," — the "Death" of American Judaism! — which Magnes wrote early in his sophomore year at the University of Cincinnati. There he argues that the "permanency of . . . Judaism" depended upon a "return to the land of our fathers," and that "the establishment in Palestine of a Jewish Church and State [is] the only salvation of our present-day Judaism."[7]

Magnes's lengthy and abundant correspondence with his family corroborates Goren's analysis and enables us better to understand Magnes's growing interest in Zionism. In addition to the 1896 essay and some of his student sermons which reflected his excitement over a Jewish return to Palestine, most critical to his inspiration were lectures in living Hebrew and Yiddish by the great popular orator, Zvi Hirsch Masliansky, which fired his soul with an insatiable hunger for the renaissant ancient tongue as well as for the savory folk language. Magnes's Zionism clearly was stimulated and deepened by his experiences in Germany, but it originated in America and not in Europe.

Upon his return from Germany, he, of course, was a confirmed Zionist. When in February 1903, Moses Mielziner, Professor of Talmud and president pro-tem died, and the historian Gotthard Deutsch succeeded him as acting president, Magnes was offered a teaching position for the second term of the 1902–1903 academic year. In several letters home, he reveals his delight over this opportunity despite his mother's grave disappointment over his failure to accept a congregational position that had been offered him. Magnes also suggests, more for his family's peace of mind than his own needs, for his modest style of living in Cincinnati seemed to suit him extremely well, that other enticing opportunities might become available for the following year. What is striking in these 1903 letters is the absence of any reflections on Reform Judaism, theology, Bible (which he was teaching), and his own academic work. Instead, he writes almost exclusively and at length about Zionism.

In response to a letter from his mother in which she wondered why he had neither been invited to preach at Cincinnati synagogues nor elected to the John Street synagogue position about which he had written his family during the winter, Magnes explained that it was the result of widespread apprehension. "The gentlemen are afraid that I shall preach too much Zionism" in a town where both reform congregations were led by anti-Zionist rabbis and laymen. In fact, already by April, two months after beginning to teach at the College, Magnes was eager to leave at the end of the term, or even earlier, if he could find a congenial position. This was true despite the fact that he registered strong doubts to his parents, after meeting a synagogue president, over whether he could ever "be able to put up with a life that must be cut out to suit such men and women," and despite his earlier excitement about the Hebrew Union College position.

The shift in Magnes's attitude — his sudden disenchantment with the Hebrew Union College — resulted from his Zionist sentiments and the reaction they provoked. In the middle of his second academic year when he taught ten hours per week in the precollegiate department, Magnes wrote home about the new President's decision to flunk a senior — "one of the best in his studies" — because he was a Zionist.

Magnes discussed President Kohler's anti-Zionism and noted that to Kaufmann Kohler, Zionism was a "red rag in the face of a bull." Nevertheless, despite Kohler's "tirades against Zionism" and, more directly, his warning to Magnes to curb his Zionist activities, Magnes even seemed to like him. Since he felt that Kohler was heavily influenced by the rabidly anti-Zionist Hebrew Union College faculty member and Cincinnati rabbi, David Philipson, he was unwilling to judge him harshly, and retained enough objectivity to conclude sagaciously that given Kohler's attitude, his own contract would not be renewed. The situation resolved itself soon enough, however, for on that very day, February 10, 1904, Brooklyn's Temple Israel put a letter in the mail offering Magnes the pulpit beginning on September 1, 1904. Having worked through his feelings about this career change very thoroughly earlier in the winter, Magnes quickly accepted the offer.[9]

Magnes's letters in these months enable us to understand what Kohler referred to when he scored Magnes's Zionist activities, activities with many parallels in Magnes's Berlin years. First, he had organized a *hevrah* of Zionist youth, the Young Hebrew Zionists, by the early months of 1904 a very active group, and also participated in the activities of the Cincinnati Ohave Zion Society. Second, Magnes became seriously interested in Hebrew poetry, published his first article on Bialik, read the Hebrew poets, and spoke Hebrew with other interested Zionists in town, at a time when the new president had banished modern Hebrew literature from the Hebrew Union College curriculum. Magnes not only argued, in his Bialik article, that Jewish life in America lacked poetry, song, religious emotion, and thought, but that the Hebrew language was the essential vehicle for a Jewish cultural revival. Three years later, he insisted that a "pagan" Jew who writes in Hebrew is a "better Jew" than an "ethical monotheist" who does not like the language of Jewish life. Already by early 1904, this strong interest in Palestine and Hebrew culture convinced Magnes that he would not fit in Cincinnati, or, for that matter, even in New York. "I am neither a Reformer of the Cincinnati brand," he wrote home, "nor a Jew of the Eastern trademark and I shall have to cut out my own way." Where he would find his own way he obviously did not know, but he informed his parents that he would surely find a following, if not at Temple Israel, "then in some other place."[10]

Third, to Kohler's dismay, Magnes had become enamored with the small but vibrant East European immigrant community of Cincinnati. He loved the Yiddish language and its culture, enjoyed his associations with the people who spoke Yiddish, and derided the negative American Jewish attitude toward its "sweet tender sounds."

A Yiddish circular announced that Dr. Leon Magnes would address the Cincinnati Ohave Zion Society and that tickets could be purchased at several stores and agencies in the immigrant community. He wrote home about a Baron Günsburg Memorial Meeting, Zionist society and Zion Club meetings, and a talk which he gave to the Rumanians. In addition, he did not forget to mention the rallies and benefits for the Kishinev victims which he attended, committee and board meetings at the Settlement house, and his active involvement with the United Hebrew Charities run by his old friend, Rabbi Solomon Lowenstein. Such activities, and the people involved with them, surely provided a supporting context for Magnes's growing interest in the Hebrew renaissance and Zionism.[11]

When Magnes finally left Cincinnati, he did not leave behind the culture and nationalism of the East European Jewish immigrants which he had so carefully cultivated during his brief sojourn there. These ingredients of modern Judaism had become an integral part of his life. As the years passed, he not only remembered his rabbinical and academic associates along the Ohio with fondness, but as new leaders emerged there, he reestablished an old relationship and chiseled out a new one.

The next time Magnes and the president of the Hebrew Union College communicated with one another, his nemesis, Kaufmann Kohler, had been succeeded by Julian Morgenstern, and by then Magnes was Chancellor of the Hebrew University. Despite Morgenstern's opposition to Zionism, their letters were very friendly. This is probably due to Morgenstern's personal affection for Magnes, who had given him "wise and helpful guidance" in Heidelberg in the summer of 1902 when Magnes persuaded him to study Semitic languages. This counsel, which culminated two years later in a Ph.D., summa cum laude, "shaped very happily the entire course of [Morgenstern's] subsequent life." More than three decades later, as Magnes's sixtieth birthday approached, Morgenstern excitedly informed him that Hebrew Union College would offer him an honorary Doctor of Hebrew Letters degree. Magnes, who thought of himself as a "fractious son," was "delighted" but even more "embarrassed," and declined the honor.[12]

The Morgenstern-Magnes relationship, however, had been resumed more than a decade earlier when the new chancellor of the Hebrew University sought to launch the Institute of Jewish Studies which had been founded in 1924, with Felix Warburg's $500,000 endowment. After being rebuffed by the Jewish Theological Seminary, Magnes asked Morgenstern to provide the Hebrew University with a visiting professor for the 1925–1926 academic year and to endow one Hebrew Union College graduate with $1,000 to $2,000 for one year of study at the Hebrew University. Morgenstern asked Jacob Marcus to serve as the first visiting professor, but Marcus, just finishing up four years of study in Germany, was eager to begin teaching at the Hebrew Union College. The president then turned to Nelson Glueck, also studying in Germany, who responded that once finished with his Ph.D., he would be delighted to go to Palestine, provided Morgenstern aided him. Morgenstern promised to do so but could not underwrite a visiting professor for the full academic year; consequently, Glueck went to Jerusalem only for part of 1925. However, Sheldon Blank, a young Bible scholar, went during the 1926–1927 academic year, Glueck went again at the end of that academic year, and Jacob Mann, a medievalist, followed in 1927–1928. Magnes wrote numerous letters to make certain each man would come and feel welcome, and he was very pleased.[13]

In the letters which Magnes and Morgenstern exchanged about visiting professors, they both had much to say about politics in Palestine, too. Rarely was there disagreement: they both supported "organized systematic work for bettering Arab-Jewish relations"; they both hoped for increased "scholarly contact between Jew and Arab"; and they both acknowledged that the Arabs had "fundamental" and "deep" rights. In one 1929 exchange, Magnes even claimed that these rights were "perhaps more basic than those of the Jewish people." The core of the program for Palestine which Magnes later presented in great detail in public speeches and private letters, is to be found in his letters of the late 1920s.

Morgenstern's promise to send Nelson Glueck, and his ability to raise funds to support him in Palestine, echoed into the following decades. Glueck, an archeologist, who spent long periods of time in and around Palestine in the two decades before 1948 as Director of the American School of Oriental Studies, became a close personal friend of Beatrice and Judah Magnes. Nelson and his wife, Helen, would have frequent Sabbath dinners at the Magnes home in Arab East Jerusalem. As the years passed, Magnes and Glueck shared their most intimate hopes and fears with one another, not only in their direct personal associations in Jerusalem, but in their correspondence in English and Hebrew that travelled between Cincinnati and Jerusalem as well.[14]

On Glueck's side, the most interesting revelation is his strong desire, even after being chosen president of the Hebrew Union College in 1947, to be Magnes's successor as the president of the Hebrew

University. More than two decades earlier, after three months at the American School of Archaeology, Glueck had written a long letter to Magnes detailing his own vision for the university. But in 1947, he boldly shared with Magnes his dream of receiving "the highest honor and the greatest office that could be extended to and filled by any Jew in the world" — the presidency of the Hebrew University.

In addition to his ambivalence about his position as the president of the Hebrew Union College, Glueck also told Magnes, and there is no doubt of his sincerity, that "more than anyone else" Magnes was the person whom Glueck wanted to be at his inauguration. He also shared in Magnes's opposition to Stephen S. Wise and to the merger of the Hebrew Union College with the Jewish Institute of Religion. Glueck's efforts, however, to persuade Magnes to accept an honorary degree on his seventieth birthday came to naught for Magnes declined, as he had a decade earlier. Yet ever eager to invoke the influence of his "genuinely American" native soil, he told Glueck how one of his schoolteachers had indelibly impressed upon him that Benjamin Franklin was the only diplomat at the French Court in plain dress and no decorations. "Why, in my old age, should I go back on the teachings of that Oakland, California schoolmaster?" wrote Magnes in his gracious letter rejecting the honor.

By reading his candid letters to Glueck, we also learn something about Magnes's inner-most feelings in the final months of his life. We learn especially of the trepidation he felt before testifying before the United Nations Special Committee on Palestine in 1947; of his desperate attempts to gain financial and political support for his political program (Ihud) for a binational state with two equal peoples, and of his attempts to convince the Arabs, the British, the Americans, and the United Nations that chaos was not the only alternative to partition; and of his consistent feeling that only his ill health, and hence inability to travel outside Palestine, doomed his political goals. In the summer of 1946, after raising $25,000 for Ihud by appealing to individual Jews all over the United States, he told Glueck that he lacked the strength to pursue further solicitations during the critical year of 1947. Clearly, one of the reasons for his frequent letters to Glueck in his last year was the latter's strong support of Magnes's binational plan. Upon learning of the United Nations decision to partition Palestine, he wrote Magnes that he felt "sick and distraught" and considered "donning sackcloth and strewing his head with ashes" over the news. Upon Magnes's death, Glueck noted in a letter of lament to Mrs. Magnes, that "all hopes for peace between Arabs and Jews have died with Judah."[15]

During his seven and one-half years in Cincinnati, Magnes deepened his understanding about issues that would be vital to him to his dying day. As a student and subsequently as an instructor at the Hebrew Union College, the budding Zionist, pacifist, and radical fretted about academic and cultural freedom. Later, as an American Zionist in Jerusalem, he worried even more over a projected Jewish state that ignored the claims of Palestine's Arabs, sharing his forebodings with his old friends on the Ohio and turning to them for support and consolation. Cincinnati was no mere waystation in Magnes's growth and development, but a place to which he could return because it was persuaded to grow along with him.

II
New York: Vortex or Void?

Figure 4. The New York Jewish Intellectuals, Magnes, Louis Ginzberg, Samson Benderly and others grouped around Solomon Schechter, Tannersville, New York c. 1907. (*Courtesy of Hava Magnes*)

3

A New American Judaism

DEBORAH DASH MOORE

Looking backward, a chronic habit of historians, certain points in time assume a saliency and vividness that other years do not. One year merges with another, until suddenly a cluster of events fall into focus and call out for recognition. Of course, historians know that there are no abrupt departures in history, that precedents can always be found, yet the urge is irresistible to pinpoint the moment when a movement took shape, when a new vision of the world achieved acceptance, even when institutions had their genesis. Yielding to that temptation, I suggest that the birth of a new American Judaism occurred in 1905, a year   *1905* of pogroms and revolution in Russia, massive immigration to the United States, and frantic efforts by American Jews to organize overseas aid to support the self-defense efforts of their Russian brethren.[1] A crucial year, 1905 also marked the emergence of the historical self-consciousness of America's Jews, a self-awareness that found expression in the celebration of the 250th anniversary of Jewish settlement in America. Indeed, the anniversary celebration itself highlighted the arrival of a new group of American Jewish leaders, identified with the premier immigrant city of the Jewish world, New York.[2]

Their fortunes linked to New York's rise to preeminence, these men and women asserted simultaneously the city's national importance and their hegemony over American Jewry. Their New York power base rested on their personal integrity sustained by a fresh ideology of American Judaism. Challenging an older network of American Jewish organizations, they turned New York into the capital city of American Jewry.[3] During the next six years, New York became the vortex of an emerging Jewish world whose outlines were becoming visible to men and women of foresight. Drawn to the city as by a magnet, native-born American Jews — Louis Marshall from Syracuse, Henrietta Szold from Baltimore, Louis Lipsky from Rochester, Judah Magnes from Cincinnati, Leo Levi from Galveston, and Cyrus Adler commuting from Philadelphia — joined forces with immigrants — Israel Friedlaender, Solomon Schechter, Hayim Zhitlowsky, Samson Benderly — to lay the foundations for a new American Jewish consensus.

The mass migration of Russian Jews to the cities of the United States provided the impetus for such collaboration. Aware that "no era in Jewish history exceeds the present in importance and solemnity" and convinced that "to play a proper role therein is a high privilege and a higher duty," a new group of leaders innovatively responded to the crises of the times.[4] These young people aspired to the leadership of a "mighty American Jewry" which they believed was bound to evolve from the union of "masses" and "classes," cemented to a new American Judaism. With Leo Levi, the president of B'nai B'rith, they anticipated that "in a few years we shall see on this continent a reborn, rehabilitated, virile, powerful Jewry, enriching the world with its virtues, its energies and its genius."[5] The times called for fresh strategies to co-opt the immigrants and create consensus through an ideology sufficiently broad to contain the spectrum of Jewish opinion and advance the cause of Judaism in America. Confronting the challenge of mass immigration with its attendant social disorganization and spiritual ferment, these aspiring New York Jews buried their antagonisms and crafted an alternative American Judaism to Reform.[6] Unlike its equally ambitious predecessor, the new American Judaism welcomed Jewish religious diversity because it perceived Judaism as the creative culture of the living Jewish people. By shifting the emphasis away from the Jews' religion to their ethnic identity, the new American Judaism skirted divisive debates over ritual that had plagued reformers. Advocates of the new American Jewish religious ideology encouraged various forms of collective expression. In their efforts to preserve the Jews as a people, they combined cultural Zionism with a reconsidered traditionalism. The latter derived from an appreciation of what Israel Friedlaender called the "spiritual goods" of the Russian immigrants.[7] Threatened by immigrant radicalism and self-segregation, and fearing a secular nationalism unrestrained by religious norms, the elite leaders of New York Jewry accommodated the cultural Zionists' nationalist posture with its enthusiasm for a flexible Jewish religious culture.[8]

Having travelled from the western United States to its eastern edge, Judah Magnes not only entered New York City's maelstrom, but stood briefly at its center.[9] There he encountered intersecting circles of men and women: Zionists like Louis Lipsky, Henrietta Szold, and Bernard Richards; teachers at the Jewish Theological Seminary like Solomon Schechter, Israel Friedlaender, and Mordecai Kaplan; Jewish social service workers and educators like David Blaustein, Samson Benderly, and Solomon Lowenstein; immigrant socialist intellectuals like Hayim Zhitlowsky, David Pinski, and Leon Zolotkoff; elite Jewish leaders, members of Temple Emanu-El like Louis Marshall, Jacob Schiff, and Felix Warburg; and wealthy East European Jewish philanthropists like Israel Unterberg, Harry Fischel, and Bernard Semel. All of them shared a sense that American Jewry stood at a crossroads. In the chaos of Jewish life caused by mass immigration, they sought for an order that they hoped would rescue Judaism from the corroding acids of modernity. Given the diversity of their backgrounds, it is remarkable that these people could forge a common ideology of American Judaism. Yet for a brief span of time they not only shared similar values but cooperated in building schools, settlement houses, modern synagogues, and Jewish communal organizations. Until their conflicting ultimate goals drove them apart, they responded creatively to the needs of the moment and laid the foundation for the future consensus of American Jews. They were the first generation of American Jewry as we know it today who attempted to draft both a declaration of American Jewish independence and an articles of confederation.

The historian Evyatar Friesel has argued that the development of a new American Judaism and the organized American Jewish community derived from an ideology of optimism shared by all segments of American Jewry. This ideology resonated nicely with the ethos of American progressivism. It assumed "that America, being a land of human equality and freedom, held a brilliant future in store here for Jews and Judaism — even more, . . . that it could be realized if the right steps were taken."[10] Such was the power of this assumption that it united American Jews despite sharp class and ethnic differences and spurred them to cooperative communal activity with its future-oriented, hopeful attitude. Yet in 1911, even such an optimist as Friedlaender assessed American Jewry in dismal terms: decentralization, petrification, and centrifugal tendencies plagued New York — and by extension American Jewish life.[11] Magnes shared the same view. In 1904, he noted in his diary:

> the utter anarchy and helplessness and anchorlessness of our Jewish life. We do not know what we are, what we stand for, if the future is to see us alive or dead; our present is without a point of view; we are drifting, and we do not seem to care much whither.[12]

In Friedlaender's opinion, Jews in the United States were poorly equipped to turn the conditions of political freedom and economic opportunity characteristic of American society to their advantage, especially to the advantage of Judaism. It was, therefore, encumbent upon those who led American Jews to project a coherent new Judaism-under-freedom upon the formless present.

This task assumed greater urgency because of its inherent difficulties. The men who strove to lead American Jews assumed that a genuine American Judaism would not be imposed by an elite but would be the untrammelled expression of free Jews. As Magnes wrote, "because we American Jews are free, . . . we shall therefore work out our salvation as Jews (salvation meaning for me of course, our national salvation)."[13] Caught in the dilemma of imagining an optimistic future that would evolve creatively out of a pessimistic present, the proponents of a new American Judaism argued in dialectical terms. Friedlaender put it picturesquely in 1905:

> Jewry is dangerously ill; assimilation proposed suicide; Zionism recommends transportation to a healthy climate. But the patient has still too much vitality to commit suicide and too little energy to bear transportation. The only remedy, therefore, which he is in a position to accept is one which will not take him out of his place, and yet enable him to maintain his life.[14]

In short, New York City was to be the keystone of the Jewish future. The young ideologists' dialectics led them back to their starting point: immigration. They divided the past into such dualities as a rigid Orthodoxy versus an emaciated Reform and responded to the present with centrism: a vision of a scattered, diverse Jewish people unified by a spiritual center of either land, language, community, or ideology.

Magnes sounded this dominant theme with great clarity in a letter to his close friend and communal coworker, Solomon Lowenstein, upon David Blaustein's death. Asked to honor Blaustein at a memorial meeting as both a Zionist and a supporter of the New York Kehillah, Magnes proceeded to explain his dual role:

> Although the Zionist organization and the Kehillah are absolutely distinct entities, there is a direct relationship between them making it proper for one person to represent both organizations. . . . The idea common to both of them is that of the Jewish Centre. The Kehillah is endeavoring to establish itself as the Jewish Centre of the million Jews of New York City. The Zionist movement is endeavoring to establish the Jewish Centre for the Jewish people in the Jewish land.

Magnes went on to reflect on how Blaustein had attempted to establish a Jewish center for the immigrant quarter at the Educational Alliance, but had failed because he thought that "all that was necessary was to imitate . . . the Christian settlements . . . ." In the past, wrote Magnes, "the Synagogue was the only Jewish Centre which the Jews had." But in modern times the synagogue had lost its primacy and now every building with Jewish activities held the potential to be a Jewish center. Nevertheless, despite the fragmentation and compartmentalization characteristic of contemporary Jewish life, "it is significant of the trend of the times that the old idea of having a single Jewish Centre, in which should be gathered all kinds of Jewish activities is again becoming fashionable."[15]

If Magnes saw a correlation between building a local Jewish center in New York City and a national one in the land of Israel, Friedlaender argued also for the importance of the United States as the Jewish center of the diaspora.

> America is fast becoming the center of the Jewish people of the Diaspora. . . . America is already the center of the Jews. As regards the number of its Jewish population it is second to none but to Russia, which is in a state of dissolution. . . . But America has every chance of also becoming the center of Judaism, of the spiritual life of the Jewish people in the Dispersion. . . . It has the numbers which are necessary for the creation of a cultural center. It possesses the economic prosperity indispensable for a successful spiritual development. The freedom enjoyed by the Jews is . . . the natural product of American civilization. . . . In short, this country has at its disposal all the materials necessary for the upbuilding of a large, powerful center of Judaism."[16]

The concept of a Jewish center with its promise of synthesis fired the imagination of New York's ambitious Jewish thinkers even as it legitimated their claims to leadership.

The young rabbis, teachers, publicists, and politicians of New York Jewry who espoused the ideology of a new American Judaism challenged older influential American Jewish organizations, especially the B'nai B'rith, the international Jewish fraternal society, and the Hebrew Union College, the intellectual center of American Reform Judaism. Located in the Midwest, in Chicago and Cincinnati respectively, they were led in 1905 by Adolph Kraus, president of the B'nai B'rith, and Kaufmann Kohler, head of Hebrew Union College. The recognized leaders of organized Jewish life by virtue of their positions, Kraus and Kohler stood for a liberal, rationalist, and universalist interpretation of

American Judaism that viewed the Jews as a religious community, inspired by a mission to the Gentile world, by a commitment to ethical monotheism, and by a sense of "noblesse oblige" toward their less fortunate "coreligionists."[17] Dr. Myer Solis-Cohen translated these tenets into popular faith in his description of Philadelphia as a city "full of people who regard Judaism as a belief in the unity of God and a beautiful code of morality and a 'high family life' . . . "[18] Speaking to Philadelphia's section of the National Council of Jewish Women, Magnes decried this "exclusive emphasis of the idea of religion" because it defined "the Jewish Community as the 'Universal Church,' and it tended to make of the Jewish religion a creedless ethicism, of which, indeed the Society for Ethical Culture, or at the most Jewish unitarianism, is the unvarnished, logical outcome."[19]

The most promising, if problematic intellectual weapon against this Jewish ideology of radical acculturation and against its spokesmen and communal organizations turned out to be Jewish nationalism. Magnes first articulated this theme in a sermon on Isaac Mayer Wise, the institutional leader of American Reform in the nineteenth century. Magnes prophesied that in response to the ideologically motivated dismissal of three Zionist professors from Hebrew Union College "there is to be a new contest, a new battle between those who wish the preservation and the development of the Jewish community and those who wish to remain at ease . . . ." Implying that he was more worthy of Wise's mantle than were the present leaders of Reform, Magnes promised to "hold to the spirit of real progress."[20] He elaborated his dual commitment to a revival of religious traditionalism and a reaffirmation of Jewish nationalism in his plan for the reconstruction of Reform Judaism outlined in 1910. In his sermon on "A Reform of Judaism upon a Nationalist Basis" Magnes made Jewish nationalism the foundation stone, insisting that "only on the assumption that we are a nationality, or a people, or a race, is change in our religious life at all possible."[21]

Nationalism became the cutting edge of the new American Judaism. In 1906, Schechter's influential statement on Zionism called it "the Declaration of Jewish Independence from all kinds of slavery whether material or spiritual."[22] Though Schechter's statement prompted a rebuttal by Jacob Schiff, committed Zionists like Friedlaender, speaking of Schiff, privately expressed "pity that a man who is such a good national Jew (without the name) should stop just one step away from us. But," Friedlaender concluded, "he is not the only victim of the Golus . . . ."[23] The diverse group of Jewish intellectuals who accepted Magnes's invitation to gather for regular meetings of the Ahvah Club in 1910 resolved to restrict membership to "adherents of National

Judaism."[24] Exponents of a cross-section of Jewish ideologies, the men shared a common desire to solve the problems plaguing contemporary Jewish life. According to the historian, Moshe Davis, the club represented the first major effort to merge intellectual leadership with organizational activism. Its members rallied to the banner of national Judaism, symbolically identifying themselves while agreeing to disagree regarding the substance of their affirmation. Jewish nationalism was "an orientation," in the words of Max L. Margolis, one of the three Zionist professors who left Hebrew Union College for its new rival, the Jewish Theological Seminary of America.[25]

National Judaism did not merely unify supporters of divergent ideologies vis-a-vis an older American Jewish establishment but served as a rationale for the vigorous communal activities of its New York adherents. As Friesel has observed, American Zionists were far more committed than their European counterparts to diaspora work. Building Jewish communal institutions in America was no less a Zionist commandment than rebuilding the national home in Palestine. American Zionists sought to create a vigorous frame for the body as well as the soul of American Jewry.[26] Friedlaender expressed this argument most eloquently in his 1910 speech to the Zionists of Canada where he explicitly recognized that it would be the new world Zionists who would "be called upon to solve the great problem of the relation between the duties of the Jew towards the land of his adoption on the one hand, and towards the land of his ancestors on the other. There is an extreme section within our movement," he warned,

> which, wholly disbelieving in the possibilities of Judaism in the Dispersion, would fain transfer every particle of Jewish energy to Palestine. This tendency born of skepticism and despair will never find a foothold in the New World. The Zionists of this continent, toward which the centre of our people in the *galut* is gradually shifting, fully realize the great tasks that devolve upon them in consequence of this momentous transformation. The Zionists of America will take an active, and, wherever possible, a leading part in making this hemisphere an attractive home for those of our people whom Providence has led hither, and in founding, at the same time, a resting place for Judaism, for our Torah and culture . . . . But, while doing their full duty towards the lands of their adoption, the Zionists of America will never forget their allegiance to that land which is and will never cease to be, the land of 'Klal Yisroel.' They will prove to the world that the Zionist ideal, far from checking the efforts of the Jews on behalf of the countries of their abode, serves rather as an ever-flowing source of stimulus and inspiration for such efforts, insures for them success and stability, and raises them to higher levels and nobler standards.[27]

The establishment of the Jewish Theological Seminary under Schechter's guidance or the New York *Kehillah* under Magnes's supervision or the Young Israel movement under Friedlaender's inspiration, or the creation of various experimental proto-Jewish center synagogues such as Goldstein's Institutional Synagogue, Kaplan's Jewish Center, and Wise's Free Synagogue served as innovative institutional platforms for New York Jewish religious leaders. Through them, the leaders reached beyond the immigrant quarter to challenge successfully the hegemony of the Reform establishment.

As ideology motivated the creation of institutions, so the growth of a vibrant organized Jewish community in New York City encouraged its leaders to compete with the Midwesterners for the mantle of leadership of American Jewry. With an alternative rabbinical school, an alternative religious center, and an alternative political organization — the American Jewish Committee — New York Jews could claim authority over the B'nai B'rith and Reform-Alliance Israelite Universelle in the area of world Jewish affairs. Furthermore, the New York City organizations, merely by virtue of their location, preempted the Midwesterners in speaking for the immigrant masses. Additionally, by placing at the top of their agendas immigrant Jews' needs and concerns — from self-defense monies for Jews in Russia to better Jewish educational facilities to fighting immigration restriction in Congress — the New York organizations appeared able to co-opt the support of the masses. The willingness of Jacob Schiff, Felix Warburg, and Louis Marshall to underwrite these organizations and to collaborate with their leaders suggests the New Yorkers' relative tolerance of Zionism or national Judaism as compared to their peers in Cincinnati and Chicago.[28] Friedlaender even grounded some of his optimism regarding the Jewish future in America in his belief "that Schiff's outlook on Judaism is far broader and his attachment to Judaism far more intense than among the Jewish upper four hundred abroad. Schiff is no doubt a national Jew," he assured Harry Friedenwald, president of the Federation of American Zionists, "while Judaism abroad is considered a mere church."[29] And Schiff later admitted to Friedlaender that "I do not think that we are apart so very much personally" even while he continued to quarrel with Friedlaender over the true meaning of Jewish nationalism.[30]

The new American Judaism also embodied a vision of a democratic America that promoted the harmonious cooperation of its varied nationalities through cultural pluralism. These views coincided with the opinions of secular Jewish nationalists. In an editorial in *The Maccabean* in 1909, Louis Lipsky attacked Reform Jews as hypocrites for celebrating such national holidays as Pesach, Purim, and Hanuk-kah. "There are no Americans by race," wrote Lipsky. "America is the meeting-place of the nations of the world." Drawing conclusions for the Jews, he continued: "In order to occupy a place in the America where the races of Europe meet, the Jew, as a self-respecting citizen, must claim that he is a Jew by nationality. If he does not do that he is an American citizen with a blemish."[31] Hayim Zhitlowsky, the socialist ideologue and ardent advocate of diaspora Yiddish nation-alism who immigrated to America in 1908, had visited the United States in 1904 and had quickly plunged into the arena of ideological prescription for America. Like Magnes, he rejected the message of "The Melting Pot." In two lectures given on the future of the nation-alities in America, Zhitlowsky astutely pointed to resistance to assimilation in the "unconscious devotion to language and habits and manners that become traditional and are involuntarily observed in the family" and in "national institutions, like churches," where the native tongue is used. Zhitlowsky recognized that since the nationalities were segregated in America, they retained the consciousness of "not being . . . true American but . . . hyphenated American." The return of the immigrant intelligentsia to the masses would lead to "equal recognition for all languages and cultures of all peoples of the land . . . ."[32] As the historian Abraham Karp has pointed out, Zhitlowsky argued that "America could act as an example and a challenge to the world," by offering a model of "nationalities living in peace and cooperative harmony." His democratic ideal was "A United States of United Peoples," his ultimate ideal, a United States of the World.[33]

Unlike earlier Jewish adherents of democratic pluralism, the religious spokesmen of New York Jewry argued for an interpretation of American diversity as primarily national, not religious. Magnes in 1909 entitled a sermon honoring the centennial of Abraham Lincoln's birth, "A Republic of Nationalities." There he stressed that "America must, in order to be true to its high conception of liberty and of equal-ity, seek to gather within its borders the representatives of all national cultures of every civilization."[34] To emphasize the extent to which this notion departed from accepted canons of religious pluralism, Magnes chose as his examples of desirable integration the Japanese and blacks, two groups deemed most alien to American society and culture, while Friedlaender addressed this theme in a more lyrical vein: "The true American spirit understands and respects the traditions and associa-tions of other nationalities, and on its vast area numerous races live peaceably together, equally devoted to the interests of the land." To be sure, Friedlaender admitted, "in blending Judaism with Americanism the edges and corners will have to be levelled on both sides. Compromises will be unavoidable. But," he concluded reassuringly, "the happiest of marriages is a series of mutual compromises."[35]

When Friedlaender presented these theories before the Ahvah Club in 1911 several members criticized him for minimizing the idea of the state in American nationalism. Kaplan, already leaning toward a view of nationalism as the modern form of religion, and Lowenstein also questioned Friedlaender's optimistic assessment of the open-endedness of American culture. They worried, too, that the influence of Americanism upon Judaism was more pervasive than Friedlaender realized. However, Friedlaender located the problem for the future of American Judaism not in American cultural nationalism, but in what he considered a specious Jewish Americanism, an ideology that projected America as the exclusive center of the future Jewish world and that rejected Zionism and its Jewish center in Palestine. In short, the greatest danger threatening the new American Judaism was "provincialism," the thinking that a qualified Judaism, limited as American Judaism necessarily was, sufficed. Only if American Jews retained their vital links with the "Jewish" Judaism of Zion in the spiritual center in Palestine and refused to isolate themselves from world Jewry, would they avoid a withering death. This was one task facing Jewish nationalists: to ensure the survival of American Jews. It complemented a second goal advocated by Bernard Richards and supported by other American Zionists, namely, "to judaize and missionize America."[36] To the growing politicization of American culture, Richards responded by urging Jews to preserve Judaism's Hebraic core and spiritual content.

But as indicated by the brief outlines of this debate over the character of American culture and nationalism and the corresponding position of a national Judaism, the consensus achieved by New York's Jewish intellectuals concealed substantial differences of opinion regarding Jewish nationalism and religion. Even the religious exponents of national Judaism differed in their interpretations of Zionism. At times, as when he reported to the eleventh convention of the Federation of American Zionists, Magnes defined Zionism in such broad terms that it could be equated with Judaism. There he said, "Our Zionism must mean for us a Judaism in all its phases. Zionism is a complete and harmonized Judaism."[37] At other times, he pictured it as a "romance of the Jewish national frontiersmen" accomplishing the feat of making "heroes and heroines of modern Jews."[38] Yet beneath both notions lay Magnes's understanding of Zionism as the ideal vehicle for religious statesmanship, an aggressive strategy for preserving and deepening Judaism in an age of ideologies when Zionism brought all the forces of modernity to the aid of a beleaguered tradition. Each Jew converted to Zionism, as Magnes himself had been, became a *baal teshuvah* to a revitalized Judaism.

Zionism also encouraged Jews to pick up the prophetic vocation again. As Rabbi Eugene Kohn, a future follower of Kaplan and supporter of the Reconstructionist movement, wrote about the nationalism of the prophets, it "had infinitely more of a definite religious content than that of most Zionists." For the prophets, "a Judaism without a Jewish nation was as inconceivable as a Christless Christianity would be to a Christian. But equally inconceivable to them was a Jewish nation without a Judaism. We Zionists are often inclined to taunt our opponents with having invented a mission for the Jewish people," Kohn admitted. "But the prophets, too, believed in the mission of the Jew . . . . Nationalism, being a premise in their thought rather than a conclusion, was not regarded as an end in itself, but as the means of bringing about the kingdom of God on earth."[39] Magnes concurred in Kohn's assessment and had "no quarrel with the idea of a mission . . . . If the world's redemption is ever to come," he told a meeting of the Council of Jewish Women," it will come . . . through the agency primarily of the Jewish people." For Magnes, one of Zionism's great virtues was its frank recognition of that need and its sanctioning of political means to secure a Jewish center.[40]

Ever concerned with the issue of religion, Kaplan inclined to reverse Magnes's understanding of Zionism as religious politics and to portray Zionism instead as a political religion. In an address given before a 1909 meeting of Jewish Theological Seminary alumni, Kaplan discussed a theme common to these Jewish thinkers, "Judaism and Nationality," arguing that "the Jewish national genius distinguished itself in the recognition that life must be consecrated to God by being consecrated to man." Kaplan warned that "the whole fabric of the purely nationalist Jew is bound to be the product of a mere feeling of proud chauvinism . . . unless it take on the same expression as it has done through the three thousand years of our history, namely, the religious . . . ."[41] Kaplan's ideal Jew was a "religious-national type." Kaplan hyphenated the two words in 1909 because the modern amalgamation of nationality and religion, which he expected to follow on the heels of the separation of church and state, had not yet occurred. In the past, Judaism had functioned as a national religion; in the present, Zionism guaranteed the return to that synthesis and assured the eternity of Judaism. However, "the real Zionist platform," he wrote during World War I, "is not the one formulated in the Basle program, but the prayer in our ritual which reads, 'Let our eyes behold Thy return to Zion.' "[42]

Confronting these similar but opposing views of Zionism, Friedlaender employed a dialectical method to search for a synthesis. In an essay on Simon Dubnov's theory of diaspora nationalism Friedlaender insisted that "Zionism must, first of all, be based unconditionally upon the recognition of Jewish Nationalism . . . ."[43] But as he explained in a letter to Schiff, "when Jewish Nationalists speak of the Jews as a Nation, this does not at all imply that they have, or should have a political government." Friedlaender defined a nation as "a community bound together, not only by ties of religion, but also by the bonds of common birth," although he recognized that this was not standard American usage. New world Zionists who did not draw their inspiration "from misery and persecution" but from "hope and idealism," could never accept a "mere *Nachtasyl* [temporary asylum], destined to shelter the homeless of our people" nor "a philanthropic solution of our present material problem."[44] Rather, Zionism ideally represented the "consummation of the great national aspirations that Israel has cherished from generation to generation."[45]

As a cultural Zionist committed to seeking consensus, Friedlaender tried to combine the opposites of political religion and religious politics. Turning his attention also to the political ideal of the prophets, he defined politics as "devotion to the commonwealth" and the prophets of Israel as essentially politicians dedicated to perfecting the state to achieve righteousness, the human ideal of holiness. While the prophets did not achieve their ultimate goal, they did turn Israel's political superiority into religious or spiritual supremacy. As a result, Zion became the political expression of Israel's religious superiority, the focus of its spiritual aspirations. The prophets were true spiritual Zionists. Later he wrote that "the Jewish state was not to be an end in itself, but merely the material means for a spiritual end, the political framework for the great moral truths which were to be embodied in definite human institutions."[46]

Friedlaender also attempted to balance the claims of the diaspora advocates of national Judaism with those of the Zionists by urging his famous formula: Zionism plus Diaspora, Palestine plus America. As "a strong believer in the future of American Jewry . . . equally American and Jewish," Friedlaender dreamed of the time when "American Judaism will be as great and as glorious as was Judaism in Spain." Nonetheless, he saw no contradiction in also believing that one or two million Jews will settle in Palestine under Turkish suzerainty and will "live the life of a free people, will build up our historic home, will speak our historic language, will cherish our great religion with its historic institutions and will foster our lofty historic ideals . . . ."[47] America promised to solve the Jews' material problem, but Palestine was needed to solve the spiritual problem of Judaism. "In the Dispersion," he wrote, "we can and must aim at the preservation of Judaism, at the adaptation of Judaism, but we scarcely dare hope for a creative Judaism."[48]

Yet, of course, Friedlaender and his associates did hope for a creative Judaism in America, and by 1911, many signs were pointing to future triumph. Magnes had reached the peak of his influence through the *Kehillah* and its bureau of Jewish education, its crime-fighting apparatus, its rabbinical board, and its initial successes in labor arbitration. The *Kehillah* appeared to be on the verge of doing the impossible, namely, bringing all of the diverse and antagonistic elements of New York Jewry into a single institutional framework and a posture of cooperation. Yet under the surface of this success lay fissures that would soon shatter Magnes's fragile efforts at community construction.[49] Similarly, in 1911, the American Jewish Committee, with which the *Kehillah* was allied and which included Zionists and Orthodox East European Jews on its governing committee, scored its most dramatic success to date in lobbying for the abrogation of the Russian-American commercial treaty. A second legislative triumph was pending: the passage of the New York Civil Rights Act prohibiting discriminatory resort advertising.[50] But overshadowing these significant gestures by federal and state governments loomed the Dillingham Commission report on immigration to the United States with its invidious characterization of "new" immigrants (including Jews) as opposed to "old" ones, and its recommendations of restriction.[51]

Signs of future conflict surfaced as well among the religious organizations in New York City. In 1911, taking a step toward denominationalism and away from consensus, Schechter began to consider fortifying the Seminary with an expanded organizational structure. He broke off his relationship with the Educational Alliance, one of the potential model local Jewish centers, and turned instead to proposals for a congregational union that would culminate in the United Synagogue in 1913.[52] Schechter also increasingly viewed the *Kehillah's* bureau of Jewish education as a competitor which diverted funds from the Seminary, while experiments in popular elementary Jewish education appeared to threaten the chance of building the great institution of higher Jewish learning in America which Schechter envisioned.[53] The broad ideological program for developing a new American Judaism in the great new American Jewish center lacked the strength to overcome intramural rivalries, once the initial goal of legitimacy and leadership vis-a-vis the old establishment had been achieved. Efforts to provide intellectual coherence by the Ahvah Club proved fruitless, and in 1912, it disappeared from the New York scene.

Among the Zionists, changes in the leadership of the Federation of American Zionists foreshadowed renewed conflict between the political Zionists and the cultural Zionists.[54] National Judaism no longer seemed to be a sufficient banner around which to rally. With the growing prominence of New York City as the new heart of American Israel, the New York beneficiaries turned increasingly to their disparate organizational concerns rather than to the common cause that might unite them. Having won temporarily the battle for consensus, Jewish leaders girded themselves for the next round of combat.

The conflict came perhaps more quickly than anyone had anticipated, and it came in varied forms. In 1913, B'nai B'rith bid to regain its place as the leading American Jewish organization by founding the Anti-Defamation League in opposition to the American Jewish Committee.[55] In 1914, the movement for an American Jewish Congress attracted widespread support among the Jewish masses and its rhetoric of American Jewish democracy endangered the growing moral authority of national Judaism, for, by definition, its ideology embraced purely secular organizations and movements.[56] Finally, in 1917, the elaboration of a New York Jewish philanthropic network provided a secular communal alternative to the *Kehillah's* religious community. Yet the Federation provided only minimal support for Jewish education, one of the central concerns of the *Kehillah*.[57]

With the outbreak of World War I, the ideological consensus that sustained the new American Judaism suffered further erosion as the easy equation of Judaism and Americanism, religion and nationalism, and America and Zion fell apart. In a world at war where nationalism demanded 100 percent Americanism, even Friedlaender's genius for conciliation failed him. Writing in 1915 on the crisis in American Jewry, he prophesied that

> the interaction of the heterogeneous elements of American Jewish life would resolve itself in a great and strong harmony. America bade fair to become an ideal Jewish center, where the practical wisdom of an emancipated Jewry and idealistic intensity of Ghetto Jewry would be merged in one united community, fully conscious of its duty as the future leader of the Jewish Diaspora, and acknowledging its indebtedness to the center of all Jewry in the Land of our Fathers.

Yet he went on, opposing groups fighting over the issue of an American Jewish Congress threatened to wreck "what promises to become the greatest Jewish center in the history of the Jews since their dispersion." In his anguished analysis of the situation, Friedlaender called on Zionism to be neutral, to include all Jews, and not to degenerate into a movement exclusively of the masses. As the "driving force" in American Jewish life, Zionists nonetheless needed their "backbone" of support, the non-Zionists, for both had a common enemy — assimilation. In the battle against this foe, insisted Friedlaender, there should be room for all who work for the preservation of Judaism.[58]

But Friedlaender's evocation of the old common foe scarcely muted New York Jewry's civil war. Only the pressure of external events, especially the war, eventually forced the combatants to compromise. While the dream of American Jewish hegemony was salvaged through worldwide philanthropy, it would take longer for American Jews to reclaim the vision of a consensual new American Judaism that might serve as the "common ground of all American Israel."[59]

Figure 5. Ch.N. Bialik and Ahad Ha-Am with H.M. Ben Ammi and J.H. Ravnitzky, Tel Aviv, 1926. (*Courtesy of the Central Zionist Archives*)

4

Between
"Priest and Prophet"

ARTHUR A. GOREN

At first sight, the twists and turns in Judah Magnes's varied and stormy career make it difficult to find a unifying theme for his public life. Louis Marshall, Stephen Wise, Louis Brandeis, and Chaim Weizmann — whose paths and swords he crossed — practiced well-defined vocations which they effectively combined with their communal callings. Marshall's experience as a lawyer and civic activist shaped the role he played as spokesman of the German Jewish elite and defender of Jewish rights. Brandeis's standing in American political affairs and his role as a corporation lawyer turned "people's attorney" helped catapult him into prominence as the champion of Jewish mass organization and the advocate of democracy in Jewish life. Stephen Wise turned the rabbinate into a vehicle to national Jewish prominence, his image as rabbi in Israel clothing him with the moral authority which he used so effectively in his public endeavors. Weizmann's international reputation as a scientist gave the Jew from Motl the impeccable credentials of a new type of modern leader, the antithesis of the *luft-mensch*, that equipped him to deal with world leaders. All four earned their livelihoods from their professions. When rebuffed or defeated in public life, they were able to retreat to their professional callings.

By contrast, Magnes did not pursue a clearly defined vocation. Trained as a reformed rabbi, between 1904 and 1912 he held three pulpits, leaving each in turn in a storm of controversy. During the next ten years, he served in a score of communal capacities. The position he held longest, however, was an elected one as chairman of the New York *Kehillah*, an organization that was moribund by 1918.[1]

A closer look at Magnes's American years adds weight to these first impressions of a career that lacked a base. An entrepreneur of good works, he launched movements, programs, and institutions, shifting restlessly from one to another: the Jewish Defense Association in 1905, a proposal for a Jewish congress in 1906, the Society for Jewish Art in 1907, a Yiddish art theater in 1908, the Ahvah CLub (an exclusive society of Jewish intellectuals) in 1909, the Society for the Advancement of Judaism in 1912, a "reputable" new Yiddish daily, *Der Tog*, in 1914, which soon slipped out of his control, and the "Group" — a replica of Ahvah — in 1920. In 1916, in the midst of all of these activities, Magnes asked Jacob Schiff to fund a Foundation for the Advancement of the Jewish Spirit, suggesting the Rockefeller Foundation as a model. Beginning in 1917, a score of radical and pacifist causes as well absorbed his energies.[2]

His more substantial contributions to American Jewish life also reflected the same breadth of Jewish interests, audacity, and lack of organizational tenacity. For a brief season, Magnes was a center of ferment and agitation on the Jewish religious scene. At Temple Emanu-El, he called for a reconstruction of Reform Judaism while simultaneously mulling over plans to launch a people's synagogue movement. Then, briefly, before abandoning the rabbinate, he poured his energy into the emerging organization of Conservative Judaism. More impressive was the imprint he left on American Zionism. Vaulting to the leadership of the movement on the wings of his oratory, he set out to recast Zionism in a popular American mold. During his three years as honorary secretary and virtual head of the movement, he changed its direction by emphasizing the cultural aspect of Zionism, supporting practical work in Palestine, and calling for a Zionist fraternal order. But before he had consolidated his position, Magnes moved on to the *Kehillah* experiment. In conception, and in some measure in execution, his direction of the *Kehillah* was a communal entrepreneurship of a brilliant order. During the early, promising years, the *Kehillah* lifted Magnes to the peak of his influence. But, as he admitted himself, when the United States entered the war, a new cause — pacifism — absorbed his best energies and proved to be the death-knell of the *Kehillah*. During these years, Magnes also filled key positions in the newly established American Jewish Committee and the Joint Distribution Committee. Many years later, Louis Lipsky, Magnes's old rival, proffered an explanation: "Magnes could not be kept down to routine. He was greatly excited by life. He liked to be free and to change his music." Solomon Schechter put it more pungently: "Magnes has to have a movement every day."[3]

In considering the peculiar configuration of Magnes's public career, one must account particularly for the pivotal turn in his life which made him a maverick among twentieth century Jewish leaders: his decision in 1917 to abandon the consensual leadership he uniquely enjoyed for some years for the dissenter's role. In 1917, the founder of the Jewish Defense Association became the preacher of radical pacifism; the favorite of bankers Jacob Schiff and Felix Warburg entered the lists in defense of Soviet Russia, Eugene Debs, and Tom Mooney; and the brilliant Zionist orator of an earlier day attacked the Balfour Declaration as an imperialist ploy. Later, after eschewing controversy in his new position as the first chancellor of the Hebrew University, Magnes emerged once more as a preacher on the unpopular and perhaps impractical political theme of a Zion to be redeemed in justice for all, and became, in the eyes of many, a saboteur of the Zionist cause.[4]

If Magnes "liked to be free and to change his music," one, nevertheless, finds coherence and an inner consistency in his life. Magnes, to the end, essentially remained a rabbi in the tradition of American Reform Judaism. During his formative years, from the time he arrived at Hebrew Union College at age seventeen, to his return to America after completing his post-graduate studies in Germany at age twenty-five, Magnes made a major commitment to a rabbinical career. But more important, in Cincinnati he imbibed the notion of the rabbi as a bearer and interpreter of prophetic Judaism, no less than as pastor, pillar, and builder of a congregation. Converted to Zionism in Berlin, he envisaged the broader possibilities of the rabbi as communal leader in the service of a great cause whose prestige and skills would enable him to become a mobilizer of political power. Merging the two roles of preacher and social activist he mirrored the Social Gospel in American Protestantism, a movement to which young Reform rabbis responded with alacrity. A third component reinforced this synthesis: the influence of Ahad Ha-Am, in whose person Magnes found a model to emulate and in whose writings Magnes discovered a credo for prophetic leadership. By 1917, Magnes was transformed from a progressive *shtot rov* (town rabbi) to a protester and admonisher who was shaped by these three strands: Reform Judaism (Cincinnati), Zionism (Berlin), and prophetic leadership (Ahad Ha-Am). In large measure they explain the pattern of his public life.

When Magnes arrived in Cincinnati in 1894 to begin his studies at Hebrew Union College, his aspirations were undoubtedly pitched far higher than his peers. The college drew most of its students from poor families in small midwestern cities who were enticed by the award of free tuition and living expenses. For most of them, the opportunity to earn a bachelor's degree at the University of Cincinnati concurrently with studies at the College held out the prospect of a profession and a modest livelihood as rabbi of a small congregation. Magnes had other choices. He could have attended the University of California, a street-car ride away from his home in Oakland. Moreover, the rabbinate for Magnes was not simply a poor boy's path to respectability. He nursed higher aspirations. Although his father was a struggling dry goods merchant, Magnes's maternal uncle, Julius Abrahamson, served as president of Oakland's First Hebrew Congregation and was a partner in one of the city's large department stores. Jacob Voorsanger, rabbi of San Francisco's Temple Emanu-El, the leading Reform congregation in the West, had taken a special interest in the youngster, tutored him in Talmud, urged him to study for the ministry, and subsequently aided him in many ways. His mother, especially, looked upon service by her son in a prestigious pulpit with great favor.[5]

By the 1890s, an American rabbinical elite existed to which a talented, ambitious, and proud young man could aspire. Renowned representatives of this select group were the venerable Isaac Mayer Wise, president of the college, practicing rabbi, and publisher of the *American Israelite*; Emil G. Hirsch, rabbi of Chicago's Sinai Congregation, editor of the *Reform Advocate*, and professor of Rabbinic Literature at the University of Chicago; and, of course, Voorsanger himself, who in addition to serving in the pulpit, served as the first professor of Semitic Languages at the University of California and published the weekly *Emanu-El*.[6] Each assumed the multiple roles of preacher, pastor, scholar, publicist, communal leader, and social activist. The source of their standing and influence remained, however, their rabbinical position as ministers to wealthy patrician congregations.

Upon his graduation in 1900, Magnes took a critical step to prepare himself for this elite rabbinate. Encouraged by Voorsanger and his teachers at the college, he left for Berlin to pursue post-graduate work at the Lehranstalt für Wissenschaft des Judentums (better known as the Hochschule), the renowned institute for advanced Jewish studies, and to earn a doctoral degree at a German university. In the winter of 1902, Magnes returned to the United States with a Heidelberg Ph.D. in Semitics, the aura of having studied at the Hochschule, and a new Jewish Weltanschauung, Zionism.[7]

The Zionism he discovered in Berlin — "it is my *Lebensprogramm*," he remarked — profoundly influenced his conception of the rabbinate: "I no longer picture myself a liberal preacher whose chief duty is to preach goodness and to minister tenderly to a congregation of wealthy Jews," he informed his parents in a heated reply to their fears that his Zionism would jeopardize his career. "My Zionism," he explained, "makes me more than a preacher or community leader. It makes me a worker for the preservation of the Jewish people as a whole and for their greater glory and better life in their own land. It makes me a politician." In another unpublished letter, he described the scorn he felt for "the pastors, priests, ministers, and preachers" who "draw pay for their being religious and for their being moral." What enabled him to compromise himself and accept the paid position of rabbi — there were financial and moral debts owed to those who had supported his studies — was "my conception of Judaism, my nationalism." He would enter the pulpit "not as a conductor of services, but as a student and worker for the reviving of a Jewish culture." In 1904, when he agreed to be rabbi of Temple Israel, the foremost Reform congregation in Brooklyn, New York, he set two conditions: freedom of the pulpit to preach his message of Jewish cultural revival, and the opportunity to work with the Jewish immigrants, the yet unsullied bearers of an authentic Judaism.[8]

This was, of course, his Berlin program which accorded not only with his view of the rabbi as communal leader but with his understanding of Reform Judaism as well. He subscribed no less than did the Cincinnati Reformers to the notion of Judaism's universal message. Israel was "the servant bringing mankind closer to its idea of brotherhood and righteousness," and its dispersion among the nations was providential. Indeed, the concept "prophetic Judaism" popularized by the Reformers resonates throughout his personal writings, for his quarrel was not with "Reform Judaism" but with "ossified Reform Judaism," the consequence of assimilation and denationalization that would be reversed by a Jewish renaissance and a renewal of the spirit. "The basic element of every theory of Jewish life is the continued existence of the Jews," wrote Magnes, and Zionism was the best guarantee of survival. Magnes would support any undertaking or movement which contributed to this end.[9] For them, group survival and cultural revival were religious as well as national imperatives.

As a rabbi, his task then was to teach and exhort not only his own congregation, but the entire congregation of Israel. Concurrently, his ecumenical approach enabled him to serve a large variety of Jewish causes, many essentially secular and political. The high rabbinical standing associated with his Emanu-El post clothed him with the authority and prestige that enhanced his effectiveness beyond the temple, but ironically, within it, brought him little sympathy for his larger aspirations or for his hopes to revitalize the congregation. Beginning in 1912, Magnes devoted himself solely to the wider pulpit of the *Kehillah* that he had created three years earlier.[10]

Nevertheless, on resigning from B'nai Jeshurun in 1912, the last pulpit he filled, Magnes and his supporters found it desirable to create for him a surrogate congregation of sorts, the Society for the Advancement of Judaism, which paid him a salary and met annually to be addressed by him. On its establishment, Magnes informed the public: "With the aid of several men of this city, I shall have the opportunity of devoting myself to those problems of Jewish religious organization and Jewish education, without being attached to any particular synagogue. A society for the advancement of Judaism has been formed, and I expect through this society to be given complete freedom and added energy to devote myself to Jewish work in this city." In fact, as Schechter put it caustically, Magnes was "rabbi-at-large," and New York was his congregation.[11]

New York's "rabbi-at-large" occupied an anomalous position. Scoffers called him chief rabbi of the Lower East Side, while Orthodox malcontents described him as the Cincinnati seminarian without whiskers who tried to control *kashrut* and the Talmud Torahs. However, the Reform rabbi did bring together demoralized Orthodox rabbis in an attempt to stem the erosion of rabbinical authority. He also gave advice and support to those who came to him seeking encouragement and help in establishing the Young Israel movement. But Magnes's greatest commitment — anchored in the *Lebensprogramm* that he embraced in Berlin — was to the creation of a modern Jewish educational system to ensure the spiritual and cultural uplift of American Judaism.[12]

Early in Magnes's career, the boundaries between the preacher and the political leader had become blurred. Addressing Jewish radicals at meetings of the Jewish Defense Association and American radicals fifteen years later at meetings of the People's Council and Civil Liberties Union, Magnes appeared in the dual capacity of political activist and Jewish minister. In this respect he resembled the social gospel ministers, who in the late nineteenth and twentieth centuries insisted on applying Christian teachings to social problems and who refused to recognize a wall between religion and politics. In a burst of optimism and righteous wrath, liberal Protestant clergymen sought to wed morality and power. In 1917, when Magnes joined the pacifists, he forged intimate ties with the radical wing of the social gospel movement. He not only shared antiwar platforms with Norman Thomas,

John Haynes Holmes, Hollingsworth Wood, John Sayre, and others, fought with them for civil rights, and preached anti-imperialism, but shared as well, a close affinity with them as ministers of religion. Norman Thomas recalled how members of the American Union Against Militarism were overjoyed when Magnes joined them, enabling the Union to continue to have a leading rabbi among its spokesmen, for he replaced Stephen Wise, who in supporting America's entry into the war had become a renegade to the cause. But it went beyond that. Thomas, an important figure in the Fellowship of Reconciliation, the radical Christian peace group, invited Magnes to its meetings, and on one occasion suggested that Magnes organize a concurrent Jewish group to affiliate with the Fellowship. On another, after informing Magnes of a forthcoming meeting of the Fellowship where the idea of God in the modern world would be discussed, Thomas added in a postscript — "more close to your theology than I am to my friends."[13]

In his sympathy for the social gospel movement, Magnes resembled Stephen Wise, who followed a strikingly similar path. Until 1917, Magnes directed his energies on behalf of social and cultural change inward to the Jewish community, while Wise was active mainly on the larger American scene, winning attention by his involvement in one social reform cause after another. First Magnes and then Wise rose to prominence through their wide-ranging public activities to become the model for the twentieth century American rabbi as national leader. For Magnes, however, the brilliant, tumultuous early years ended abruptly. The dual function of the rabbi as moral guide and political leader generated tensions that impelled him to take up the mantle of the protester, albeit a protester of a special kind — unaffiliated with party, group, or sect. The American milieu only partially explains the sources and complexion of Magnes's nonconformism. Unlike Wise, another influence, in the person and teachings of Ahad Ha-Am had also captured Magnes's imagination and was guiding his behavior, and informing his thinking.[14] Ahad Ha-Am's ideas not only informed Magnes's thinking, but they influenced and sanctioned his public behavior. Scholars, most notably Evyatar Friesel, have examined the impact of Ahad Ha-Am on the circle of cultural Zionists to which Magnes belonged. Friesel has pointed out that on such cardinal questions as the interaction of religion and Jewish nationalism and the attitude toward the diaspora, the American cultural Zionists acknowledged him as their mentor but, unlike the secular and pessimistic Ahad Ha-Am, they considered the link between Judaism and Zionism as fundamental and believed also in the viability of the American Diaspora.[15]

While these questions are significant in their own right, another

aspect of Ahad Ha-Am's influence is more pertinent to our understanding of Magnes. It is sufficient to consider Ahad Ha-Am's two best
known essays to perceive his full import for Magnes. In "Priest and
Prophet," published in 1893, and in "Moses," an elaboration of the
first essay, published in 1904, Ahad Ha-Am explicated the centrality
of the prophetic tradition in Judaism as he understood it. "The fundamental idea of the Hebrew Prophet was the universal dominion of
absolute justice," he proclaimed in "Priest and Prophet." And farther
along, he wrote,

> These prophets of Righteousness transcended in spirit political and
> national boundaries and preached the gospel of justice and charity for
> the whole human race . . . . Their national ideal was not a 'kingdom
> of priests,' but, 'would that all the people of the Lord were prophets.'
> They wished the whole people to be a primal force, a force making for
> Righteousness, in the general life of humanity, just as they were
> themselves in its own particular national life.[16]

And in "Moses," he declared:

> The Prophet has two fundamental qualities which distinguish him
> from the rest of mankind. First, he is a *man of truth*. He sees life as it
> is with a view unwarped by subjective feelings; and he tells you what
> he sees just as he sees it; unaffected by irrelevant considerations. He
> tells the truth not because he wishes to tell the truth, not because he
> has convinced himself after inquiry that such is his duty, but because
> he needs must, because truth-telling is a special characteristic of his
> genius — a characteristic of which he cannot rid himself even if he
> would.
>   Secondly, the Prophet is an *extremist*. He concentrates his whole
> heart and mind on his ideal in which he finds the goal of his life and
> to which he is determined to make the whole world do service without
> the smallest exception. There is in his soul a complete, ideal world; and
> on that pattern he labors to reform the external world of reality.[17]

In the personal journals of Magnes, one repeatedly encounters the
agony and the agitation of an earnest man seeking to translate those
prophetic ideals into political realities, in Ahad Ha-Am's analysis an
impossible task, for the prophet cannot reform the world according to
his desires, nor can he delude himself by shutting his eyes to its
defects. In Ahad Ha-Am's paradigm, the priest's task is to confront
reality, to mediate between contending forces, and to transmit the prophetic ideal as best he can to a recalcitrant people. Of necessity, he
must compromise.

Priest or prophet, communal functionary or charismatic leader, salaried official or preacher beholden to no one, statesman or dissenter — these were the choices Magnes struggled with throughout his life and never resolved. Moving from one to the other, he ever sought to combine them somehow. In one journal entry, after listing the ways one might strive for social justice, he concluded that gradual reform supported by government or revolutionary upheaval were both corrupting. Yet, one must act — "I do not want to be condemned to quietism. More, I *will* not be."[18]

No mere juxtaposition of Ahad Ha-Am's strictures with Magnes's behavior can explain Ahad Ha-Am's effect on Magnes. One must also recall that Ahad Ha-Am remained an aloof and Olympian figure in the Jewish world, refusing to join party or faction for fear of compromising his freedom. His moral authority stemmed precisely from his distance from the tacticians and intriguers who peopled the organization executives and the congresses. *Lo zo ha-derech*, this is not the way, is the echo, if not the voice of the prophet. Magnes was a witness who became a disciple. When he resigned from the Provisional Zionist Council in 1915, he turned to Ahad Ha-Am for advice, and took his first long step towards his new role, begging Ahad Ha-Am to vindicate his break with the movement. He charged the American Zionist leadership with a bid for power that was destroying American Jewish unity and sacrificing Zionism's authentic goals. Central to his accusation was the moral question raised by the movement's political goal. "In the Zionist sense, the war cannot give Palestine to the Jews," he wrote to Brandeis in his letter of resignation. Jews could expect only free immigration and equal rights with the other occupants of the land — an equal opportunity to build the land, but no more, he insisted. Again in 1917 and in 1920 at a time when Ahad Ha-Am was moving in a similar direction, Magnes wondered whether it was possible to make "short shrift of the principle of self-determination whenever it suits the needs of the conqueror."[19]

For Magnes, the prophetic creed was a universal one, and he saw it as his duty to cry out against the injustices of war and imperialism. Indeed it was his Jewish duty to do so, and, even more, as a rabbi, it was doubly incumbent upon him. In biting mockery he derided the leaders of Reform Judaism — formulators of the spiritual mission of the Jews to the nations — who in the midst of the bloodletting held their peace. Only in the antiwar sentiments of the Lower East Side did he find the authentic Jewish voice, blending the universal and the particular so that out of the Jewish historical experience there arose a spontaneous pacifist and radical cry for justice, a cry which transcended the boundaries of the Jewish people. Defending himself in a letter to Mayer Sulzberger in October 1917 against accusations that his pacifist militancy fomented anti-Semitism, he wrote:

This is not the first time that the Jews have been threatened with, or have had to suffer from, anti-Semitism because of their convictions. That the anti-militarist outburst on the part of the Jewish masses and in their elemental passion for peace is a conviction, or at any rate, the outcome of the Jewish tradition, you will admit. I regard it as one of the glories of Jewish life that the Jewish masses have expressed themselves as they have. It is a justification of the Jewish religion. It saves Judaism from the bankruptcy which has overtaken Christianity. It distinguishes the Jewish prophetic nationalism from the heathen nationalism of the Christian nations. It shows the Jews to be the true international people, made so by their very national tradition. That I have been able to express some of this, however weakly, is a privilege of which I am hardly worthy. I have never felt myself so much at one with the Jewish people, and with the Jewish religion.[20]

Contempories early sensed the dilemma and even the tragedy of Magnes as prophetic leader. A week before he sailed for Palestine with his family, in May 1922, Mordecai Kaplan recorded in his diary the impressions that a farewell dinner for Magnes made upon him:

The gathering presented a sobering contrast to those that used to take place in [Israel] Unterberg's house seven, eight, and nine years ago when Magnes was in the prime of his glory, when he was the cynosure of all who had been hoping that he would bring order out of the chaos of Jewish life. Is this anticlimax in his career evidence of his inability to lead or Jewry's inability to be made to function normally? Here is how he diagnosed his own case: 'Despite the numerous friends it has been my privilege to win I have felt lonely. My friends who are identified with Jewish religious activity could not sympathize with my yearning for freedom to express my passionate desire for righteousness and peace. My radical friends failed to see why I loved Jewish traditions, Jewish history, and the Jewish land with a consuming intensity. At one time I contemplated establishing a platform where totally unattached to any organization, I could express myself freely. But it is in order to refrain from carrying out that purpose that I am leaving, for I know that I might have in that way saved my own soul, but I would have said things that might have hurt or might have prejudiced the cause of the Jewish community' . . . . He possesses traits which in another age might have led to his gathering about him a band of ardent disciples and he would have gone down in history as a Jewish seer . . . . The only way to be effective as a prophet nowadays . . . is to suffer martyrdom, like the Sinn Feines [sic], IWW leaders, and the pacifists who are languishing in the prisons years after the armistice has been concluded. But to have Warburg praise you as a delightful fellow, and to be in a position to throw off all responsibilities and go travelling and observing the world is not compatible with the martyrdom that we usually expect from the prophets.[21]

Nevertheless, he did gather about him, if not in America, then in Jerusalem, a small band of admirers — Hugo Bergman, Gershom Scholem, Ernst Simon, Martin Buber, Gavriel Stern, and others. Observing the courage of this innocent American as he challenged the realpolitik of the establishment, these German intellectuals, the products of an Old World skepticism, were moved to join him in the effort to reconcile ethical ideals with political activism.[22]

Neither priest nor prophet, Magnes lived with the dilemmas and stresses that Ahad Ha-Am had delineated in his analysis of the two archetypical models of Jewish leadership. During the last twenty years of his life while serving as chancellor and president of the Hebrew University, he expressed his predicament almost daily in what was at once a symbolic gesture and a homily. Upon greeting the frequent visitors to the university in his office on the roof of the library, he would point out and explain the sites to his guests as they gazed at the panorama below. To the south was the Temple Mount where the priests had conducted the temple service in the presence of thousands of pilgrims, and to the north, just beyond the ridge of Scopus, was the Arab town of Anatot, the birthplace of Jeremiah. On the one hand, the eye was moved by the splendor and power of the establishment, and on the other by the humble village of the prophet.[23] Suspended between the two, in the midst of his university, stood Magnes with his guests. Built with stone and mortar, peopled with officials, scholars, and students, it was all made possible by compromise and sometimes by unsavory politics. A teacher, preacher, and organizer — and often a dissenter in Zion — at the Hebrew University he had built a spiritual center for the Jewish people and also, at last, the free pulpit to which he had always aspired.

Figure 6. Magnes, Max Schloessinger, Harry Friedenwald and other members of the Federation of American Zionists, Tannersville, New York. c. 1905. (*Courtesy of the Jewish National and University Library*)

5

Magnes:
Zionism in Judaism

EVYATAR FRIESEL

Judah L. Magnes's ideas on Zionism were elaborated mainly during the years before World War I when he was living and working in New York City. True, he had already become a Zionist before moving to New York, and his experiences during World War I and his life in Palestine after 1922, added an extra dimension to his ideas in general, and to his Zionism as well. But the New York years were the most creative and successful ones in Magnes's life, and they should be considered the most important years for the development of his thinking about Zionism. Even when new features later were added, we shall see that his outlook did not basically change.

Magnes's first Zionist stirrings came early. In 1896, one year before the first Zionist Congress, when he was still a rabbinical student at the Hebrew Union College in Cincinnati, his article "Palestine — or Death" incorporated many Zionist ingredients. Where the San Francisco lad had picked them up remains a matter for speculation.[1]

Upon graduation in 1900, he went to Germany to pursue his doctoral studies. Although he registered at the University of Heidelberg, he spent most of his time in Berlin where he attended the Hochschule, the well-known liberal rabbinical seminary.

At the beginning of the twentieth century, Berlin was the foremost intellectual center of West European Jewry and a powerful magnet for Jewish immigrants from the East, from Posen, Poland, and Russia. At the time Magnes arrived, Berlin, with more than one hundred thousand Jews, was a throbbing center of many different Jewish ideas and influences. Most notably, it was the center of the German Zionist movement, which meant that then, as later, it was the center of Zionism in Western Europe. Given its heterogenous Jewish population, its high proportion of Jewish immigrants, its role as a meeting place between East and West, and its highly animated Jewish life, Berlin, in many ways, resembled another city that Magnes would later come to love — New York.

Berlin also was one of the important European centers for Jewish students who had been denied admission to Russian universities because of the *numerus clausus* (quotas for Jewish students) in effect there. The Jewish student colony was a hotbed of ideologies, especially of Zionism and socialism. During the years before World War I, a whole generation of Zionist leaders was bred in the German student organizations.

It was almost inevitable that Magnes would be absorbed into so stimulating a milieu. He attached himself to a congenial group of students at the Hochschule, and it was there that he became a Zionist.[2] Overwhelmed by his new beliefs, Magnes felt that a new world of ideas had opened before him. In October 1901 he wrote to his family:

> I can simply describe [Zionism] by saying that it is now my whole philosophy. It is my *Lebensprogramm*, and to stick it in a corner would be the same as sticking myself in a corner. Since I have become a Zionist, my view of life has changed; my view as to my calling has changed; my view as to my future has changed; my hopes, my prayers have changed.[3]

In October 1901, together with a group of his fellow students, among them Arthur Biram, Emil Cohn, Max Schloessinger, Eugen Taeubler, Isidor Zlocisti, and Gotthold Weil, who later would become well known in Zionist and Jewish circles, Magnes formed a Zionist society called the "Jewish-National Society of Students at the Hochschule in Berlin," better known by its briefer Hebrew name, *Aguda Le-umit*. Max Schloessinger was elected president. The Society was the main organizational forum for Zionist activities. In his memoirs, Gotthold Weil tells us that Magnes kept away from the German Zionist Federation and from the other large Jewish student organizations then active at the University of Berlin. His correspondence of that period shows intensive thinking about the questions of modern Jewish life, considered from a Zionist perspective. Yet his Zionism was still general and unelaborated.[4]

At the beginning of 1903, after Magnes returned to the United States and accepted a position at the Hebrew Union College, he resumed his Zionist activities despite the militant anti-Zionism of the new head of the college.[5] When, early in 1904, an opportunity presented itself to fill a pulpit in Brooklyn, he gladly accepted, and in September settled in New York.[6]

There Magnes leaped eagerly into the ebullient Jewish life and quickly established relations with Jewish activists and intellectuals of virtually every shade of thought and orientation. In June 1905, he was elected secretary of the Federation of American Zionists, the central organization binding together most of the Zionist societies in the United States that had been founded in 1898. In 1904, the Federation, led up to then by Richard Gottheil and Jacob de Haas, both good friends and faithful followers of Theodor Herzl, began to undergo a change in leadership. After Herzl's death, in June 1904, Gottheil left the presidency of the Federation, and Harry Friedenwald, a well-known opthalmologist from Baltimore, was elected president. Since Friedenwald lived in Baltimore, and the strong-minded de Haas continued to administer the Federation in New York, nothing much changed. In 1905, de Haas decided to lay down the secretaryship of the Federation, and Magnes was elected secretary, a position he was to hold until 1908. Magnes's election completed the transition: a new Zionist group had established itself at the head of the Federation, a group whose members would introduce significant changes in American Zionism, especially on the ideological level.

Jacob de Haas, the outgoing secretary of the Federation, had been a difficult personality to deal with, but he was certainly an outstanding administrator. Furthermore, he had fulfilled his position as a professional (together with the editorship of *The Maccabean*, the official organ of the Federation of the American Zionists), while Magnes was only honorary secretary, and his position in the Federation was only one of his fields of activity. To continue de Haas's level of work was, from a purely administrative point of view, a difficult challenge. Nevertheless, the Federation was well administered during Magnes's secretaryship. On the other hand, Magnes brought with him assets that were unique. During the next three years he became a well-known public figure among New York Jews. He developed close contacts with the Jewish socialists, who were a major force on the Lower East Side. In 1906, he was appointed associate rabbi of Temple Emanu-El, the most important Reform congregation in the United States. In 1908, he strengthened his ties with the German-Jewish establishment when he married Beatrice Lowenstein, Louis Marshall's sister-in-law. They were married by Solomon Schechter, the head of the Jewish Theological Seminary, a man who exerted a deep influence on Magnes. Indeed, the group of Jewish intellectuals connected with the

Seminary or gravitating about Schechter, formed another focal point, and a most important one, in Magnes's Jewish life.

Altogether, there was no one among the American Jewish leaders in New York, and certainly no one in the American Zionist movement, who maintained ties with so many different and often mutually antagonistic segments of the Jewish community. The new position he was to fill after 1909 as president of the *Kehillah* of New York City, would enhance even more his standing as an American Jewish leader. In spite of his relatively young age — Magnes was only twenty-nine years old in 1906 — until the appearance of Louis D. Brandeis on the Zionist scene in 1914, Magnes was the only figure of truly national standing in American Zionism.

As had been the case during de Haas's last year, the fact that Harry Friedenwald, the president of the Federation of American Zionists, lived in Baltimore left the secretary of the movement much latitude of action. Magnes not only administered the Federation of the American Zionists, but also formulated matters of Zionist policy that were very much at the center of attention in European Zionism. That also had been the situation in the past: a major crisis in the European movement like the Uganda Controversy, proposing a territory in East Africa for "Zionist" colonization, reverberated only faintly in the United States. The much mentioned observation that "America is Different," found here one of its baffling expressions, for if we examine the correspondence between Zionist central headquarters in Europe with the New York office of the Federation we become aware of a curious dissonance.

A typical example is found in the correspondence between Magnes and David Wolffsohn, the head of the World Zionist Organization from 1905. At Magnes's request, in late June 1906, Wolffsohn sent a congratulatory message to the ninth Annual Convention of the Federation of American Zionists, held in Tannersville, New York. In his letter, Wolffsohn also explained his policy, stressing heavily the "political" character of his administration.[7] Magnes replied as follows: "At the convention . . . we shall pass a resolution along the lines of your letter, namely: first, emphasizing the fact that our movement has been and must remain a political movement in the full sense of the term; and second, that we are in favor of immediate and intense activity in Palestine."[8] This was a most peculiar interpretation of Wolffsohn's letter, for Wolffsohn was the last man to advocate "immediate and intensive work in Palestine." But, Magnes went on: in spite of the importance of political action, there was little that American Zionists could do in such matters. On the other hand, ". . . all our strength lies in practical work in Palestine. We are of the opinion that such a thing would find an echo in the Jewish masses of this country."[9] In other words, Magnes was adopting the very opposite of the Wolffsohn administration's position, at least as far as the activity of the American movement was concerned. He was not alone in his attitude. Different leaders of the American Federation stressed during these years the necessity of practical work in Palestine, not as a principle of Zionist policy, but as an answer to the specific conditions of American Zionism.[10] The apparent incongruence between Wolffsohn's message and Magnes's response occurred again and again in their relations. It represented more than a problem of mutual understanding. It reflected the fact that each was working out of a different Jewish reality, and consequently formulating Zionist policy in different terms.

The Zionism Magnes brought back from Europe was still open, broad, and quite unencumbered by the ideological discussions going on in the European movement. Nevertheless, his inclinations were already clear. Like Ahad Ha-Am, Magnes from the very beginning showed a tendency to concentrate on the problems of Judaism, rather than on the problems of the Jews. Indeed, it seems clear that during his stay in Berlin, Magnes became acquainted with the ideas and writings of Ahad Ha-Am, and acknowledged him to be his master. Later, when back in the United States, he wrote about him and tried to open a correspondence with him.[11]

In New York, Magnes became a member of the sophisticated group of Jewish intellectuals gravitating about Solomon Schechter, the distinguished and colorful head of the Jewish Theological Seminary. All of them — Israel Friedlaender, Alexander Marx, Eliayahu Abraham Lubarsky, Louis Ginzberg, Max Schloessinger, Max Margolis, Henry Malter, and Henrietta Szold — were "cultural" Zionists, sympathetic to the view of Ahad Ha-Am.[12] Magnes already knew Schloessinger from Germany and Margolis and Malter from his Hebrew Union College days. Recognizing Magnes's rare gifts, they all welcomed him into their midst. Writing to Ahad Ha-Am in 1906, Lubarsky described Magnes as "our jewel, a child captured by the 'heathen' and saved from them by a miracle."[13]

Magnes's manifold interests would later also bring him into contact with other Jewish social and intellectual circles.[14] Nevertheless, the group around Schechter remained of special importance for him for two reasons: first, some of the members of that group — and Magnes among them — were undergoing a process of religious development that would lead them from Reform Judaism to what later would be called Conservative Judaism. Indeed, it may be said that Magnes was among the first American Jews to explore and move in the conservative direction,[15] although he still belonged to the Reform rabbinate. Second, it was among the members of that group that the new cultural Zionism was being elaborated during this first decade of the new century. Since Magnes was one of the outstanding exponents of cultural Zionism, it is important to analyze his thought in detail.

A careful examination of Magnes's ideas justifies the conclusion that his Zionism must be understood as one component in his larger conception of Jewish life, which also included the additional elements of Jewish nationalism and Jewish religion.

"Zionism is the name of the attempt on the part of the Jews to bring the Land of Israel into the center of Jewish life," was the definition, dating from 1911, which established the place of Zionism in Magnes's larger conception of Jewish life. To revitalize Jewish life, given the conditions and problems of modern society as understood by Magnes, was the principal aim of all his endeavors, and the Land of Israel was one of the means to attain it.[16]

In affirming his commitment to Zionism, Magnes also rejected a major postulate of European Zionist ideology, "the negation of the Galut," the Zionist idea that the Jewish diaspora had no future. In a letter to Chaim Weizmann in June 1914, he explained his position.

> The Despair theory of Zionism does not appeal to me. I have not despaired of the Jewish people, and I believe in its eternity even without Palestine. To me Palestine seems to be the cornerstone of this people, or the crown, the heart, the center, or whatever we may want to call it. The people will continue to live without Palestine, and continue to develop its total culture. With Palestine the people will live better and develop its total culture more hopefully and with more achievement. The entire people must be organized, in different forms, in different countries. Palestine should be the connecting link, the summit of organized [Jewish] life. The Jews of the world influence Palestine; Palestine influences the Jews of the world.[17]

Why Palestine? Because, he wrote in 1911, Palestine was

> ". . . the land of our origin, the land in which our Bible was produced, the land towards which our People has turned throughout its entire history. Here . . . Judaism may develop in its own atmosphere and upon its native soil. Here, at least, the Jews may be a majority and not as everywhere, a minority. Here they may be concentrated and not dispersed. Here they may have a territorial center with some degree of

political autonomy . . . . Here they may have a spiritual center, and the Judaism here developed may in many ways be authoritative for, and enrich the Judaism of, the Jews in other parts of the world.[18]

The other major component in Magnes's position was Jewish nationalism. Magnes defined himself as a Jewish nationalist, and the Jews as a people, a nation, but the concept as used by him, had clear delimitations: "Very often a nation is confused or made synonymous with a political state and with a continuous territory. But it is just this idea of nationality that we wish to combat from the beginning."[19] To explain his case, he cited the many examples of national groups without states, or who lived beyond the borders of their states, or states with no uniform national composition, and concluded "that the existence of nationality is by no means absolutely dependent upon political statehood."[20] All of which made it clear that the Jews, although without a territorial center, comprised a nationality. Among their national characteristics, Magnes pointed to race, since they intermarried mostly among themselves; to their two national languages, Hebrew and Yiddish; to a consciousness of their common history; to a common enemy, anti-Semitism; to a "national religion [that] was up to very recent days the great stay and support of Jewish nationality"; and, showing the influence of Ahad Ha-Am, to a specific Jewish culture that had developed inside and outside the synagogue. Last, but certainly not least, Magnes pointed to the most important of all the attributes of Jewish nationality, the "existence of the Jewish will to be a Nation," largely subconscious, but expressing itself in the many organized forms of Jewish life. "Every Jewish club, every Jewish society, every Jewish home is an expression of this will."[21] It therefore turned out that even the opponents of Jewish nationalism, like the very members of the Reform congregation before whom Magnes was delivering his sermon, were Jewish nationalists of a sort. In its more developed form, Jewish nationalism expressed itself in movements and ideologies, of which Zionism was the most radical.

There was an obvious interplay between Magnes's ideas on Jewish nationalism and his understanding of Jewish life in the United States. Magnes rejected the idea of the American "melting pot," as described by Israel Zangwill in his popular play for it implied a type of Americanization that would bring about the "de-judaization" of the Jews.[22] In the political sense, every American citizen owed loyalty to the United States, but not in the cultural sense. "In America, where the grouping of Jews politically has no place, it is primarily for religious and cultural purposes that the Jews are beginning to form themselves into organized communities."[23] At the same time, exhorted Magnes, each American must also "saturate himself with the dominant culture of the land, which is English. Our language is English, our history, our literature, our laws, our institutions, our ideals are almost entirely English." But why, then, should the Germans, the Irish, the Jews, and all the other national groups in America hold on to their original national culture, together and parallel with the dominant culture of the land? Because it was the natural thing to do, replied Magnes, and it was also necessary:

> The hiatus between the traditional national culture and the new surroundings is often so great that it leads to degeneracy of many kinds. The children of minority nationalities are all too often not the equals of their parents in those things that have permanent value, because the chain of tradition has been broken and the accumulated wisdom and beauty of ages is set at nought.[24]

Here Magnes was identifying with the advocates of "cultural pluralism," a concept subsequently elaborated by Horace M. Kallen, also a Jew and a Zionist, but already much-discussed in the United States during the first decade of the century.[25]

The third component of Magnes's conception was Jewish religion. Although religion was an indispensable element in his view of Jewish life, he recognized that modern conditions had led many Jews to lose their attachment to the Jewish religion, or that certain forms of Jewish religion had fallen into a state of "petrification."[26] Jewish cultural nationalism, therefore, may fill the void in Jewish consciousness arising from the weakened ties to religion among the younger generation of Jews.[27] "Zionism has given birth also to the idea of a Jewish Culture, . . . apart from religion, in the narrower, technical sense of this term . . . [which] has given many a Jew his place in Jewry."[28] But in the long run, insisted Magnes, the revitalization of religion was a major task of modern Jewry, intrinsically connected with the revitalization of Jewish national life in general, and a central theme in his Zionist credo:

> It is in the domain of religion itself that Zionism has exercised the greatest influence . . . . It is the experience of Zionism that once the Jew becomes loyal to Israel, he becomes a devotee of Israel's religion. His early ardour may be for the Jews alone; thus aroused, it strengthens into interest and affection for all things Jewish; increasing knowledge and intimacy lead inevitably to the climax — devotion to Jewish religion.[29]

Or, as he put it somewhat differently in a letter to Rabbi Joseph Stolz on May 23, 1909:

> I hope for new [religious] values in the future. That, too, is why I am a Zionist — because I believe the new values can best be created in a Jewish center — I think that there are thousands of American Jews like me at the present time — neither 'orthodox' nor 'reform,' but actively and intensely Jewish and ready for a form of religion and national Judaism that will be loyal to the past — its national and religious elements — and hopeful of the future.[30]

Magnes's ideas on Zionism were congruent with the cultural Zionism developing among members of the Jewish Theological Seminary group during the first decade of the twentieth century. Like others in that circle — Schechter, Friedlaender, and later, Mordecai M. Kaplan — Magnes considered himself a disciple of Ahad Ha-Am, although, like them, he too altered several elements in Ahad Ha-Am's formulation. Magnes's attitude towards Jewish life in the Diaspora was much more positive and intrinsically religious — while Ahad Ha-Am's was intrinsically secular. Almost all the American cultural Zionists, including Magnes, were either indifferent or unsympathetic to the possibility of future statehood in Palestine, while for Ahad Ha-Am it was never excluded in principle. The deep-felt revulsion against political means and aims that later characterized Magnes's position may have been reinforced by his type of cultural Zionism, although it mainly represented his own personal experiences during World War I, both in the United States and in Europe.[31] Later, when Magnes was living in Palestine, his distrust of political Zionism would influence his activities with regard to Jewish life in the country and to Jewish-Arab relations.

There were several differences between Magnes's position and that of his fellow American cultural Zionists. Solomon Schechter's Zionism was much more strictly dependent upon his religious beliefs, which again were much more traditionalist than Magnes's. The very mention of the idea of "Jewish nationalism" was enough to enrage Schechter.[32] Friedlaender's Zionism, on the other hand, was more America-inspired. His famous formula, "Zionism plus Diaspora, Palestine plus America," meant to him that in the American Diaspora there was a future for Jewry and Judaism, while in Europe this future had become a dubious proposition. Of the three, it was only the American-born Magnes who meant by "Diaspora" the European Diaspora as well, even if during these years his field of Jewish activity and interest lay in the United States.[33]

Last but not least, although similar to the other American cultural Zionists, Magnes, in his formulations, gave another aspect special weight: the issue of Diaspora-oriented activity. Israel Friedlaender, perhaps the profoundest thinker in the group, had stated ". . . that America is destined to become in the near future the leading Jewish center of the Diaspora, and that it is the duty of American Jewry to live up to the great obligation placed upon it by history."[34] Indeed, *all* the American cultural Zionists were active in many American Jewish enterprises. In spite of their declared Ahad Ha-Amism, the American cultural Zionists, without being quite aware of it, were close in their thinking to the historian Simon Dubnow's autonomistic conception of Jewish life, which stressed the centrality of the historic "Jewish centers" in the development of Jewish life.[35] Magnes, who apparently neither mentioned nor showed any awareness of Dubnow, expressed ideas which were virtually identical with Dubnow's:

> *Galut* is more than a geographic term. *Galut* means the bulk and body of the Jewish people . . . the suffering and striving and achievement of the Jewish people in the history of the last two thousand years, and try-ing to determine the part the Jewish people can play in the troubled life of the present day. Eretz Israel will have to be judged by whether or not it can help the Jewish people to do its work and determine its function in this larger world.[36]

His positive approach to Jewish life in the Diaspora found empha-tic expression in Magnes's Zionist activities. "It is due largely to the influence of Zionism that the Jews in various parts of the world are beginning to organize for the advancement of Judaism," he wrote in his essay, "What Zionism Has Given the Jews," in 1911. Magnes himself not only participated in almost every Jewish enterprise in New York City that asked for his help, but assumed that his Zionist beliefs ought actually to lead him to such activity. When, in 1908, he left the secretaryship of the Federation of American Zionists in order to dedicate himself to building up the *Kehillah* of New York City, his explanation, given at the annual convention of the Federation, was highly significant:

> I feel . . . that I shall be able to do more for our Federation and our movement if I am relieved of the duties which have been mine during the past three years. Our Zionism must mean for us Judaism in all of its phases. Zionism is a complete and harmonized Judaism. Nothing Jewish, whether it be the Jewish land, the Jewish language, the Jewish religion, the Jewish people, can be foreign to a Zionist. We may differ

in many of our views, but we are all agreed in our love of Jewish life and in our hopes for the redemption of the Jewish spirit. Zionism must use every legitimate means for the accomplishment of its end: the revival of the Jewish people, its spirit and its land.[37]

American cultural Zionism, of which Judah L. Magnes was so outstanding a spokesman, crystallized into a definite ideology during the years prior to World War I. It was not the only Zionist approach that developed in the United States in those days. Richard Gottheil and Jacob de Haas, the American Labor-Zionists, and Louis Lipsky — all contributed ideas to American Zionism that had their measure of interest and originality. And after 1914, Louis D. Brandeis and his followers again explained Zionism in America in their own way. The importance of the "cultural" approach advocated by Magnes, Friedlaender, Schechter, Kaplan, and others, was that more than any other position in American Zionism it withstood the acid test of time and of the fast-changing conditions of American Jewish communal life. Not only does their kind of cultural Zionism remain valid today for a large segment of American Jewry, but it has played a most significant role in the penetration of Zionist ideas — Zionist ideas according to their point of view — among all American Jews.

Since Magnes was active until the very establishment of the State of Israel, a summation of his position allows us to draw conclusions regarding the strengths and weaknesses of American cultural Zionism as a whole. Young Magnes, upon his Zionist awakening in Berlin in 1901, had declared that Zionism was his "life program." But later on his Zionism was transformed, not into an ideology in its own right, but into one of the elements of a larger conception of Jewish life, which included his ideas on Jewish cultural nationalism and on Jewish religion.

Judged in ideological terms alone, it seems that Zionism was actually the least important among the components of Magnes's conception of Jewishness, coming after religion and even after Jewish nationalism. But when evaluating his Zionism, one has to pay attention to the contradiction between his theory and his practice. The fact is that Magnes spent endless time and effort on Zionist issues, and he was one of the few leading American Zionists to actually settle in Palestine. Among the leaders of the American Zionist Federation, he and Henrietta Szold were the only ones to do so.

Nevertheless, in Magnes's conception, Zionism was only the means to an end, never an end in itself. Magnes never subscribed to any of the major goals of Zionist ideology, whether in the Diaspora or in Palestine. Regarding the Diaspora, he rejected the principle of "negation of the *galut*." As for Palestine, he was opposed to Jewish statehood. It is worth noting that in the 1940s and 1950s, these were also the postulates of Mordecai M. Kaplan, the last member of the original group of American cultural Zionists.[38]

The goal of Magnes's Jewish endeavors, that very general idea of the "revival of Jewish life," appeared to be related to the somber view of Ahad Ha-Am about the condition of the Jewish people, but in reality it was imbued with a quality of optimism which came from very different sources. One was rooted in the nineteenth century hopes regarding the future of Jewry, characteristic of Jewish society undergoing acculturation in the general environment. The other source was the positive outlook among American Jewish leaders about the future of the Jews in America that developed around the end of the nineteenth century and the beginning of the twentieth century. That optimism, an essential element in American cultural Zionism, encouraged Magnes and his friends to glide too easily over too many unanswered questions, like the future of the Jewish national culture they spoke about and the contradictory relationship between the American majority and the Jewish minority cultures, especially when considered in light of the assimilationist trends of second and third generation American Jews. In addition, Magnes and some of his colleagues saw nationalism in a way that was unrealistic, for it retained all of its glitter, but none of its vibrancy.

All this was understandable. It reflected the time, the place, and the conditions in which American cultural Zionism had arisen. But Magnes and his friends never revised their basic premises — or perhaps they were unable to do so — even when the darkening clouds on the horizon of Jewish existence made them less and less credible. In Magnes's case, his abhorrence of violence, his suspicion of everything political, and his untiring efforts in later years to bring about an Arab-Jewish understanding, gave his endeavors a personal character which should not obscure the fact that he was still acting along the broader ideological lines crystallized years before in the circle of Solomon Schechter. The impact of life in Palestine, after 1922, did not change Magnes's basic thinking. From the 1920s through the 1940s, in lectures, letters, and discussions, he held to the ideas adopted decades earlier.[39]

Whether looking at the Jews as a group in their own terms or considering them as a living entity in relation to other groups, the American cultural Zionists, and Magnes outstandingly among them, were unwilling, or perhaps unable, to overcome the conceptual barrier that led logically to Jewish political independence. Magnes had written in 1911 that "the main contribution of Zionism to the modern Jews is the conception of the Jews as a people." There is reason to doubt that he ever drew the ultimate conclusion to his definition of peoplehood in the light of the ideologies and the realities of the twentieth century.

III
The First American Zionists

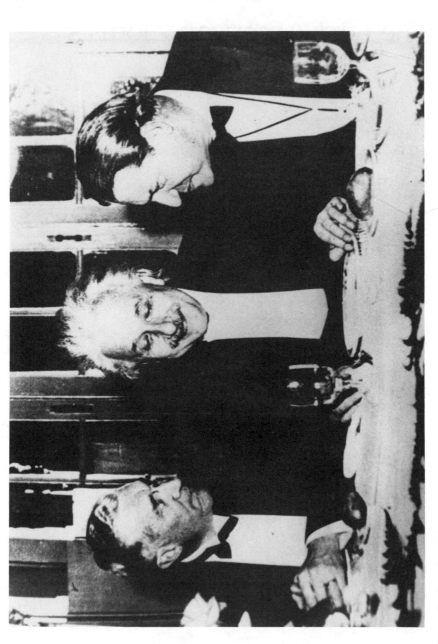

Figure 7. Stephen Wise, Albert Einstein, and John Haynes Holmes at the Hotel Astor, New York, March 17, 1934. (*Courtesy of Rosemary Krensky*)

6

Two Paths to Zion:
Magnes and Stephen S. Wise

MELVIN I. UROFSKY

At the turn of the century, Zionists in the United States recognized that the needs and perceptions of Jews in the New World differed significantly from those in the Old World, especially in the heartland of Jewish culture and piety, eastern Europe. There the hope for redemption in Eretz Israel derived from numerous factors, including messianic fervor, cultural isolation, and anti-Semitism, all of which were either greatly diluted or absent in this country. For a strong Zionist movement to grow here, its ideology would have to be Americanized, and its organization headed by new leaders, men and women bred in this country who could bridge the gap between Zionism's European roots and the interests of the fastest growing Jewish community in the world.[1]

No two men seemed more suited to these needs than Judah L. Magnes and Stephen S. Wise. Magnes, born and reared in California, had attended the Hebrew Union College, and then took a doctorate at the University of Heidelberg, where he became familiar with the Wissenschaft des Judentums and a number of its leaders. Upon his return he made his way to New York, already the Jewish capital of the country, and in 1906 became associate rabbi of Reform's cathedral synagogue, Temple Emanu-El. A fine orator, he could speak effectively both to the *Yahudim*, the established German-Jewish elite to whom he was to become related by marriage, and to the *Yidn*, the downtown Jews. His espousal of Ahad Ha-Am's concept of Zionism as a cultural and spiritual renaissance not only struck fire with the new immigrants, but also proved minimally acceptable to many of the anti-Zionist *Yahudim*, who feared the implications of Theodor Herzl's political Zionism upon their status as American citizens. Through his leadership of the New York *Kehillah*, Magnes seemed to be in the right place at the right time to build bridges among the different communal groups, and to make Zionism an accepted part of the American Jewish scene.[2]

Stephen Wise, although born in Hungary, had been brought to the United States at an early age and grew up in New York. He received his Jewish training from his father and his father's friends, including the renowned scholars Gustav Gottheil and Alexander Kohut, and his secular education in the New York public schools, City College, and Columbia University. Instead of enrolling at Hebrew Union College, Wise went to Vienna and there received *semicha* (ordination) from Adolf Jellinek, one of the leaders in the movement for the scientific study of Judaism. Upon returning to the United States, Wise earned his doctorate at Columbia University, held the pulpits first of B'nai Jeshurun in New York and then Beth Israel in Oregon; in 1907, he returned to New York to found the Free Synagogue. Considered by some the greatest Jewish orator of his generation, Wise's audiences included nearly every segment of New York's varied Jewish population; in addition, he was among the first rabbis to engage in what later came to be called Jewish-Christian dialogue. Like Magnes, Wise also struck the European leaders of Zionism as the sort of American who could popularize the movement and make it acceptable in the United States.[3]

Wise and Magnes shared more than just a superficially similar background, and it is worth looking a bit more closely at how they were alike before examining how their paths diverged.

First, Magnes and Wise shared a deep love for the United States, especially its democratic ideals. Both had typical city boyhoods, one on the country's east coast, the other on the west; both loved baseball; and both gloried in the beauty and power of the English language. But above all, America meant freedom, democracy, and equality. Magnes, for example, refused to accept awards, and in turning down an honorary degree from the Jewish Theological Seminary in 1936 he explained:[4]

> I have never been able to bear the thought of medals and honorary titles — at least, as far as I am myself concerned . . . . Perhaps it is because I was born in the free West. I recall how my first teachers used to talk of the glories of the real America — no badges, no titles, no special uniforms, etc. I know it is somewhat different at the present time in America, but I am sure that the true America still feels the same way.

Wise, in the darkest days of World War II, expressed a credo with which Magnes would have easily sympathized:[5]

> I am doubly an American, because I am foreign-born. It may be that native-born Americans take America for granted. We look upon American citizenship as the most precious and sacred of boons. We understand what it is that we have left behind us — of denial of the freedom of man, and we know what it is that has come to be our high destiny, to be a sharer in American freedom, to be a bearer of American responsibility, to be a devotee of the American Democracy, to use American freedom not for one's own advantage but for the service of the American Democracy . . . .
>
> I am an American, I thank God that my parents brought me to this country. I thank God that my children and children's children have been born in this country. They have entered into and become sharers in the most precious heritage which can fall to the lot of man, and I have faith that they will prove equal to and worthy of the high opportunities of life which American citizenship affords. They, like me, will give their deepest, truest loyalty to the America which is today, to the greater, freer, nobler America that is to be on the morrow.

Their commitment to America also informed their views of the ministry. Magnes saw the pulpit as crippled by restrictions, yet laden with opportunity. He heaped scorn on those "pastors, priests, ministers and preachers [who] draw pay for their being religious and for their being moral."[6] He entered the rabbinate not only to serve but self-consciously to lead, and in all the rabbinic posts he held between 1904 and 1912 — Temple Israel, Emanu-El, and B'nai Jeshurun — he tried to instill in his congregants a new Jewish fervor. After he left B'nai Jeshurun he toyed with the idea of a People's Synagogue or a Society for the Advancement of Judaism for a while. He sought a framework centered not only on a single building, but around groupings of people and interests, with the rabbi coordinating communal efforts to revivify the faith. The *Kehillah* was, in many ways, a manifestation of Magnes's rabbinic strivings. As Aryeh Goren notes, Magnes

> endeavored to invest the *Kehillah* with a higher purpose: the spiritual and cultural uplift of Jewish life. Thus the modernization of Jewish religious education became the organizations's most ambitious undertaking. The *Kehillah* indeed was Magnes's *Lebensprogramm*: community as the expression of Jewish peoplehood rooted in historic Judaism, a Jewish renaissance linked to group survival in a pluralist America, and a renewal of national life in the ancient homeland. Scoffers called him

chief rabbi of the Lower East Side while his own self-image was more akin to minister of the congregation of New York's Jews.

Similarly, in founding the Free Synagogue, Wise envisioned a ministry which would succor both uptown and downtown Jews, rich and poor, native-born and immigrant, businessman, professional, and laborer. He hoped, among other things, that he would be able to bridge the growing gap between *Yahudim* and *Yidn*. While Wise paid relatively little attention to speculative theological questions, one can locate the lodestar of his religious thought in the concept of *klal Yisrael*, the unity of the Jewish people. Unlike Felix Adler's Ethical Culture movement, the Free Synagogue would be unremittingly Jewish. "We mean," he said, "to be vitally, intensely, unequivocally Jewish. Jews who would not be Jews will find no place in the Free Synagogue, for we its founders wish to be not less Jewish but more Jewish in the highest and noblest sense of the term."[8]

The Judaism which Wise cherished and defended, however, derived not from a rigid ritual but from the prophetic demand for justice. It stood unafraid of the future, for while the essential ethical core remained valid for all ages, a living Judaism accepted the challenge of change. It also accepted the challenge of diversity, of differing views, because it required intellectual acceptance, not rote obedience. Orthodox, Conservative, and Reform Jews mingled with atheists and free thinkers, socialists, and agnostics, all drawn by Wise's oratory, eager to hear what he and his hundreds of guest speakers throughout the years had to say. They did not always agree, nor did Wise expect them to; he once quipped that any sermon which did not lead at least one congregant to resign in protest had been a failure. But he did expect them to think, and then to act. The Free Synagogue pioneered in making social service a central part of its program. "I could not abide the reproach," he later wrote, "that in most synagogues social service is left to the sisterhoods."[9] The Free Synagogue would, therefore, be Jewish, democratic, socially conscious, and active, as well as free.

A third area of congruence between the two men was their admiration of Eastern European Jewry, which they recognized as the source of so much that they found admirable in Jewish life. They did not accept, of course, the orthodoxy which most Eastern Europeans followed, nor did they believe that all the traits of ghetto and *shtetl* life could — or should — be transferred to the New World. After his first encounter with them while a student in Germany, Magnes wrote home "what a remarkable people these poor, starving Jews are. How they cling to life and hope — what a fine intellectuality they all have, and what a tremendous spiritual power is in them."[10] Wise uttered almost identical words when, after a walk on New York's Lower East Side, he told his wife that despite their wretched surroundings, these people had within them a "soul life."[11] For both of them, *Yiddishkeit*, that sense of Jewish being, flowed strongest in the men and women who fled Eastern Europe seeking a better life.

Perhaps the greatest thing Magnes and Wise shared was Zionism, yet they differed significantly in their views of Jewish redemption and how Eretz Israel could be restored. Both men brought great talents and enthusiasm to the cause, yet their paths only merged for a short time. In their Zionist efforts we can see traits and beliefs which fully marked their entire lives and careers.

One of Magnes's earliest known essays, entitled "Palestine — or Death," appeared while he was a student at the then very anti-Zionist Hebrew Union College. In it, Magnes warned that American Jewry faced extinction through assimilation, and to ensure the permanency of Judaism, a "Jewish church and state" had to be established in Palestine. Although published in January 1896, a month before the appearance of Herzl's *Der Judenstaat*, the theme of redemption through political means was not dominant.[12] Magnes does not seem to have fully embraced Zionism until he studied at the Berlin Hochschule, but once embraced, it proved an overriding passion for the rest of his life. To his parents he wrote:[13]

> Since I have become a Zionist, my view of life has changed; my view as to my calling has changed; my view as to my future has changed; my hopes, my prayers have changed. The questions concerning the Jewish people — and the Jewish religion is but one of those questions — are the questions that are consuming my days and nights . . . . My Zionism, however, makes me more than a mere preacher or community leader. It makes me a worker for the preservation of the Jewish people as a whole and for their greater glory and better life in their own land . . . Zionism . . . has given rise within me to some of the best thoughts and noblest feeings I have yet had.

Although, in a letter to David Wolffsohn, Magnes acknowledged that Zionism "has been and must remain a political movement in the full sense of the term,"[14] from the start Magnes adopted the ideas of Ahad Ha-Am and regarded Zionism as a cultural and spiritual reawakening of the Jewish people. More than any other American Jewish leader of his generation, Magnes worked to carry out this ideal, especially at the institution with which he later became so identified, the Hebrew University in Jerusalem. As early as 1901, he wrote that "Zionism has an answer: not alone must we relieve our oppressed;

we must again put all our energies to work, as a people, in order to create a Jewish culture."[15] In discussing an early proposal for the University, he told Chaim Weizmann that of all its goals, the University must be "at the heart of that spiritual center which we have been constantly talking of establishing in Palestine."[16]

Magnes's role in organizational Zionist life accelerated when he moved to New York. In June 1905, the Federation of American Zionists elected him secretary, which gave him the responsibility of running daily affairs. During his tenure, he wanted to emphasize "practical work," anticipating the philosophy of Louis D. Brandeis, who within a decade would utterly transform the movement in the United States. Actually, Magnes, like most of the American-born Zionists, had little use or patience for the ideological nit-picking endemic among the European groups. Americans in general have never been interested in ideology; they see a problem and want to solve it. For Magnes, Wise, Julian Mack, and others, the issue was the "Jewish Problem," with redemption in Palestine the answer; all that concerned them was determining the most expedient and effective way to implement that solution. After the establishment of the *Kehillah* in 1909, Magnes's active work in the Federation trailed off as he devoted most of his time to developing the communal organization he headed. When World War I broke out, Magnes suddenly found himself caught in the middle between the new Zionist leadership of the Brandeis faction, and the older Jewish agencies, such as the American Jewish Committee, with which he had long worked.

Stephen Wise's early Zionist activities are remarkably similar to those of Magnes, although prior to 1914 the two men had little contact with each other in Zionist affairs. Wise knew of early efforts to rebuild Palestine because *meshulahim* (charity collectors) from the Holy Land were frequent visitors in his father's house, gathering both *halukah* funds for the religious institutions, as well as support for the Ohavei Zion colonies.[17] But there is little evidence that he knew or understood the different elements of Zionism, and his earliest recorded statement on the subject intimated that it might not even be necessary to rebuild Zion if the United States and other enlightened nations forced the anti-Semitic governments of Eastern Europe to stop persecuting Jews.[18]

Following the First Zionist Congress in 1897, Wise and Richard Gottheil took the lead in attempting to merge the various Zionist clubs in New York into some cohesive pattern. In December 1897, they founded the Federation of Zionist Societies of Greater New York and Vicinity, with Wise as secretary; the following year they established the Federation of American Zionists, again with Wise as "honorary secretary," a term he later described as meaning "unpaid."[19] A turning point for Wise came in August 1898, when he sailed for Europe as a delegate to the Second Congress. "For the first time in my youthful life," he recalled:[20]

> I got a glimpse of world Jewry. There I sought and met for the first time with great men who were great Jews, with great Jews who were great men . . . . Suddenly, as if by magic, I came upon a company of Jews who were not victims or refugees or beggars, but proud and educated men, dreaming, planning, toiling for their people. Veritably I suffered a rebirth, for I came to know my people at their best. Thrilled and gratified, I caught a glimpse of the power and the pride and the nobleness of the Jewish people, which my American upbringing and even service to New York Jewry had not in any degree given me. I was a Jew by faith up to the day of the Congress in Basle and little more. At Basle I became a Jew in every sense of that term. Judaism ceased to be a type of religious worship. The Jewish people became my own.

Wise also fell under the spell of the movement's founder, and as one colleague later wrote, Wise "was never able to rid himself of the overwhelming influence of Theodor Herzl and the prejudices of that early period."[21] The political Zionism preached by Herzl was central to Wise's thinking for the rest of his life, and while he came to know and appreciate labor, religious, and cultural Zionist thought, he remained above all the political activist seeking to build upon practical work.

Upon his return to the United States, Wise became one of the movement's most indefatigable workers, going on speaking tours for the Federation of American Zionists, raising money, enrolling members, and selling shares in the Jewish Colonial Trust. But he also became disenchanted with the endless ideological bickering and with European leaders whom he felt did not appreciate American Jewry as anything other than a source of funds. When Wise travelled to Europe in the spring of 1904, he was dismayed at how little the European Zionists thought of their American colleagues, and although he was a member of the Greater Actions Committee, they did not seek his views on the burning issue of the East Africa offer. He resigned in protest from the Greater Actions Committee, declaring:[22]

> I cannot and will not work with men who refuse to place in me their fullest confidence. That Herzl and his colleagues fail to take counsel with the only American member of the Greater Actions Committee then present in Vienna, touching the state of affairs in America, constitutes an indignity to which no gentleman can submit with honor . . . .

I am as much a member of the Greater Actions Committee as Herzl or any man. It was and is his duty to deal with me, with us, frankly and honestly — I am not a Russian underling nor yet a Turkish landowner who must be kept in the dark as to the real purpose of things.

Wise dropped out of active Zionist work after 1906, devoting his time to founding and developing the Free Synagogue. He was certainly aware of Magnes and the Federation of American Zionists during these years, but there is no record of contact, and if any took place, it may well have been less than friendly. Wise opposed the original charter of the *Kehillah* because he considered it unrepresentative of the city's Jewish population, and also attacked the American Jewish Committee, another agency with which Magnes had close ties, as undemocratic.[23] Wise's dormant interest reawakened, however, after a trip he and his wife took to Palestine in 1913, and he returned determined to work for the Yishuv, although not necessarily through the Federation of American Zionists. The device he chose, a fact-finding commission to evaluate needs and then plan for specific projects, perfectly reflected Wise's involvement in Progressive reforms. He raised the necessary funds, and the commission was about to sail when war broke out in Europe.[24]

World War I proved both a blessing and a curse for the Jewish people. The worst fighting on the eastern front occurred in heavily populated Jewish areas, whose inhabitants were totally uprooted. Within days after hostilities commenced, every major American Jewish organization had established a relief fund to aid their brethren in Europe, and they sent millions of dollars in cash, food, clothing, and medicine before America entered the conflict in April 1917. Zionist leaders recognized, however, that the map of Europe and the Middle East would be redrawn after the war, opening up the real possibility to secure Herzl's long-sought charter in Palestine. But, and it was a crucial point, as long as the United States was neutral, and even after 1917 so long as it had not declared war on Turkey, American Zionists had to tread extremely carefully lest they say or do anything to offend the Ottomans, thereby endangering the Palestinian settlements.

The war also brought a new Zionist leadership to power in America. Louis Brandeis of Boston, one of the nation's leading reformers and a confidant of President Woodrow Wilson, now applied his organizational genius to the problems of Jewish redemption. His motto of "Men! Money! Discipline!" transformed a loose federation of barely 12,000 members into the Zionist Organization of America, 186,000 strong, within five years. Perhaps more important, his synthesis of Zionism and Americanism created a peculiarly American Zionist ideology which proved the meeting ground upon which both *Yahudim* and *Yidn* could eventually stand and support the Jewish renascence in Palestine.[25] The tens of thousands of Jews who flocked to the new banner came primarily from the masses of recent immigrants, and they wanted not only to help their brethren in Europe and support the Yishuv, but also to carve out their own niche in American Jewish life. Brandeis, with Stephen Wise at his side, led them in this endeavor, and in doing so challenged the hegemony of the American Jewish Committee, with whom Judah Magnes had strong ties.

The Committee had, in the absence of any competing agency, assumed the role of spokesman for American Jewry in national and international affairs, and at the outbreak of the war, believed it should direct and coordinate all relief programs for the beleaguered Jews in Europe.[26] The Committee leaders, especially Louis Marshall and Jacob Schiff, looked askance when the Provisional Committee for Zionist Affairs, led by Brandeis, not only established its own relief fund, but issued a call for American Jews to unite in a new democratic organization.

The Committee had been founded upon the idea, as Adolf Kraus put it, that the masses were little better than "riffraff," and that the "best" people could and should act for the benefit of the entire community. As Horace Kallen noted, the *Yahudim*

> distrusted the rank and file . . . . [They] showed distrust of democracy, fear of frankness, a consciousness of moral and social insecurity . . . . They insisted that whatever could be done, could be done quietly, by wire pulling, by the influence of individuals, by the backstairs method of the *shtadlan* of the Middle Ages and of the Russian Ghetto.[27]

The story of the struggle to create the American Jewish Congress has been detailed elsewhere,[28] but as far as Magnes and Wise were concerned, it drove them to opposite sides. Wise, of course, had opposed the Committee leaders for several years. He had first locked horns with the *Yahudim* in his celebrated refusal of the Emanu-El pulpit, attacking Louis Marshall's position that the trustees of a synagogue held veto power over the content of rabbinic sermons.[29] More important, his philosophy both as a Jew and as an American opposed any elite which presumed to direct the affairs of the Jewish people. When Brandeis asked Wise to head the Zionist finance committee, Wise declined, explaining he had absolutely no influence with the wealthier elements of the community. "Access to them is denied me," he said, "because of the social and economic and ethical heterodoxies in my teaching which I am happy, if not proud, to say have made me wholly unacceptable to the rich Jews of New York. They do not support me in any measure."[30] Brandeis, himself no stranger to such ostracism, fully understood, but for him and for Wise, American Jewry had to be organized along democratic lines, not merely to augment Zionism, but because both men fervently believed in the right of people to rule themselves rather than to be governed by a self-perpetuating autocracy.

Ironically, Judah Magnes had originally objected to the Committee on similar grounds. In his original proposal for the *Kehillah*, he applauded the work of the Committee, but noted that "it must, however, be restricted in its usefulness because it has no mandate from the people."[31] A proper Jewish organization had to rest, ultimately, on the principles of democracy. In founding the New York *Kehillah*, Magnes envisioned that other cities would establish similar communal agencies which would then unite in a nationwide federation affiliated with the Committee.[32] Such a plan would thus democratize Jewish organizational life while retaining the influence of the *Yahudim* for the good of the community. Now, as a member of the American Jewish Committee and of the Provisional Committee, as well as chairman of the *Kehillah*, Magnes appeared as the key person who could mediate among Zionists and non-Zionists, uptowners and downtowners, *Yidn* and *Yahudim*; the role he originally hoped for in his rabbinate might yet come to pass.

Unfortunately, changed circumstances as well as Magnes's personal loyalties deprived him of this role. Without belittling Magnes, one can note that he simply lacked the personal stature to deal with the opposing forces. Neither Brandeis nor Marshall saw Magnes as their equal, and the stakes were too large to entrust negotiations to anyone in whom they had less than full confidence. Moreover, while Brandeis and Marshall recognized the practical necessity of reaching some sort of compromise, their associates did not. Jacob Schiff, for example, considered the Congress a mere facade for Jewish nationalism, and denounced the Zionists for their blatant irresponsibility, which would call the loyalty of all American Jews into question. "With the actual holding of the proposed Congress," he warned, "the coming of political anti-Semitism into this land will be only a question of time." The machinations of the Zionists would encourage Gentile Americans to look upon Jews "as an entirely separate class, whose interests are different than those of the gross of the American people." Schiff bitterly opposed an open convention where demagogues would broadcast Jewish business to the world, and with this view many on the Committee agreed.[33]

Wise deferred to Brandeis in attempting to reach agreement with the Marshall group, and at one point uncharacteristically urged caution, writing that "we must move very carefully."[34] But he doubted that the *Yahudim* were negotiating in good faith, and he believed that they would not willingly share power with the Zionists. The record also indicates that the masses wanted to push ahead far faster than their leaders, and the Yiddish press insistently demanded that the Congress meet immediately. Joseph Barondess, Gedalia Bublick, and other East Side figures literally forced Brandeis and Wise to move on the Congress faster than they had intended.

Magnes originally looked sympathetically upon the Congress proposal, and was one of the few members of the Committee who did not see democracy as dangerous. Together with Marshall and Cyrus Adler, he represented the Committee in a series of meetings beginning in the fall of 1914 to see whether the Committee and the Zionists could work together. About the only area of cooperation they could agree upon, however, was to merge overseas relief work into the American Jewish Relief Committee, which, despite its accomplishments, only convinced each side of the stubbornness and duplicity of the other.[35] Magnes tried to convince his colleagues on the Committee that a Congress would not harm Jewish interests, and in an eloquent appeal set forth the case for democratizing Jewish leadership. The Committee, he averred, could not in its present form meet the needs of either European or American Jewry.[36]

> First, because in formulating its policies, it is not in close enough touch with (a) the Jewish masses of America, and (b) the aspirations of the different kind of Jews in the belligerent lands; and second, because it has not, in its present form, what it absolutely needs in carrying out whatever policies it determines upon — the united support of large sections of the Jewish people of this country.

He pointed out that the Committee was asking American Jewry to support it when it had not, in fact, clearly determined what the best policy would be.

> Let us assume, for example, that it be decided that our best policy is to keep silent. How do you expect this to be carried out unless you give a chance to the leaders and representatives of the people to work this policy out with you, and to make them equally responsible with you in carrying it out? The people will then understand that their silence is not due to a command or to their own dumbness, but to the fact that their own leaders, chosen by them, have so concluded; and the responsibility will then be borne by everyone and silence will be secured. So, too, with every step taken to carry out any policy thus determined upon.

As to the worries of Schiff and others that demagoguery would rule at the Congress, Magnes answered in words that Brandeis or Wise could easily have spoken:

> Objection is made on the ground that intemperate words will be uttered. They are being uttered now, every day in all quarters, and the one possibiity of checking such utterances is by convening the representatives of the people, to place more responsibility upon them for their utterances and their actions. It would be a sign of demoralization and low vitality if the Jews of the country, the great majority of whom are directly affected by the war, were not excited and alarmed and eager to help by word and deed. We must take advantage of the righteous and natural excitement and eagerness, and, while being stimulated and influenced by it, convert it, into real strength and dynamic power . . . .
>
> The one hope of our coping with these problems, of doing justice to the Jews and to this country, is to set in motion a democratic, nation-wide Jewish movement that will place upon every Jew in the land a portion of the responsibility for the future . . . . The local problems of these communities, and the national problems before all of us, have a chance of being solved only if we now take advantage of the historic responsibility placed upon us and endeavor to create a genuinely democratic representation of the Jews of the country.

But it was to no avail; more than three decades would pass before the *Yahudim* finally recognized that the era of the *shtadlan* had passed.[37] Both Marshall and Brandeis believed too strongly in their respective positions; the Committee did not believe in the ability of the masses to govern themselves, and the Zionist leadership would accept nothing less. Forced to choose, Magnes cast his lot with the Committee, despite his misgivings, because of his personal ties to the *Yahudim* and because the Committee had provided his chief backing in the *Kehillah*. He turned bitterly upon the Zionists, accusing Brandeis, Wise, and the others of departing from the true goals of Zionism in venturing forth to democratize American Jewish life.[38] Charging the Provisional Committee with fostering disunity among American Jews, he turned a blind eye to the failure of the American Jewish Committee to negotiate meaningfully, a fact that many of the Committee's former allies were now recognizing. Instead of serving as the mediator to bring the various elements of the community together, Magnes now stood discredited. The Zionists no longer trusted him; the *Kehillah* was falling apart; and in the Committee his voice carried little weight. Before long, his uncompromising pacifism would alienate him from that body as well.

Magnes was wrong in believing that the Congress fight was a deviation from Zionist principles. The dominant theme in Zionist affairs henceforth would revolve upon the type of society to be created in Eretz Israel, and despite differences between various factions, nearly all agreed that the Yishuv had to be democratically organized. For Wise and Brandeis, democracy was the essence of Zionism, the meeting place between the teachings of the Hebrew prophets and the principles of American freedom. The Brandeisian synthesis, as I have called it elsewhere, combined these two strands, thereby making it possible for American Jews to support the ideal of Jewish restoration in Palestine without fear of compromising their loyalty to the United States. For Wise especially, American Zionism had to be consistent not only with Jewish ideals but with American beliefs as well.

For Magnes, of course, Zionism remained a matter of mind and spirit, and his belief that before Jews could return to their homeland as a political entity they would have to lay a foundation based on justice and spiritual development. His initial comments on the British mandate, that the "historic rights" of the Jews did not outweigh the fact that there were five or six times as many Arabs in the Holy Land as Jews,[39] anticipated his future efforts in Brit Shalom and Ihud, while his own *aliyah* and lengthy connection with the Hebrew University provided the most eloquent testimony to his lifelong commitment to the spiritual and cultural Zionism of Ahad Ha-Am.

My view is that Wise, and not Magnes, set the model for the only type of Zionism that could flourish in the United States. The millions of Jews who had fled persecution in Europe had chosen as their Zion not the ancient homeland of their people, but the new Zion, the *goldene medineh* (golden land), across the seas. This was their *aliyah*, and the *Yidn* had every intention of becoming as good and loyal Americans as the *Yahudim*. To them, America meant not just freedom from persecution, but also the freedom to live and work in a land in which democracy and participation in communal affairs were more than catchwords. For Wise, Brandeis, Mack, and others, separating their Zionist activities from their Americanism was impossible, a trait which Magnes would later exemplify so bravely in his efforts to create a binational state. But at least in these early years he appears to have been the prisoner of a misconception that somehow Zionism could and should be just spiritual and cultural. As a result, it would be men like Stephen Wise who would lead American Zionism into the era of strength and influence which the early founders of the movement in this country hoped for but could not themselves achieve, while Magnes, along with Henrietta Szold, helped ensure that American ideals of justness and equity found their place among the *halutzim* of the *Yishuv*.

Figure 8. Magnes with Henrietta Szold in Egypt, c. 1943. (*Courtesy of Hava Magnes*)

7

Doing Good in Palestine: Magnes and Henrietta Szold

JOAN DASH

When, in 1933, Henrietta Szold said, in speaking of the Arabs, that people do not necessarily want to have good done to them by others,[1] she was describing her own situation in Jewish Palestine, as well as that of Judah Magnes. Both Magnes and Szold had come there to "do good." They worked without salaries; they were efficient and orderly and incurably high-minded; and in that most politicized of countries, they remained aloof from all partisan politics.

What the Yishuv would have liked to see in them instead, was the spice of human weakness — a little greed, a spot of mendacity, of high spirits or of low humor — that might have diluted the taste of these two Western foreigners. Moreover they were also American and that was held against them for there were few Americans in Palestine during the British Mandate period, and the United States itself was regarded with deep suspicion. In the 1920s and 1930s, it was already the home of the world's most influential Jewry — those people, in other words, who intended to do good to the Jews of Palestine. For all these reasons, Magnes and Szold remained outsiders, dedicated to a community that could not like them, and connected by deep ties to another nation, distant and powerful, upon whose goodwill the Yishuv was sorely dependent.

Miss Szold arrived in Jerusalem in 1920, on the eve of her sixtieth birthday and only months before the arrival of Sir Herbert Samuel, the first British High Commissioner. She was not quite five feet tall, overweight, plain looking — having always been plain, always refusing to succumb to face powder or hair-dressers — and she wore hat, gloves, a lace collar with a lace pin at its precise center, while carrying a large purse that went with her everywhere. She was polite, prompt (no virtue in the Middle East), compulsively honest, a truth teller even to her own hurt, and addicted to overwork. She was, therefore, in appearance what she was in fact, a maiden lady and former schoolteacher. Such women were rare in the Palestine of the *halutzim*; the occasional spinsters of advanced years, when they did appear, were usually British, and the Yishuv had no affection for them either.

Her past, of course, came with her — it was part of her luggage, along with the copy of Gray's *Botany,* with which she intended to identify the wildflowers of Palestine, searching for counterparts to what she had left behind. Born in Baltimore in 1860, the first of five daughters of Rabbi Benjamin Szold, a scholar and German-speaker, she had taught for many years in a private school for girls. She was also a writer, an editor, the founder of the first American night school for immigrants, and since 1893 a Zionist. Shortly after the turn of the century, she had gone with her mother to live in New York, within the circle of the Jewish Theological Seminary.

It was in New York, on a Saturday afternoon in 1903, that there appeared at the door of her apartment, "A gentleman . . . a young man looking full of youth. He said, 'My name is Magnes, and I have been thinking we ought to know each other so I came.' "[2] She found him sunny, enthusiastic, and decisive, and she took to him immediately. When Dr. Magnes, some time later, suggested that she join a little study group of young women interested in Zionism, one he had helped to form, she immediately agreed.[3]

It was also in New York, and in the Seminary circle, that Miss Szold fell disastrously in love at age forty-two with Louis Ginzberg, a scholar and writer many years her junior. In 1909, to escape the reverberations of this unhappy romance, she went with her mother to Europe, then to Palestine, where for fourteen days they travelled by farm cart over rutted roads, visiting more than a dozen of the Rothschild colonies. Everything they saw struck them as heartbreaking and desolate, full of blasted hopes. In the cities they met filth and flies and ragged, hungry children, afflicted with trachoma.[4] It was the sight of these children that led her mother to suggest the little study circle in New York ought to do more than read Herzl and Pinsker. "You ought to do practical work in Palestine," she said.[5]

When they returned to America, Miss Szold founded Hadassah to do just that. Their earliest undertaking was to establish a visiting nurse service in Jerusalem, which later gave birth to a school of nursing. But in 1916, when World War I devastated the Holy Land, the Zionists of Europe sent a call for help to Americans. Louis Brandeis, the new leader of the American movement, then turned to Miss Szold: Could her Hadassah send a medical mission — a rescue ship? She had no doubt whatever, envisioning two doctors, two nurses, some drugs, and bandages and related supplies. To the women of Hadassah she suggested they raise some of the necessary funds by walking, instead of spending money on streetcars.

This project was to meet with so many delays, because of diplomatic hurdles connected with the war, that two years elapsed before the ship finally sailed, and by then it was no longer a simple matter of two doctors and two nurses. In the interim, Szold underwent a crisis of conscience. She was a pacifist, as she wrote to Dr. Richard Gottheil, a Zionist leader and Columbia professor of Semitics. "I am afraid you have to bracket me with Dr. Magnes and Miss [Lillian] Wald. I am anti-war, and anti-this-war, and anti-all-war . . . . My position — for me — is of the essence of my religious and philosophical makeup . . . ."[6] With her friend Jessie Sampter, a Hadassah member, she had joined an organization called the People's Council of America for Democracy. A number of well-known radicals, including Magnes, were on its executive committee.

Sampter, a semi-invalid, had been slightly crippled by polio. "She was casual about nothing, and could accept no idea or person without deep scrutiny," according to Margaret Doniger of Hadassah.[7] Her correspondence with Szold during this period illustrates the pressures put upon the two women, by Louis Brandeis and others of the Zionist leadership, to surrender either their pacifism, or their positions in the Zionist movement, for they were seen as a source of profound embarrassment, clear proof to national and international powers that important Jewish figures were pro-German. Miss Sampter wrote to Miss Szold in September 1917, "I believe we should refuse to discuss the merits of pro- or anti-war, and insist that as moral beings our moral convictions are ultimate things which we cannot subject to any authority, any more than we could steal or murder to advance the Zionist cause."[8]

Miss Szold continued the discussion a few days later:

> Why, if I think that belonging to the Peace and Democracy movement is a way of expressing my Americanism, should I sit quietly by while the Zionist ideal is being travestied, and say I will withdraw because my participation may be 'damaging to the movement?' . . . The movement has gone to war. We are prepared to win by the sword and as a conquest the land which is to be for a sign of peace and justice . . . .[9]

But when she and Sampter were formally summoned before a board of Zionist leaders their resolution began to crumble. Brandeis had already been elevated to the Supreme Court. Judge Julian Mack, Rabbi Stephen Wise, Dr. Harry Friedenwald, a childhood friend of Szold's and onetime president of the Federation of American Zionists, were men of authority, used to command. All were in agreement, insisting that the People's Council was hostile to the policies of the American govenment. Szold and Sampter could be Zionists, but not pacifists; they could equally well be pacifists but not official Zionists; they must choose.[10]

Miss Szold was severely shaken. She saw her Hadassah work and her Zionism, the cornerstones of her life now, under serious threat. Moreover it was hard for her to hold on to her convictions when men like Brandeis and Wise — learned men, whereas she had had little formal education — saw them as misguided and dangerous. In the end, she resigned from the People's Council, while assuring the group of her continued belief in their purposes.[11] It was not the first time, nor the last, that she was to find herself at odds with the male Zionist leadership. Often, but not always, she would back down, while swallowing her resentment and guilt because she lacked the courage to do otherwise.

In June 1918, the medical unit set sail for Palestine. By then it had become a miniature health department of twenty doctors and twenty nurses, along with enough equipment to outfit a fifty-bed hospital.[12] A year later, Jessie Sampter followed them, and less than a year after that Miss Szold herself set out for Palestine, as an emissary of Louis Brandeis. Dissension within the Unit, as well as the Yishuv's reaction to it, led to her mission: to see why the doctors quarrelled interminably among themselves, why the Yishuv hated them, and what could be done about it.

She had distinct misgivings about her chances of success. She was old, she said, her Hebrew was inadequate, and she doubted anyone would take her seriously there, certainly not Menachem Ussishkin, chief of the Zionist Commission, who considered it insulting that the Americans had sent a woman to represent them.[13] She had received a series of anguished letters on the subject of Ussishkin from Dr. I. M. Rubinow, the head of the American Zionist Medical Unit. Rubinow, whom Szold had chosen because of his interest in social welfare (he had tried in vain to commit the American Medical Association to health insurance) was not a Zionist and knew no Hebrew. Therefore, Ussishkin, he said, was resolved to run him out of the country.[14]

According to Ussishkin, the Unit must sever all ties with America and be placed entirely in the hands of the Zionist Commission, henceforth serving only Zionist purposes, ignoring the cities while working for the welfare of the only productive segment of society, the *halutzim* and road-builders. Szold and the Americans of the Brandeis faction believed their medical unit could serve everyone in Jewish Palestine, for indeed it was pledged to treat every citizen, regardless of religion. Nevertheless, even before her arrival she hoped to see the word "American" disappear from its title.[15]

Once she arrived, she found that not even the rigors of her earlier visit had prepared her for daily life in a country that had been, until the war, a forgotten outpost of the Turkish empire. There were no telephones. The postal service was so inadequate that most European countries had their own mailing systems. There was only one road suitable for normal traffic, and that road was rarely in full repair. At the time of British entry, neither water supply nor drainage systems existed — people depended on cisterns in towns, on wells in the villages. Typhoid, malaria, and trachoma were commonplace, as was hunger. When the rains came, the earth turned to glutinous mud; in winter, everyone froze. There was nothing to buy and nothing to read; it was a country poor to begin with, blasted by years of war, apparently consisting only of rocks and hope.

But all this faded when compared to the difficulty of human relations — the bickering within the Unit; the bitter opposition of the Orthodox to the New Yishuv; the Arab riots, which broke out soon after she came, along with Jewish resentment of America and all its works, which was accompanied by demands for more, and yet more from America. After two weeks of it, she was a wreck. "I was ready to flee back to America; I wondered bitterly whether I had devoted twenty years of my life to an ideal that had turned out to be a will-o'-the-wisp. For what is a Zionist who no longer believes in the Jewish people? . . . A voice kept shouting inside of myself: 'These are not your people. You have no part and parcel in them.' "[16]

Her greatest comfort was a circle of American friends — Sophia Berger, a social worker with whom she had rented an old Arab house in a mixed quarter; Alex Dushkin, a young teacher; Julia Aronson, a dietician whose sister was married to Israel Friedlaender of the Jewish Theological Seminary; Nellie Straus-Mochenson, a Hadassah member who settled in Palestine and married there; and Jessie Sampter.

Sampter lived in rooms on the Street of the Prophets where

members of the American group met on Saturday mornings for religious services, for no synagogue in the country permitted men and women to worship side by side. Later, she built a little house in Rehovoth and adopted a daughter; she wrote poetry and articles about Jewish life, eventually joining the kibbutz Givat Brenner. When she left for Palestine, Sampter had said in her will: "If any accident befall me, remember that I preferred that danger to my safety here."[17] For Miss Szold, Jessie Sampter was always a source of spiritual strength.

Within this English-speaking circle, Henrietta Szold felt at ease, insofar as a woman of her temperament — reserved, shy, and formal — was ever at ease. When compelled to speak Hebrew, she was always uncomfortable. Two years after her arrival she wrote, "My Hebrew flows as badly as the water in our cistern — not at all . . . . It is maddening to live in this country with an Anglo-Saxon language psychology,"[18] and even after decades there she found her thoughts constricted by the limitations of her vocabulary.

As for Dr. Rubinow, he never adapted. He left on vacation a few months after she came, unable to promise he would return, and, in his absence, Miss Szold had to take charge of the Unit. During this period, she began working closely with the *halutzim*. She established clinics in the countryside; fell in love with the young people, and saw in them the only hope for sanity amidst the chaos of Jewish Palestine.

Although Rubinow returned from his vacation, he left for good in 1922, but his Palestine experience, in spite of its difficulties, had converted him to Zionism. A few years later he became Executive Director of the Zionist Organization of America, and in the mid-1930s President Franklin Roosevelt appointed him consultant to the committee that drafted America's Social Security laws, a field in which he was an authority.

Once again, Miss Szold was in charge of the Unit — and at a time when it faced financial disaster. It was then that Magnes and his family arrived, taking up residence close by the Berger-Szolds. There were constant comings and goings from one household to the other, as well as picnics and excursions to explore the countryside. Benedict Magnes, the third of Magnes's three sons, remembers a day when a hike was planned and he was to be left behind because he was too young. The boy was inconsolable until Szold said, "It seems we're always being told we're either too young for things, or too old. People say I'm too old . . . . Well, we mustn't let it bother us." He felt better then.[19]

Two of the Magnes children attended a school in the neighborhood, run by Deborah Kallen, the sister of Horace Kallen, one of the founders of the New School in New York and a close associate of Justice Brandeis, with whom Szold had worked in the States. Now she heard accounts of an American-style school, progressive and free, that included such subjects as fingerpainting, and where the Magnes boys actually enjoyed themselves. It was not clear that they learned much, but they did look forward to school, something unheard-of in Jewish Palestine where the curriculum was rigid, monotonous, and modeled on ancient European principles to which the concept of self-expression was utterly foreign.

In Magnes, Miss Szold had at her side an old friend for whom she felt not only affection but great admiration. He came to the Unit's offices in the Hotel de France, where he set his orderly mind to the task of untangling the Unit's finances, and in March 1923, when she got sudden word that her sister Rachel was seriously ill in America, it was Dr. Magnes whom she left in charge of the Unit.

Between 1923 and 1925 she made three trips to Palestine and back, returning to Jerusalem for good in September 1925 with a new Unit head, Dr. E. M. Bluestone, an idealistic young American whose service there proved to be such an ordeal that he returned home even before the completion of his two-year contract. From now on, Miss Szold told the American women of Hadassah, they must have a Palestinian at the head of the Hadassah Medical Organization (HMO), as the Unit was now called. She said that while once it had been possible to ram a system from without down the throats of the Yishuv, that time was now past.

> Here in Palestine an organic life is being developed. You and I may not like some of its manifestations. As a matter of fact, I confess to you that some of its manifestations have aroused my indignation and destroyed my nerves. But for better or worse, that is the organic life that is being developed here by Zionists who are the bone of the bone and flesh of the flesh of our ideal.[20]

The Hadassah Medical Organization was changing. The original medical rescue ship, which had gone on to establish clinics and hospitals throughout the country, began the process of "devolution." Handing over to the Yishuv the institutions that it had built, it kept only the Jerusalem site, which remained under American authority. And since 1921, when Dr. Nathan Ratnoff of New York organized a

committee of American Jewish physicians to build a medical department at the Hebrew University, Hadassah had been looking toward
the same goal. The two organizations in partnership became the
Rothschild-Hadassah University Hospital and Medical School, formally dedicated in 1939.

Meanwhile, Miss Szold was entering a new stage in her career,
one that would have the effect of stretching her ties to America so
severely at times that they were almost ruptured. In 1927, she was
elected one of three members of the Zionist Commission, the shadow
government that ruled Jewish Palestine under the British. For two
years she served as the member in charge of education and health. It
was a time when the Jewish homeland seemed headed for bankruptcy
and dissolution, partly because American funds failed to arrive — the
result not only of the Depression, but of infighting among the
Zionists, Brandeisists against Weizmannites. Miss Szold had been
elected because Weizmann wanted her there, and he wanted her as a
hostage to America, a proof that if American money came it would be
handled efficiently. Yet the money still failed to come, for which Weizmann seemed to hold her responsible. Schoolteachers were starving,
halutzim lived for weeks on nothing but tomatoes, children fainted
from hunger in the schools, and she felt deserted by her American
friends. In her misery, she quarreled with Sophia Berger, leaving the
comfortable home in which Sophia had coddled her and entertained
for her. She wrote to her friend Alice Seligsberg, an American social
worker who had spent two years with the Unit in Palestine, "I understand the structure of an Ibsen drama through my experiences of the
last few months. Everything, everything, in my personal relations, in
my Zionist relations, has been just as hard as I feared it would . . . .
The worst of all disharmonies is that I can't get away from self-pity."[21]
Moving into a single room in the Hotel Eden, she lived out of her
wardrobe trunk from then on, certain she would be going back to
America forever once her term of office expired.

But in 1931, after a return home that proved to her she was no
longer cut out for American life, Miss Szold was back at the Hotel
Eden — summoned back, this time by the Yishuv, to establish a central
social service bureau. Jews were beginning to come to Palestine from
Germany, and, for the first time, trained social workers were in the
country, bringing with them the possibility of modern social work, in
place of the profuse, but disorganized, efforts of religious organizations. Szold began the new undertaking with relish; although past
seventy, she worked as hard as ever, even offering her services to the
British as a probation officer. Amazed and pained by what she saw in

the back alleys of Jerusalem, she began to explore the problems of delinquent Jewish youth. Among the children of North African immigrants, she discovered hordes of little thieves and pickpockets, set loose in a world that seemed to have no place for them — just as it had no place for their fathers, who consequently lost all authority over the sons. Miss Szold was one of the first to understand the implications of this gulf between Oriental Jews, formed by feudal cultures, and those of European origin. She longed to see something done for the children, an idea that had occurred independently to Jessie Sampter.[22] Later, when Miss Szold begged Hadassah to take up their cause, the Americans refused for years to have any part in it. They didn't like hearing that 10,000 children of the Yishuv never went to school. They wanted success stories from Palestine, not tales of misery and failure.

In 1933, when Arthur Ruppin, head of the Jewish agency's newly created German Bureau, urged Szold to accept the directorship of a small undertaking named Youth Aliyah, she at first declined. Its intention was to bring groups of selected German children to be educated on the kibbutzim. How can we educate children from abroad, she thought, when our own are so neglected?[23]

Yet she agreed in the end, not only because of the pressures brought to bear on her by Ruppin and others, but because one of the particular beauties of the Youth Aliyah plan was that the German youngsters would be allowed by the British to remain in Palestine permanently, thus circumventing the strict immigration laws. In time she came to believe that Youth Aliyah was her most important accomplishment, certainly the one that brought her the deepest satisfactions.

But the 1930s were a period of painful change for the Yishuv, a time of disillusion, marked by the murder of Chaim Arlosoroff, a prominent labor leader, whose death was followed by a prolonged trial of several suspects that brought labor and rightist groups into impassioned conflict; the rise of right-wing Revisionism; and increasing unrest among the Arabs that exploded into open warfare in 1936, with Arab guerillas pitted against British troops. Replying to a letter from Brandeis on the subject of "things Palestinian," Miss Szold wrote:

> Many of us have long been unhappy. We are disappointed in ourselves, that we have not risen above the level of these parlous times . . . . And of me you expect such influence upon 'transgressors' as will make them mend their ways? . . . My immediate circle has known these three years, since my return from . . . America, that I consider that our

people have betrayed their Zionist task of regeneration. Beyond that circle — it is a contracted circle — my voice does not reach at all.[24]

Brandeis sent her money for projects that were close to her heart, among them the school system and social work. In his somewhat stilted letters, he exhorted her to use her influence to strengthen the moral fiber of the Yishuv. No doubt he overestimated her influence. In any case his letters had the effect of underlining the great gap between the ideal and the real Palestine.

Perhaps the gap was most striking in the matter of Arab-Jewish relations. Miss Szold had come to Jerusalem with the deep-seated belief that the Zionist adventure made no sense unless it led to partnership with their fellow Semites, the Arabs. For this reason, she had joined Brit Shalom in the mid-1920s. Yet she saw on every hand a Palestine in which Jews and Arabs lived in watertight compartments, walled off from contact with one another. She was quick to blame the British and the Arab leaders, but even quicker to blame her fellow Jews.

In 1937, when a Royal Commission came to Palestine to unearth the causes of the Arab revolt, they concluded that it was impossible for Jews and Arabs to live together in that small country. Therefore, they proposed the creation of a Jewish state, a miniature state, while the rest of the territory would be joined to the kingdom of Trans-Jordan. At the Zionist Congress in Zurich, that summer, this partition proposal was to be voted on.

Miss Szold believed that acceptance of partition would mean a betrayal of the Zionist ideal, and she composed a speech to that effect, intending to deliver it at the Congress:

> What I see before us if we accept the *Judenstaat* of the Royal Commission is a repetition of the past. We entered the land by means of the sword, the *Judenstaat* . . . will compel us to keep the sword in our hands day after day, year after year . . . . I am not pleading for justice to the Arabs alone, I am pleading for justice to ourselves, to our principles, the sacred principles for which our martyrs gave their blood.[25]

The speech was never delivered. At the Zurich congress she heard Rabbi David de Sola Pool hissed and booed for statements like her own. At the Agency Council immediately afterward, Magnes delivered a fervent plea for fresh negotiations with the Arabs, in the hope that they would lead to an undivided Palestine, but he was almost howled down. The plan of the Royal Commission was in any case rejected by the Congress, but it declared itself willing to consider other partition schemes with more generous boundaries.

Miss Szold felt she had been a "moral coward" for failing to deliver her speech. She wrote to Magnes and his wife on October 10, 1937, "I am still quailing when I remember — and I remember often — the nastiness of the sights and sounds of the evening when I was present . . . . I cannot follow your example — standing calm and unassailable before a jeering audience . . . . There's my confession and my torture."[26]

And in the early 1940s, when former members of Brit Shalom began to meet for discussion in each other's homes — Ernst Simon, the educator, Martin Buber, the philosopher, as well as Magnes, who had never belonged to Brit Shalom but was a sympathizer — Miss Szold was there too. It was a small group, at first more interested in discussion than in action. In the spring of 1942, they began a series of regular meetings at Magnes's house to discuss the visit to America by David Ben-Gurion, chairman of the Agency Executive, who aimed to generate American support for the transformation of Palestine into a Jewish state, or commonwealth. Magnes believed such a program would inevitably lead to war with the Arabs, and also believed that the Zionist establishment had by no means exhausted all paths to Arab-Jewish rapprochement. Miss Szold's beliefs were less structured.

Past eighty, she had taken on in old age a disembodied, almost visionary, quality that saw history under the aspect of eternity. When the young people of Youth Aliyah wrote to ask her if they might take up arms with the British forces, she told them, "There are Jews who believe that if [Palestine] is captured today by our enemy, the whole Jewish people would be so injured by the loss that it could not recover. My personal faith is otherwise.[27] She could not advise them to fight, not even if the enemy should come from North Africa onto Palestinian soil.

The little circle of friends called a meeting in August 1942 of some 100 believers in binationalism and Arab-Jewish rapprochement, in order to discuss the founding of an organization they would call Ihud, or Unity. Magnes was elected president; Miss Szold one of five members of the presidential board.[28] So far they had heard nothing of Ben-Gurion's brilliant success in bringing the Jewish Commonwealth idea to America; they were also unaware that Hadassah was now wholly committed to statehood.[29]

When word of Ihud reached America, the Zionist Organization of America and Hadassah were stunned. It was especially painful for the women's organization, to whom Miss Szold was a sanctified figure, their founder, and their arm in Jerusalem for all the institutions they had built. Although Magnes was not so intimately linked to them, he had been since 1940 the head of their Hadassah Emergency Council, a group empowered to act for them on the spot whenever quick communication was made impossible by the war.

The *New York Times*, as well as the Jewish press, devoted columns to Ihud. Magnes was denounced on all sides, and his removal from the presidency of the Hebrew University demanded. Members of the Zionist Organization of America began to make similar demands, insisting upon some kind of public statement about Miss Szold so that she, too, would cease to be identified with the aims of American Jews and Zionists.

Hadassah dispatched a cable, requesting an explanation of her aims and plans.[30] She replied by letter, saying that Ihud was simply a discussion group and had no intention of speaking or acting as a representative of the Jewish people. And since when were discussions and investigation anathema among Jews?[31]

Her letter reached New York at the start of the Zionist Organization of America-Hadassah convention, which was attended by Dr. Jack Kligler, a friend of Magnes. Kligler sent back a running account of the events that followed,[32] describing the frequent use of the word "traitors," when referring to Ihud leaders. "For a while it looked as though Hadassah would split wide open, but an open breach was prevented, and now they are licking their wounds." A compromise was reached. Magnes and Szold were not read out of the Zionist movement, and Ihud was neither condemned nor condoned.

In Palestine, during this same period, some of the Ihud leaders were assaulted with stink bombs and threatened with violence,[33] and Miss Szold saw herself denounced in newspaper headlines. Yet she never altered her resolve to stand by Magnes and Ihud, while her affection for Hadassah had been so seriously shaken that for a time she considered resigning.

She was sick — worn out by dissension that came in the wake of the arrival of a large group of refugee children, originally from Poland, who had wandered into a Polish Red Cross camp just outside of Teheran. The disposal of these children within the homeland set off a religious war — a *Kulturkampf*, she called it — with Orthodox against unbelievers and Miss Szold precisely in the middle. The Ihud affair unrolled the same time as the Teheran affair. There was a series of illnesses that ended in her hospitalization in the summer of 1944. Magnes was able to obtain some sulfa for her, although it was not yet available to civilians, but nothing could stop the steady decline of a woman approaching her eighty-fifth year. She died in February 1945, with Magnes at her side. He had visited her regularly, keeping a daily diary of her final passage, recording her fears, her dreams, her hopes, and providing her with a moment of consolation when at her bedside he took the hand of Chaim Weizmann, from whom Magnes had been many years estranged. Later that day, Weizmann told him, "We must never quarrel," and Magnes replied, "No, that seems to be an injunction from on high."[34]

Figure 9. Golda Meir at Merhavia 1922. *(Courtesy of Marie Syrkin)*

8

Golda Meir
and Other Americans

MARIE SYRKIN

Zionism in the United States did not originate with Judah Magnes, Stephen Wise, and Henrietta Szold, of course. In tracing the story of the relationship of American Jews with the Zionist idea one ought to begin with Mordecai Manuel Noah, the first well-known native-born American Jew. Although best known for his fantastic Ararat project, which was to have become a Jewish state "revived, renewed, and reestablished under the auspices of the United States" on Grand Island, near Buffalo, New York, in 1825, even more significant were his Zionist writings, most notably, his *Discourse on the Restoration of the Jews*, in 1844, which antedate those of Theodor Herzl by fifty years.[1] One also must not overlook Emma Lazarus, whose Zionist writings were partly influenced by the misery of Jews in Czarist Russia, and partly inspired by the writings of non-Jews such as Laurence Oliphant and George Eliot, particularly her first novel, *Daniel Deronda*. As early as 1883 Lazarus wrote, "I am fully persuaded that all suggested solutions other than this [Zionism] of the Jewish problem are but temporary palliatives."[2] If the list were extended to include crackpots, romantics, and geopolitical realists, it would be considerable. In the 1880s and 1890s, the State Department was so plagued by proposals from Zionists that Assistant Secretary Alvey Adee complained that, "Our volumes of Foreign Relations are plentifully supplied with correspondence on the subject, from 1884–1898 . . . . Every few months we are asked to negotiate [with Turkey] for the cession of Palestine to the Jewish 'nation.' The project is chimerical."[3]

113

Clearly, my study must be limited to the discussion of Americans who in fact settled in Palestine. Yet even within these confines difficulties appear. Who is an American? The conundrum is posed early. Although Jewish settlements of varying magnitude had existed in Palestine since the dispersion, American Jews only began to be identified about 1870, and for the most part, were naturalized American citizens and their offspring. When they claimed protection from the Turkish government, American consuls lamented that these were "spurious Americans" who had been born in Russia or Poland, had spent a few years in the United States and had settled in Palestine with no intention of returning to their country of citizenship. One outraged American consul, Selah Merrill, distinguished himself by his distaste for "Russian Jews" who demanded privileges due Americans: "To call them 'Americans' is an insult to American civilization."[4] His successive estimates indicated that from 150 in 1882, the number of these naturalized American Jews in Jerusalem had risen to 1,000 in 1902. In Jerusalem, in this medley of orthodox Jews, living mainly on halukah,[6] one Polish Jew, Simon Bermann, who immigrated to the United States in 1852 and settled in Palestine in 1870, distinguished himself by his early plans for agricultural cooperatives combined with individual holdings. His book, The Travels of Simon, published in 1879, stimulated Jewish immigrants to settle on the land. Though his proposals had no practical result because of the antagonism of the halukah rabbis who feared that philanthropic funds might be deflected from their support, Bermann created something of an ideological stir. At any rate, he was dubbed the "American," a designation to which his American style of dress and his eighteen years in the United States presumably entitled him.[7] He can be viewed as a precursor of Eliezer Lippe Joffe, a Russian Jew who went to the United States in 1904 to study new methods of agriculture and settled in Palestine in 1910. His pamphlet, "The Establishment of the Moshavei Ovdim" (1919), emphasized cooperative settlements and individual initiative in cooperative settlements in contrast to the kibbutz.[8]

The question as to who can be designated an American has been arbitrarily answered by some writers on the subject who accept a five-year residence in the United States as sufficient. This is as it should be, for it justifiably includes some of the chief ornaments of the American contingent, most notably Golda Meir. If place of birth or length of residence are to be decisive, Henrietta Szold and Judah Magnes are among the few early American Zionists with impeccable credentials. Of the hundreds of American volunteers who joined the Jewish Legion after World War I, an indeterminate number remained in Palestine. Many of them, like Golda Meir, had been brought to the United States in childhood and left in youth.

Born in Kiev in 1898, she came to the United States in 1906 and settled in Palestine in 1921. Her American experience had amounted to fifteen years, but these included the formative years of childhood and early youth. Her education was the American public school where she precociously distinguished herself. Her English, like her Yiddish, the language of the poor first generation immigrants who constituted her world, was always to remain better than her Hebrew. She never looked back on Milwaukee with the nostalgia of Henrietta Szold for the flowers of Baltimore, but she had been shaped as much by free America as by the Tsarist oppression that terrified her early childhood. The never-healed trauma of the five-year old cowering in fear before an imminent pogrom had determined her future beliefs, but by a fortunate alchemy she had been able to transform the suffering of Russia and the opportunities of the United States to her purpose. The American pioneer struggle and the country's achieved liberties were all signs of the possible. The reality of the American dream emboldened her Zionist vision. When she signed Israel's Declaration of Independence without truculence, her quiet assurance among the rich and titled, owed something not only to her character but to the democracy in which she had grown up. When, at the end of her life, she went back to be honored in the Milwaukee public school from which she had graduated, she acknowledged the American link in her strength.

Nor did Zionist pioneers of other nationalities allow her to forget that she was American. On the Mediterranean crossing, her group of twenty young Labor Zionists encountered Lithuanian *halutzim* who were travelling on deck, Mediterranean-style steerage. Golda characteristically persuaded her fellows to give up their luxurious third-class cabins to join the Lithuanians. Despite some protests at Golda's "moralistic" leadership none of the Americans balked. But the sacrifice had been in vain. The Lithuanians spurned the comradely advance: "We don't want Americans."[9] The Lithuanians were well-versed in Hebrew and trained in agriculture; the Yiddish-speaking Americans with no agricultural skills were dismissed as bourgeois and dilettante. The Americans conscious of their ignorance and their enjoyment of American comforts, humbly accepted the role of a lesser breed.

Even in the early months at Merhavia, the kibbutz Meir and her husband joined, her American background was suspect. While waiting in Tel Aviv for admission to the kibbutz, she had given English lessons; her critics charged that she should have chosen housework instead of a soft intellectual occupation. During the trial period at the kibbutz she betrayed a number of American refinements, such as skinning the herring, a kibbutz staple, and ironing her dress — she was always compulsively neat. These were potential bourgeois deviations. However, her physical energy, capacity for work and enthusiasm finally defeated the skeptics.[10]

I mention these seemingly insignificant matters because the distinction early made between "spoiled Americans" and other immigrant streams was to persist. Skinning the herring was symptomatic of a future cleavage. In the case of Golda and her fellow voyagers, the description "spoiled" could only be comparative. Her family never made the transition from poverty to the middle class; her older sister Shana, who with her two young children recklessly joined Golda on the S. S. Pocahantas in 1921, had contracted tuberculosis in girlhood as a factory worker. Worse privation was to be endured in Jerusalem after Golda left the kibbutz at her husband's insistence. To get a notion of the poverty endured by the young family — her two children were born in Jerusalem — two examples will suffice: for six months she did the washing for a nursery school, heating the water pail by pail and scrubbing clothes on a rough board. And when a neighbor warned the milkman not to extend credit to the destitute Myerson menage, she caned the meddler in outraged fury: "No one will take milk from my children."[11]

But there was never any danger that her Zionist resolution would weaken. What she wrote shortly after her arrival in Palestine to her brother-in-law, who had stayed behind temporarily in the United States to earn money to send to his wife (Shana showed me the letter when I was writing the biography of Golda), remained valid till her death almost sixty years later:

> Those who talk about returning are recent arrivals . . . I say that as long as those who created the little that is here are here, I cannot leave and you must come . . . . Of course this is not America and one may have to suffer a lot economically. There may even be pogroms again, but if one wants one's own land, and if one wants it with all one's heart, one must be ready for this . . . . Get ready. There is nothing to wait for.[12]

From this simple credo she never wavered.

In the same letter, the twenty-three year old woman ventured some political observations: "I am no politician and cannot exactly describe to you the politics of England. But one thing is clear to me.

If we will not go away, then England will help us. England will not choose the Arabs instead of us to settle Palestine." These less than prescient words from the woman who would become one of the chief protagonists in Jewish Palestine's struggle against the British twenty-five years later were the measure of her innocence. She had neither personal sophistication nor academic training; her power lay in her limitations; and her absolute espousal of two articles of Faith: First, that Jews must have equality as a people; and second, that all human beings must have social and economic equality. The synthesis of these beliefs was Socialist Zionism, whose banner she had raised in Milwaukee and was never to drop. In time, Golda would become an astute politician although not a geopolitical theorist or intellectual. She would never lose the sometimes alarmingly simple yet wonderfully persuasive force of her elementary convictions. They transformed her into a world leader.

Her career, so rich in drama that it might have been plotted by an overimaginative second-rate Hollywood script writer determined to place his heroine at the center of every world crisis that affected her people and with the temerity to add the familiar family versus career conflict as a tearjerker, is well-known. I will concentrate on that aspect of her activities of greatest contemporary interest: her views on the Arab problem. First, let me dispose of a current canard. As evidence of her egregious lack of sensibility, she has been repeatedly charged with denying the existence of Palestinians. Her actual words were: "There is no Palestinian people; there are Palestinian refugees."[13] In the 1980s, such a distinction is damning; within its historic context it is not at all so. When Golda arrived in Palestine, the only avowed Palestinians were Jewish pioneers. Arab nationalists stridently rejected the designation of "Palestinian" as an attempt to fragment an ideal Arab unitary state. From the Versailles Conference until the Partition debate at the United Nations, Arab spokesmen insisted that Palestine was southern Syria and that to confer independent status on this territory, cherished in Jewish history, infringed on the Arab nationalist vision. As late as 1956, Ahmed Shukairy, subsequently head of the Palestine Liberation Organization, argued at the Security Council that "it is common knowledge that Palestine is nothing but southern Syria." Golda took her adversaries at their word.[14]

Only in the 1960s did the Palestine Liberation Organization come forward with the demand that Arab refugees be renamed a homeless Palestinian people. Since that time, the distinction has become archaic. So completely has the new nomenclature triumphed that when some years ago the Herzl Press, of which I was editor, reissued two Zionist classics, one *A Palestine Diary*, written in the 1880s by Chaim Chissin, a Bilu pioneer, the other *Memoirs of Palestinian Women Pioneers*, originally published in 1932, fears were expressed that the titles would be misleading. I am happy to say that we stood our ground, perhaps to the confusion of librarians. But Golda saw no reason to comply with a revision of history that she viewed as an astute tactical ploy directed against Israel.

Not that she ever underestimated the force of Arab nationalism or the urgency of the Arab refugee question. Well known are her eloquent demonstrations of Arab responsibility for the plight of the 550,000 refugees who joined the Arab exodus in 1948 and her numerous proposals, when a member of the government, to reach a constructive solution for that plight.[15] In time, she accepted the fact that the changed vocabulary of Arab nationalism represented not merely a semantic trick but a sobering political reality, however spurious in its origin. This did not alter her view of the justice, *absolute not relative*, of Israel's cause; nor would she make peace with the facile formula that two homeless peoples, the Jews and the Palestinians, were battling for the same land. In weighing the claims of Arab and Jewish nationalism, she put in one scale Jewish need and the compromises already made through the whittling away of the original compromised homeland by the successive amputations of Trans-Jordan, in 1922 and the Partition Resolution in 1947; and in the other, the rich gratification of Arab nationalism in twenty-one independent new states with vast territories and rich natural resources.[56]

These arguments are standard Zionist exposition. What gave Meir's rhetoric its extraordinary force was that she had suffered each stage of the debate in her own experience and that her attitudes derived directly from that knowledge, not from polemical theorizing. She remembered keenly the young years when *she* was the *Palestinian* and recognized as such. She did not have to study British census figures to know that her coming had not displaced a single Arab. The barren fields of Merhavia she helped make habitable between bouts of malaria, the dahlias and apricots her daughter would in time send her from the Negev kibbutz of Revivim, gave her the assurance to challenge adversaries with the proud declaration that Jewish toil had created more living space for both Arab and Jew. In her capacity as Foreign Minister and Prime Minister, she mastered the appropriate diplomatic terminology and learned how to negotiate toughly in the international arena just as she had been a tough labor leader in the

Histadrut and a shrewd party politician in Mapai. But the moral core of her conviction, in its pure, some would say simplistic clarity, was what sustained her.

Between such an approach and Judah Magnes's early perception of the immediate critical need for Arab-Jewish conciliation, there was no meeting point. No mention is made of Magnes in her long autobiography. Nor do her close associates of the prestate decades in Palestine recall any discussion of Magnes with her. In the 1930s, when she was secretary of the Histadrut, the great labor union of Jewish Palestine, she might well have had dealings with Magnes in his capacity as administrator of a university that employed many workers. Recall, however, that Magnes was away from Palestine in 1946 which was the time of Golda's rise to prominence as a political activist. But there is little doubt as to her disagreement with the Magnes political program. Like Magnes, she opposed partition when it was first proposed by the British Royal Commission in 1937, but she changed in response to the catastrophe of the Holocaust when partition became the official policy of the Jewish Agency. Her views on Brit Shalom or the Ihud are easy to deduce.

Golda's political mentors were Ben-Gurion and Berl Katznelson, the spiritual teacher of pioneer Palestine whom she venerated. Both men were involved with Magnes in negotiations with Arab Leaders — a process Ben Gurion describes in his book, *My Talks With Arab Leaders.* As early as 1924, at a meeting called by Brit Shalom, Ben-Gurion stated his opposition to a binational state on the grounds that Jewish national independence could be enjoyed only in the tiny area allotted whereas Arabs had vast unpopulated territories for settlement and dominance.[17] However, Ben-Gurion early favored parity, and throughout the 1930s the cooperation of Magnes in arranging meetings with Arab notables was often enlisted. As related by Ben Gurion, the tortuous discussions form a disheartening record.

Whether there was any realistic possibility of accommodation between the opposing viewpoints of the parties is not within the scope of this essay to assess. Both Ben-Gurion and Katznelson espoused binational parity in the legislative bodies to prevent domination of one national group by the other. Katznelson was a passionate advocate of this position, however, with one proviso: Parity would come when Jewish independence had reached full development. A break with Magnes came in 1938 when it was reported to the Jewish Agency that he had negotiated with Nuri Pasha in Beirut on the possibility of a Jewish agreement based on a minority status for Jews in Palestine and a fixed ratio for Jewish residents, supposedly a third, in relation to other inhabitants of Palestine. In answer to this charge, Dr. Magnes wrote to Ben-Gurion that he had advocated a temporary, not a permanent, minority status for Jews, a reply that despite Ben Gurion's professions of personal esteem for Magnes was not likely to placate the Jewish Agency.[18]

In 1947, during the hearings before the United Nations Commission on Palestine in Jerusalem, the Ihud delegation headed by Magnes, proposed, in contrast to the Jewish Agency's demand for a Jewish state, a United Nations trusteeship and Jewish immigration to Palestine till numerical equality between Jews and Arabs had been achieved. Obviously, Golda, by then head of the political department of the Jewish Agency and totally committed to a Jewish state that even if truncated would be able to authorize the free immigration of the survivors of the Holocaust, would find little to applaud in such a proposal.

Unlike the Revisionists who were maximalists in their demand for territory — a Jewish state on both sides of the Jordan River — Golda was a maximalist in her concept of national independence. She was realistic enough to accept territorial compromise as in the Partition Resolution, but she insisted that within the confines agreed to as a painful but necessary sacrifice, freedom to act in behalf of martyred Jewry should be untrammelled.[19]

That the longed-for Jewish state brought not only national independence that at last opened the gates barred by the British, but also unending hostility baffled and grieved her; but it never shook her faith in the necessity and goodness of what had been achieved. When in the euphoria of Israel's dazzling victory in June 1967 she declared to a huge Madison Square Garden audience gathered to celebrate with a sadness that haunted her hearers, "The last thing that Israelis want is to win wars. We want peace,"[20] she was voicing her deepest disappointment. As her repeated public appeals to Arabs from 1948 on indicate, she was tormented by a sense of lost opportunities, and by the tantalizing awareness of how much Arab-Jewish cooperation might achieve for both peoples in the Middle East. And with maternal intensity, she mourned the waste of young lives in sterile warfare. But this did not weaken her insistence on full national independence and on "secure borders," an insistence that her critics regarded as short-sighted and inflexible, but that her admirers viewed as high-minded and hard-headed. She could, with equal sincerity, reach the ethical nobility of her much-quoted statement, "When peace comes, we will perhaps be able to forgive the Arabs for killing our sons, but it will be harder for us to forgive them for having forced us to kill their sons,"[21] and she could also reply sharply to those who feared that Israel might become militaristic, "I don't want a fine, liberal, anticolonial militaristic, *dead* Jewish state."[22]

In June 1967, in a private conversation, I asked her what would happen to the newly conquered West Bank. Her answer was instantaneous, "What would we do with a million Arabs!" The concerted refusal of the Arabs to negotiate with Israel changed what might have been a temporary occupation into a continuing presence. And there is no denying that with the passage of time and constant Arab belligerence the Israeli mood hardened. However, as Prime Minister, Golda advocated the Allon plan, still the program of the Labor Party, that calls for withdrawal from most of the populated West Bank, while opposing a separate Palestinian state.

The idealistic girl matured into an adroit stateswoman, skilled in negotiation, temperate in argument, yet granite in action and desire. Her sometimes despairing outcry, "We wanted to be good farmers, not good soldiers," did not weaken her will for what seemed to her the ultimate good: Jewish national survival in a just society. To the end, she believed that the national and social visions of her youth would be fulfilled despite the failures of which she was bitterly aware. Among these, American Jewry's refusal to settle in Israel in significant numbers rankled keenly. "You are ready to die with us, why don't you live with us?" she asked young American volunteers in one of Israel's wars. That was her wound as well as the wound of Zionism.

Although Golda was the most illustrious of the early American Zionists, others should not be overlooked. First come those who accompanied her on the aptly named S. S. Pocahantas. In 1961, forty years after the arrival of the original contingent, Foreign Minister Meir invited her old comrades to a celebration of the anniversary. Of the original nineteen only eight came; some had died, some were ill, one had returned to America. However, children and grandchildren, blond, blue-eyed sabras and dusky Yemenites whose presence testified to the authentic melting pot of Israel, filled Her Excellency's drawing room. To the bewilderment of one American guest, the young folks preferred to sing popular American songs rather than the well-worn pioneer lyrics of their grandparents.

Of those who achieved eminence besides Golda, one ought to name Dov Joseph, a Canadian who enlisted in the Jewish Legion and settled in Jerusalem in 1921; and who would come to be known as

Joseph, the Provider, for his heroic role as military governor of Jerusalem during the siege of the city in 1948. Another notable recruit of the Jewish Legion to settle in Palestine was Gershon Agronsky, known as Gershon Agron, editor of the *Palestine Post*, later the *Jerusalem Post*. Among those who also ought to be included are the poet Jesse Sampter who settled in Palestine in 1919 and the educator, Deborah Kallen, sister of the distinguished American Jewish philosopher, Horace Meyer Kallen.

Throughout the thirties small organized groups of He-Halutz went to Palestine after receiving agricultural training in preparatory farming communes in the United States. Ein Ha-Shofet and Kfar Blum are among the first kibbutzim established by Americans.

Various memoirs of the period written by members of Ha-Shomer Ha-Tzair or Habonim, describe the particular difficulties of American workers. Ben-Zion Ilan, born Benjamin Applebaum,[23] who in 1931 at age nineteen left the Bronx to spend his life in the kibbutz of Afikim, dwelt not only on the physical hardships but on what he calls the "cultural gap," a phrase that would echo in a different context in the future, for few Americans knew Hebrew. There was the further disadvantage of what Ilan called, "The light in darkness," the American passport, a temptation and escape hatch for the socialist pioneer in the Emek (Valley of Jezreel), just as it would be in later years for the middle-class American in Jerusalem or Tel Aviv, who would cite a favorite horror story about the imbecilities of Israeli bureaucracy. In the 1920s and 1930s, the individual could blame only his personal inability to endure danger, disease, and backbreaking toil.

Unlike later doubts, in these early memoirs, the conviction of the splendor of the ideal embraced shines forth. Strikingly absent are the realistic misgivings of the intellectuals of the Magnes circle. Was this difference due solely to deficiencies in maturity and comprehension? Part of the explanation may lie in the difference between the life of a university scholar and that of a kibbutznik draining a swamp in the Huleh valley. Young Benny Applebaum and his comrades were, like Golda, convinced by their daily labor that their activities were socially productive and nationally redemptive. Their lives confirmed their ideology. If Arab marauders from a neighboring village attacked an installation obviously beneficial for the country and all its inhabitants, then as socialists and Zionists these pioneers could deplore blind obstructionism instead of doubting the righteousness of their cause. In that Zionist dawn, Golda and her comrades saw the creation of the homeland within the parameters of their initial concept. It gave them the uncritical assurance to dismiss the shadows and misgivings already perceived on Mount Scopus. It also gave them the spiritual energy to create the state.

IV
The Hebrew University

Figure 10. Hebrew University opening, 1925, with Chaim Weizmann at Magnes's right. *(Courtesy of Weizmann Archives)*

9

The Idea of a
Jewish University

DAVID BIALE

Judah Magnes will be remembered for many varied achievements in the history of the Jews of the twentieth century, but undoubtedly his most enduring contribution was to the creation of the first Jewish university, the Hebrew University of Jerusalem. Although Magnes had never served previously as a faculty member at an academic institution — a fact which caused considerable controversy — he left an unmistakable stamp on the new institution. In many ways, Magnes's conception of the university symbolized his general political and philosophical position just as the university as a whole can be seen as a symbol for some fundamental tensions in the Zionist movement. In these remarks, I address both the idea of a Jewish university and its relationship to Zionism and, more specifically, Magnes's contribution to the history of the idea.

The idea of a Jewish university actually originated at the end of the Middle Ages. In 1466, the Sicilian Jewish community petitioned the Sicilian King John II to allow them to establish a university similar to those of the time, but for Jews only. This idea was stillborn, despite official sanction. Such was also the fate of a similar project in the city of Mantova. In the eighteenth century, Jean-Jacques Rousseau in his *Émile* proposed a Jewish university that would be part of a free Jewish state. But it was only with the emergence of Jewish nationalism in the 1880s that the idea of a Jewish university began to win a real following. The first to propose such a project was Hermann Schapira, one of the earliest activists in the pre-Zionist Hovevei Zion (Lovers of Zion) movement, and a professor of mathematics at the University of Heidelberg, who, in 1882, wrote two articles in the Hebrew periodical *Ha-Meliz*, in which he proposed establishing a Jewish university consisting of faculties of theology and the natural sciences. As with many of the other projects of the Hovevei Zion, Schapira's proved premature and had to wait the establishment of Herzl's Zionist movement in 1897. At the first Zionist Congress, Schapira again raised his suggestion, but it was taken seriously only in 1901 by three young Zionists: Chaim Weizmann, Martin Buber, and Berthold Feivel.[1]

In 1902, these three published a pamphlet in German calling for the establishment of a *Jüdische Hochschule.*[2] This pamphlet is worth examining carefully, for it tells much about the initial impetus for a Jewish university. All three authors were from Eastern Europe and were acutely aware of the quota restrictions imposed on Jews in Russian gymnasia, universities, and technical schools. The *numerus clausus* was causing many young Jews to emigrate to Central Europe in order to continue their educations. But even in countries such as Germany and Switzerland, which had no formal governmental quotas for Jews, hostility to foreigners had begun to have an impact on university admissions. After an extensive review of the difficulties facing young East European Jews in acquiring higher educations, the pamphlet's authors concluded that many of their generation were, at best, "half-educated" and thus incapable of fully realizing their potential.

A Jewish university was necessary to counter one of the consequences of modern anti-Semitism. In addition, here is found a desire to use education as a means to modernize Jews. As such, the proposal for a Jewish university fell squarely in a long tradition of Jewish *Bildung*, that is, the argument by enlighteners from Western and Eastern Europe that the Jewish educational system must be thoroughly reformed and that only by exposing Jews to modern languages and science would integration in the modern world become possible. The educational program of the Russian *Haskalah* and the work of the Alliance Israelite Universelle were based on this belief in education. By the beginning of the twentieth century, disillusionment with the hope of integration had changed the focus of this educational movement to national rebirth but the goal of modernizing Jews remained the same. Although the authors of the pamphlet were all committed Zionists and favored establishing the Jewish University in Palestine, they were prepared to locate their school in Switzerland or England if Palestine proved too unpromising. Thus, their commitment was first and foremost to educating Jews and only secondarily to building up the land of Israel.

Interestingly, the 1902 pamphlet, which included a detailed organization and budget for the university, mentions a department of Jewish studies only in passing. Certainly, no one could accuse Martin Buber of lack of concern for Jewish education. But even if unwittingly, the pamphlet thus suggested one extreme interpretation of the idea of a Jewish university: a university meant for Jews, but one without any particular Jewish content. The university in this form addressed the problem of the Jews, but not the problem of Judaism. As any student of Zionism knows, this was a critical issue which Zionism as a whole had to confront and which remains very much alive today. Not surprisingly, a Jewish university in a national setting would necessarily have to wrestle with this problem daily, for in a university, cultural questions also involve practical matters of budgets and institutional priorities. It is amusing that the mathematician, Edmund Landau, in an argument for establishing a faculty of mathematics, called mathematics the "cheapest and most Jewish of the sciences."[3] For much of the next decade, little progress was made toward the university, but when the project was revived in 1912 and 1913, this tension over the character of the future university continued. Under the influence of Chaim Weizmann and Judah Magnes, the Eleventh Zionist Congress adopted a resolution in September 1913 instructing the Actions Committee to "undertake the preparatory work necessary for the foundation of a Hebrew university in Jerusalem." In January 1914, Weizmann persuaded Baron Edmon de Rothschild to support the project, but Rothschild initially favored only a scientific research institute in place of a university. Magnes, on the other hand, advocated first establishing an institute of archaeology as a way of emphasizing the Jewish nature of the university. Rothschild was eventually convinced by Weizmann to abandon his opposition to a university and other philanthropists were enlisted to finance the project.[4]

The outbreak of World War I in 1914 effectively aborted plans to found the university immediately, but in 1918, directly on the heels of the British army's conquest of Palestine, the foundation stones of the university were laid on Mount Scopus. This ceremonial act was largely symbolic since neither the money nor the infrastructure of the university would be ready for another seven years. In 1925, however, the university was finally ready to open its doors. As a result of a contribution from the American philanthropist, Felix Warburg, the Institute for Jewish Studies became the first academic unit of the university. In giving Jewish studies an honored position at the Hebrew university, the founders made it clear that the university would be a Jewish university as well as a university for Jews.

Those who gave the university this clear direction were influenced by the philosophy of Ahad Ha-Am for whom Zionism was to revitalize Judaism on a secular, cultural basis. In a letter to Chaim Weizmann upon the opening of the Hebrew University, Ahad Ha-Am emphasized the connection between the new university and the creation of a new Hebrew culture in Palestine.[5] This point was made even more strongly by Chaim Nachman Bialik in his address at the opening of the university on Mount Scopus. Bialik argued that the Jews had survived for so long through their devotion to spiritual life. In the modern world, the university came to replace the *heder* and *bet-hamidrash* whose time had passed. Bialik thus saw the university as carrying on a tradition of Jewish education in a national setting. For Bialik, the crucial element in the university was the Hebrew language which he believed would revitalize Judaism in an almost magical way. Bialik argued that the university had to fit into the new Zionist conception of the necessary connection between material and spiritual life:

> The Land of Israel is necessary for the continuation of the survival of our people. For, there has occurred a shift in our fundamental conception of the relationship between the material and spiritual survival of the nation . . . . We [no longer] argue for a separation and distinction between material and spiritual life, just as we [no longer] argue for such a division between Jew and human being . . . . In the consciousness of the nation, a new concept of culture has taken hold which is all-inclusive and humanistic. [This concept] has replaced the theological concept of 'Torah.'[6]

Zionism was to break down the diaspora distinctions between materiality and spirituality, just as it would erase the divisions between Jews and other nations. The university, as part of this secular national enterprise, would not be an ivory tower, but rather a force for the realization of a new concept of culture. For both Ahad Ha-Am and Bialik, the university would therefore serve the cause of "normalization" of the Jewish people. For the cultural Zionists, such normalization meant not the assimilation of Jewish culture into some abstract Western culture, but rather the reconstruction of Jewish national culture on a humanistic basis.

An important contribution to this interpretation of the university was an essay by Zalman Shazar, who was to become the third president of Israel. In 1917, Shazar wrote in Martin Buber's periodical *Der Jude* of the attempt by Leopold Zunz to establish a chair of Jewish studies in a German university.[7] Zunz, who was one of the founders of the *Wissenschaft des Judentums* or school of scientific study of

Judaism, believed that the emancipation of Jewish studies had to be part of the emancipation of the Jews. But just as the emancipation of the Jews had largely failed, so the attempt to integrate Jewish studies in the universities had come to nothing. Shazar pointed out that only in faculties of theology, where Jews were not welcome, did any study of Judaism — although only biblical Judaism — take place. The only discipline which interested non-Jewish scholars in secular institutions was Hebrew philology and it is interesting to note that for this reason, the philological approach to Jewish texts assumed an important place in the Hebrew University, a place which it still holds today. Although Shazar did not specifically mention the need for a university in Zion, he concluded his essay with a call for revitalizing Jewish studies in the context of the renewal of the Jewish nation.

Shazar's essay suggested the importance of a secular approach to Jewish studies. The followers of Ahad Ha-Am believed that such an approach was only possible as a result of Zionism. The application of critical methods to the study of Jewish sources was already a century old by the time the Hebrew University was founded. Yet, as Gershom Scholem argued in his famous essay in 1945 on the Science of Judaism, apologetic concerns severely biased the work of the nineteenth-century scholars. As he wrote in his biting style, the apologetic needs of the *Wissenschaft des Judentums* had caused it

> to remove the irrational stinger and banish the demonic enthusiasm from Jewish history through exaggerated theologizing and spiritualizing. This was actually the decisive original sin. This terrifying giant, our history, is called to task . . . and this enormous creature, full of destructive power, made up of vitality, evil and perfection, must contract itself, stunt its growth and declare that it has no substance. The demonic giant is nothing but a simple fool who fulfills the duties of a solid citizen and every decent Jewish bourgeois could unashamedly bid him good-day in the streets of the city, the immaculate city of the nineteenth century.[8]

While not all the cultural Zionists were as revolutionary as Scholem, his animus against the nineteenth-century Jewish historians certainly struck a nerve. Even if one does not accept Scholem's belief in the "demonic" in Jewish history, it is clear that an unbiased and comprehensive examination of all aspects of Jewish history, which was part of the original program of the *Wissenschaft des Judentums*, was impossible in nineteenth-century Europe. Caught by the need to answer anti-Semitism and to gain admission to European "culture," the historians were forced to show how *similar* Jewish history was to that of Christian Europe rather than to explore what was unique to the Jews.

It was the hope of the cultural Zionists that Zionism would free the Jews from the need for apologetics and make possible an objective study of Judaism. Again, to quote Scholem:

> The new valuations of Zionism brought a breath of fresh air into a house that seemed to have been all too carefully set in order by the nineteenth century. This ventilation was good for us. Within the framework of the rebuilding of Palestine it led to the foundation of centers where Judaic studies, although central, are pursued without any ideological coloring. Everyone is free to say and to teach whatever corresponds to his scholarly opinion without being bound to any religious (or anti-religious) tendency.[9]

To be sure, just what content a secular Judaism might have was a question which Ahad Ha-Am and his followers never fully answered. Perhaps Scholem's personal credo would serve best: "Nothing Jewish is alien to me." Indeed, Scholem's own appointment to a chair of Jewish mysticism when the Institute of Jewish Studies was created proved that the founders of the university did not allow themselves to be restricted by either an orthodox or rationalist interpretation of Judaism.

Yet, the secular character of the university was not a certain matter for all the founders. Chaim Weizmann feared that Judah Magnes might turn the Institute for Jewish Studies into a theological seminary.[10] Weizmann was unfortunately motivated by extreme personal hostility to Magnes, a subject to which we will have to return. His fear was largely unwarranted and indeed, today, the Hebrew University represents one of the few places in modern Israel where secular and religious Jews work together under generally accepted scholarly canons. The credit for this achievement goes to the founders of the university who were, for the most part, trained in the universities of Central Europe and brought with them a secular approach to scholarship. The Hebrew University was a product of what has been called the "secular movement" in Jewish history, that spectacular period when writers and artists who had deep roots in Jewish tradition were trying to create a Jewish culture in Hebrew and Yiddish without a specifically religious basis.

Magnes himself played a significant role in determining the secular character of Jewish studies at the new university, Weizmann's fears notwithstanding. Perhaps as a result of his American background, Magnes took a broad approach to Jewish learning. An interesting example of this was his enthusiasm in trying to bring Walter Benjamin to the university in 1928.[11] Benjamin was an iconoclastic German literary critic whose connection to Judaism was largely through his friend, Gershom Scholem. In 1928, Scholem arranged a meeting between Magnes and Benjamin in which Benjamin spoke of his desire to turn his literary and theological interests to Jewish sources. Magnes agreed to give Benjamin a stipend to learn Hebrew after which it was hoped that he would find a place on the university faculty. Unfortunately, Magnes made the mistake of sending Benjamin the stipend in Germany instead of waiting for him to show up in Jerusalem. Benjamin, who was desperately short of money, used up the stipend and never followed through with the plan, partly, it seems, because of his increasing attraction to Marxism. What this story illustrates about Magnes was his willingness to encourage eccentric approaches to Jewish sources which had little or no basis in traditional Judaism.

I have alluded to Magnes's conflict with Weizmann and we cannot avoid discussing the great controversy between Magnes and his supporters on one side and Weizmann and Albert Einstein on the other.[12] This controversy shook the university for a number of years in the late 1920s and early 1930s until, in 1933, Magnes was, in his own words, "kicked upstairs" to the honorific position of president and stripped of his academic responsibilities. To read the documents of this dispute today is a melancholy undertaking for it does not reflect well on any of the principals, all men of great achievements, and, sad to say, even greater egos. I do not wish to devote attention to the personal side of the controversy which undoubtedly played a major role. What is important, in light of our subject, are the principles at dispute. Magnes argued for control of the university by people living in the Yishuv, while Weizmann and Einstein favored supervision by outsiders. This was not solely a question of academic governance but also reflected the larger conflict between the Yishuv and the Diaspora Zionist movement. Weizmann represented the interests of the World Zionist Organization, which wished in general to maintain control over events in the Yishuv while the leaders of the Yishuv, such as Ben-Gurion, were already in the 1920s determined to govern themselves. Thus, the Magnes controversy was really a teacup tempest symbolizing a basic issue in Zionism: control by the Yishuv or by the Zionists in the Diaspora.

Weizmann and Einstein considered Magnes no more than a lackey of American Jewish money and a man with no genuine academic credentials. It is certainly true that Magnes seemed to have a prejudice against the natural sciences and, as chancellor, he ruined his relationships with the scientists. From an academic viewpoint, concerning matters such as promotions and selection of faculty, Magnes was probably not the right person for the job. Yet, Magnes on his side had an equally legitimate concern about Weizmann. Fearing Weizmann's political opportunism, he wrote in his journal: "It is his moral quality that is questionable. He is through and through a politician. He is constantly playing a game, very cleverly and one does not know what he is after. His statement to me recently that he would resign if Einstein did, is part of some game calculated to bring him advantage . . . ."[13] He feared that Weizmann would politicize the university by bringing it under the aegis of the Zionist Executive. He also believed that Weizmann was trying to obtain academic appointments for political cronies. As a result of his American upbringing, Magnes was keenly sensitive to the importance of academic freedom and he fought vigorously to keep the university nonpartisan and unpolitical. At a time when the Zionist movement was politicized on almost every question, Magnes's view of the university was virtually unique. In the Yishuv during the 1920s and 1930s, almost every aspect of life from sports to health care was organized and dominated by political parties as they created the infrastructure of the future Jewish state. In the long run, Magnes's success in keeping the university out of the hands of political functionaries was a signal contribution to a society which has remained balkanized by politics.

Magnes's hostility to the mixing of politics with education was rooted in his anarchistic tendencies. He wrote to Felix Warburg concerning Weizmann's designs:

> One of the great evils of the present day is, in my opinion, the authority which the State exercises over religion and education. The modern state presumes to be higher than a man's conscience and the modern state has destroyed the old *res publica* of learning. Everything is subservient to the State . . . . Coming to Palestine: one of the evils of the educational system is its absolute dependence, financially and spiritually, upon the Zionist political machinery. The fact that the University is, fortunately, independent of this is helping us to create a true University.[14]

Magnes's fear that the university would be used for political purposes and subverted by extreme nationalism is reflected in his journal entries as early as the university inauguration in 1925.[15] He did not believe the university should be connected to the Balfour declaration and thus with what he considered British imperialism. Instead of using the university inauguration as an occasion for Zionist propaganda, Magnes saw the university as reaching beyond nationalism. In one of his journal entries in which he reflected on the relationship between nationalism and universalism, he noted that the university would be the first universal institution in Palestine.[16] For the Jews to foster universalism required first education in Judaism: thus, the need for a Jewish university. But, for Magnes, the idea of a university excluded pure nationalism or chauvinism. He hoped that the university, thus conceived, would become a meeting place between Jews and Arabs and serve as a means for reconciling the two nations.

Magnes's vision of a Jewish university as a stepping-stone to universalism reflected both his American Jewish training and his Zionist political position. Magnes brought with him to Palestine the belief that Jewish nationalism was only justified if it served a universal aim, a stance which may be seen as a nationalist variant on classical Reform's universalist teachings:

> The doctrine of the Reform Jews was universalism. Who can quarrel with the doctrine? It is the doctrine of the prophets . . . . But while preaching this doctrine, they were all the while trying to escape from their Judaism . . . . They uprooted much of their wholesome, vital *Volkstum* and proved themselves false to the very doctrine of universalism they preached. For the most part they remained part-Jews, and in every country became chauvinistic and super-patriotic.[17]

Thus, for Magnes, the universalists who deny their Jewish roots end up as rabid chauvinists in the countries in which they live. Only a universalist stance linked to genuine national roots can succeed: "The Jew who has so thoroughly grounded himself in his Judaism that his universalism becomes the development and crown of his Judaism."[18] This interpretation of Jewish nationalism in general and the role of the Hebrew University in specific was out of harmony with most Zionist thinking. Most Zionists had rejected universalism as too abstract and utopian: a Jewish obsession not shared by any other nation. In their desire to normalize the Jews, they saw the Hebrew University as one institution among many in the national movement rather than as a beacon standing above the national struggle. It was surely utopian of Magnes to believe that any Zionist enterprise established during this period of crisis and tension could remain aloof from nationalist passion.

A good example of Magnes's utopianism was his support for the Brit Shalom group and his later leadership of the binationalist Ihud.[19] The Brit Shalom originated in the mid-1920s in response to the increased Arab hostility to Jewish immigration and it proposed a retreat from the Zionist goal of a Jewish majority in the land of Israel.

Given the small number of Jews in the country and the lack of urgency for a Jewish state which only would be felt after 1933, the Brit Shalom's program was not so unrealistic. But the Ihud's call for binationalism in the 1940s, in the wake of the Holocaust and the Arab riots of the 1930s, was an idealistic exercise in futility if not naivité.

Both of these movements drew heavily on university faculty members for support, and even though the majority of the faculty opposed them, the university acquired a reputation as an iconooclastic institution. In the final analysis, this image of the university, to which Magnes made perhaps the signal contribution, gave Zionism a less monolithic character than one might expect of a nationalist movement.

Magnes also had to fight on another front for his idea of a Jewish university. The very name "Hebrew University" implied something different from "Jewish university." In the vocabulary of Jewish nationalism, the new Hebrew man was to be a reincarnation of the Hebrew of the Bible: close to nature, capable of defending himself and scornful of the *galut*.[20] If for some like Bialik, a Hebrew university meant a university conducted in the Hebrew language, for others it meant something much more radical: a rejection of the scholarly tradition of exile and adoption of a revolutionary, nationalist ethos. Among some faculty and students, this ideology inspired direct action to turn the university into a battleground for Hebrew nationalism. Thus, in 1932, a group of right-wing students succeeded in disrupting a lecture by Norman Bentwich, who had been Attorney-General for the British Mandate and was sympathetic to the Brit Shalom.[21]

A particularly revealing incident occurred in 1927 over the question of establishing a chair of Yiddish at the Hebrew University. Magnes had raised a substantial sum from a New York Jew to finance the chair, but he ran into vociferous opposition from nationalist elements. Here seemed to be a direct challenge to their ideal of a new Hebrew culture divorced from the "jargon" of the diaspora. Public demonstrations were held by the Brigade for the Defense of the Hebrew Language, *Gedud Meginei ha-Safa ha-Ivrit*, with the war-cry *tzelem ba-heikhal* ("there is a crucifix in the Temple"). Faculty opposition came from Menachem Ussishkin and Joseph Klausner. Klausner threatened to lead a group of students to break up the lectures of anyone appointed to fill such a chair. A committee of the faculty was formed consisting of Magnes, Ussishkin, Gershom Scholem, Bialik, Hugo Bergman, and Moshe Schwab to deliberate upon the question. Magnes was afraid that the Yishuv might boycott the University if the chair was inaugurated and it was decided to quietly bury the whole project. Fortunately, these ideological battles calmed down by the time the State of Israel was founded and the chair of Yiddish was finally established in 1951 with Professor Dov Sadan as its first occupant. But Magnes himself did not live to see this vindication of his desire for a truly Jewish university and not just a sectarian Zionist institution.[22]

The battle over Yiddish thus represented a fundamental argument over the place of a Jewish university in Zionism. Nationalism threatened to impose its own agenda on the free and open investigation of Jewish life. Gershom Scholem, writing on the twentieth anniversary of the founding of the Institute for Jewish Studies, bitterly criticized some of his colleagues for the sin of nationalist excess:

> We came to rebel but we ended up continuing [in the same path] . . . . All these plagues have now disguised themselves in nationalism. From the frying pan into the fire: after the emptiness of assimilation comes another, that of nationalist excess. We have cultivated nationalist 'sermons' and 'rhetoric' [melitza] in science to take the place of religious sermons and rhetoric.[23]

Scholem's fears over the effect of nationalism on the university — fears which Magnes shared — have largely proven unfounded. Yet, in a subtle way, the problem of nationalism remains in the very structure of the university. The study of Judaism is not integrated into the departments of humanities but is instead a separate institute within the faculty. Instead of studying the Jews as part of general history and culture, students see the Jews as separate and different. One might legitimately ask whether this approach serves either good scholarship and teaching or the larger universalist goals posed by Magnes.

In the final analysis, the question of a Jewish university cannot be divorced from the question of a Jewish state. In a world still hostile to Jewish national aspirations, it is exceedingly difficult to rise above political passions as Magnes urged. Whether a Jewish university can help to revitalize Judaism and the Jewish people without succumbing to the worst excesses of nationalism remains an open question. In recent years, the university has once again become the scene of political battles between different conceptions of Zionism. A university does not exist outside of its society and the questions with which it must grapple remain questions for the society as a whole.

Figure 11. Magnes and Martin Buber c. 1945. (*Courtesy of the Buber Archive, Jewish National and University Library*)

10

The Appeal of the Incorrigible Idealist

PAUL R. MENDES-FLOHR

In the spring of 1922 exhausted, deeply aggrieved but unrepentant, Judah L. Magnes departed for Palestine. He had been ostracized by the established American Jewish community, which remained unconvinced that his pacifism and radical politics were not only consistent with, but also dictated by, the pristine teachings of Judaism. On the eve of his journey, he wrote to his lifelong friend Max Schloessinger:[1]

> As to myself, I have become what you might call *ziemlich radikal*. For example, while not myself a member of the Socialist or Communist Party, I sympathize deeply with what the Soviets are trying to do in Russia, and with what the *Betriebsräte* (industrial councils) are trying to do in Germany. In short, I am one of those innocents who believe in the possibility of a new world, and both as a Jew and a human being I should like to do whatever I can to bring it about . . . .

In Jerusalem, the forty-five year old Magnes soon found a community of mostly Central European intellectuals, who shared not only his radical politics but also his profound conviction that the renewal of Judaism sponsored by Zionism could only be sustained by a religious or, more correctly, by a Biblical humanism. This community, although relatively small in number, occupied a prestigious position within the Yishuv and provided Magnes with what sociologists would call a "plausibility structure:" sharing his fundamental perceptions of the world, his deepest sentiments and symbolic discourse, they granted his worldview a necessary sociopsychological credibility, without which he would have courted the peril of a debilitating cognitive and spiritual solipsism. Confirming his worldview, they thus encouraged Magnes to continue, with renewed resolve and energy, to promote his conception of Israel as a primary agent in creating a just and compassionate world.

Yet, there was much, it should be noted, that estranged Magnes from his Jerusalem colleagues. They often found his rhetoric sermonic and platitudinous, the exposition of his ideas superficial, and his general learning wanting. Indeed, true to the intellectual traditions of their Central European education, Magnes's colleagues tended to view matters in more complex, dialectical terms than he, developing their thoughts in a philosophically more nuanced fashion. Moreover, one suspects that Magnes remained in their eyes an American, and even with respect to him they found it difficult to overcome the supercilious disdain for *Amerika* that European intellectuals were then wont to cultivate. Despite his Heidelberg Ph.D. and fluent, albeit faulty German, it seems all too evident that Magnes neve quite passed as a *yekke*, a German Jew, in Israeli slang. Nonetheless, they found him to be a compelling figure, who elicited their respect, affection, and even loyalty.

An insight into the nature of their affinity to Magnes may be gained from a novel by Hermann Hesse, *Das Glasperlenspiel (The Glass Bead Game)*.[2] Published in 1943, after a gestation of nearly twenty years, Hesse addressed in this his last and perhaps greatest work, the most urgent issue facing European intellectuals of his age: the relation of intellect to life. In a sense the novel is an autobiography of the Central European intellectual — especially from the *fin de siècle* through the protracted anguish of World War I to the restless confusion of the 1920s and 1930s. The intellectuals, or more precisely *die Geistige*, fancy themselves to be denizens of the *Universitas Litterarum*, the province of *Kultur* and genuine spiritual quest. But Hesse detects in this league of the elite a recurrent failure to authentically relate *Kultur* to the mundane, troubled existence of ordinary men, to a world they had grown to distrust as being fundamentally alien to spirit, and all that is noble.

In the wake of World War I, Hesse notes in his novel, intellectuals became increasingly aware that their self-indulgent isolation was morally untenable and that they had an irrefragable responsibility to contemporary social reality. On the other hand, the Great War also led to an eclipse of bourgeois optimism, to terrible doubts and despair. Hesse is alarmed by the attendant cynicism of many intellectuals, but clearly he is more troubled by the rejection of *Kultur* and the nihilistic adoption of the *vita activa* of those eager for social commitment.

Hesse finds a glimmer of hope in Joseph Knecht, the principal protagonist of his novel, who represents a small but heroic counter-movement of intellectuals who affirm the moral imperative of the *vita activa* without, however, abandoning the *vita comtemplativa*. These votaries of what may be called a new humanism — among whom, incidentally, Hesse would have undoubtedly included his dear friend, Martin Buber[3] — seek to ground the life of social responsibility in *Kultur* which despite the gnawing doubts of their age, they uphold to be the realm of humanity's most refined moral and spiritual sensibilities.

After World War I, a small but distinguished band of Central European Jewish intellectuals gathered in Jerusalem. These highly cultured individuals, many of whom were to join the faculty of the fledgling Hebrew University, may be numbered among Hesse's heroic upholders of the countermovement for a new humanism, who came to Zion to participate in the Jewish cultural renaissance, especially as understood by Ahad Ha-Am and Martin Buber.[4] For them, the active commitment to creating a modern Hebrew culture meant a liberation from the moral and spiritual faculty of bourgeois culture. For the cultural venture of Zionism addressed not only the inner spiritual life of the Jews but also their concrete, communal existence. Zionism was thus conceived as the matrix of a new Jewish humanism, a humanism that would exemplify to the community of nations that national existence need not be fostered by militarism, *realpolitik* and chauvinism, forces these intellectuals held responsible for the First World War and its demonic fury. Indicative of their idealism was an ultimately stillborn effort in 1921 and 1922 to found a "Jewish Society for International Understanding" (*Jüdische Gesellschaft für Internationale Verständigung*).[5] The society, which included among its charter members such leading Zionist personalities as Martin Buber, Chaim Nachman Bialik (then living in Berlin), Robert Weltsch, Nahum Goldmann, and Jacob Klatzkin, envisioned not simply the elimination of strife between peoples through *Nichtkrieg*, the absence of war, but by the establishment of a new type of relationship between nations based on mutual respect for the integrity of each. This ideal was to be pursued not by the politics of power but by "a powerful fidelity to reality and religious power," the power of faith and pristine religious ideals of justice and mercy. This short-lived society was initiated by Hans Kohn of Prague who was to emigrate to Palestine in 1925 where he was to become one of Magnes's first coworkers on behalf of a new Jewish humanism.

These intellectuals encountered in Magnes, in the words of Gershom Scholem, a figure who was at once "puzzling and attractive."[6] An incorrigible idealist, Magnes, writes Scholem who settled in Jerusalem in 1923 at age twenty-six, struck "us youth . . . as a remnant from the nineteenth century" — an individual firmly committed to moral slogans that had become "for us the generation of the first World War" hollow and banal.[7] But Scholem and other young intellectuals from Central Europe who were to join Magnes in various endeavors, soon realized that behind his anachronistic moralism was the soul of a genuine radical. Magnes's very personality "radiated" an unique "inner freedom" which Scholem and his comrades were to recognize as the ultimate ground of an authentic radicalism. It is a freedom of an inner discipline and responsibility before the moral law of conscience — a freedom that is manifest in a readiness to draw the most "militant conclusions" that conscience may dictate. Scholem is careful to distinguish the "inner freedom" of Magnes from the "anarchic freedom" of the revolutionary. The freedom of the latter is based on the destruction of the old order, on an "easily" achieved "negation of values." Thus, Scholem notes, in the life of the Yishuv which was dominated by a revolutionary ethos, Magnes was an uncommon figure. Indeed, Magnes was not a revolutionary, but a radical — and as such he was in a sense, as Scholem put it, a "conservative," for he did not demand of society — of Judaism — that it negate its fundamental values but, on the contrary, that it take these values with utmost earnestness and seek to authenticate them in the life of the community.[8]

Magnes spoke of goodness, justice, mercy — citing Scripture, enjoining the name of Israel's prophets — without, as Scholem again observes, "evoking laughter."[9] In Magnes, the teachings of the prophets gained a new authority, a new power, one might say an existential authenticity. In his fearless, unbending, single-minded commitment to moral truth, these teachings ceased to be merely edifying words — words often rendered tedious and trite in the mouths of ordinary men — but commandments determining his very existence. Because he was manifestly willing to stake his life on these teachings — to draw unpopular conclusions, to bear the scorn of the many who opposed him, even to court physical danger — Magnes served his small but determined following as a leader. A leader, however, not by virtue of his intellectual, political, and organizational wisdom — indeed, many of his colleagues who were clearly his superiors intellectually found his political and organizational judgment wanting. Magnes rather served his followers as a leader in the sense that the German philosopher Max Scheler called a *Vorbild*, a leader who embodies in an exemplary manner the values and self-image of his following.[10] This role of Magnes as *Vorbild* of a new Jewish humanism — a humanism of civil courage and moral responsibility — was recognized by Martin Buber. In an unpublished letter to Magnes on the occasion of his sixtieth birthday, Buber writes:[11]

> . . . [T]hese days we feel nearer than ever to you, and to what you represent. In the near future, I believe, the existence of men like you, men of truth and responsibility, will become even more important than hitherto. The 'front,' which you represent, the front of individuals, the 'unpopular,' seemingly the weakest of all, will prove to be the only invincible front. It is a joy to know that you are in this world; it is a consolation to be aware of the fact that one is fighting with you a common battle. May you enjoy the latent blessing of this quality of yours which has become so rare: the courage of 'civil disobedience.' . . .
> Yours, Martin Buber

Although Buber wrote this letter in German, he cites *civil disobedience* in English — a term he expressly associated, as we learn from other writings of his, with the famous essay by Thoreau.[12] This great dissenter from nineteenth century New England represented for Buber since his youth the best of the American ethos. The civil disobedience that Thoreau taught and practiced was as Buber understood it, "in fact obedience, obedience to a law superior to that which is being disobeyed here and now."[13] So understood, civil disobedience is a matter of an individual's moral and existential integrity. As Buber expressed it on the occasion of the centenary of Thoreau's death:

> "The question [of civil disobedience] is not just about one of the numerous individual cases in the struggle between a truth powerless to act and a power that has become the enemy of truth. It is really a question of the absolutely concrete demonstration of the point at which this struggle at any moment becomes man's duty *as man* (zur Pflicht des Menschen *als Mensch*) . . . ."[14]

What is interesting is that Buber identified Magnes as an American with Thoreau and the ethic of civil disobedience. He undoubtedly drew great inspiration from Magnes's effort to translate this ethic into a Jewish context: the struggle to create in Zion a truly just society.

Clearly it was the force of Magnes's personality — his compelling moral sincerity and exemplary commitment — that held sway over the Central European Jewish Intellectuals who gathered under his banner. It is, however, misleading to conclude therefrom that the attraction to

Magnes was only visceral, and that it was void of an intellectual dimension. Magnes, after all, was the founding chancellor of the Hebrew University — an institution with which most of his comrades were associated. And his importance for the Hebrew University was not only administrative and financial. As chancellor, Magnes had a very refined sense of the university — both as a center of learning and disciplined reflection, and as a fulcrum of the cultural and spiritual renewal of Judaism. As he emphatically put it in a letter to Leon Simon, the biographer of Ahad Ha-Am: "The great mission of Judaism to build up an ethical society in the spirit of the Prophets of Israel can be furthered by the Hebrew University in Zion."[15] Quite early in his tenure as the head of the Hebrew University, Magnes's comrades recognized his conception of the University as compatible with their own. Indeed, even prior to establishing the Hebrew University, there were intimations that the individuals who were to form Magnes's circle in Jerusalem already viewed him as an important ally in their struggle to shape the intellectual countenance of the future university. In June 1924, on the eve of a crucial meeting in London of the Board of Governors of the still embryonic Hebrew University, Robert Weltsch, the editor of the *Jüdische Rundschau*, the prestigious Berlin weekly prominently identified with cultural Zionism, wrote Martin Buber urging him to attend the meeting primarily in order to meet "Dr. Magnes, *der Vertrauensmann der grossen Geldgeber.*"[16] Weltsch elliptically suggests that Buber — who was, aside from the ailing Ahad Ha-Am, at the time the most respected representative of cultural Zionism — should endeavor to strengthen Magnes's hand in the meeting that was to set the final plans for the formal opening of the university. Weltsch confides in Buber a deep anxiety about two contending groups seeking to shape the university in their image. Both must be neutralized. On the one hand, Chaim Weizmann envisions a faculty of the natural sciences as the crown of the university; on the other hand, Baron Edmond de Rothschild and his friends wish to give priority to a faculty of Jewish Studies, but one which to their mind should be a kind of Rabbinical seminary, and which would promote academic Jewish learning in the discredited mold of nineteenth century *Wissenschaft des Judentums*. Should either the camp of Weizmann or Rothschild prevail, it would prevent the University from becoming a "vital center for Jewish spiritual and intellectual life" (*einer lebendigen Stätte jüdischen geistigen Lebens*). We must, Weltsch gravely emphasizes, prevent the University from being "degraded into a typical *Golusinstitution*" (institution in exile). Buber was unable to attend the meeting, but nonetheless Magnes returned from London at the helm of the nascent institution. En route home to Jerusalem, he triumphantly wrote Ahad Ha-Am concerning the establishment of the University's first academic department, the Institute for Jewish Studies: "We have reached a nice formula, I think we can grasp and put into it all our aspirations for strengthening and expanding the concept of Judaism . . . ."[17]

Parenthetically, Buber and Magnes first met one another in 1927, and they "hit it off" marvelously. Magnes was most eager to bring Buber to Jerusalem, initially offering to share the Chancellorship with him, delegating to the famed philosopher the administration of the University's academic affairs.[18] The offer, which Buber considered seriously, was rescinded when it was vetoed by the University's Academic Council.[19] Although he joined the faculty of the Hebrew University only in the spring of 1938,[20] Buber remained Magnes's close collaborator and colleague. Indeed, Buber was associated with virtually all of Magnes's most significant cultural and political endeavors since the late 1920s. Again, it should be noted that this friendship endured despite a certain intellectual asymmetry. In a 1928 article he contributed to a *Festschrift* marking Buber's fiftieth birthday, Magnes quite candidly admits that he had difficulty with Buber's writings. With respect, for example, to Buber's philosophical meditation, *Daniel*, Magnes writes: "*Ich habe es zu Ende gelesen und — nicht verstanden* (I have read it to the end and did not understand)."[21] What brought them together, according to Magnes, was their shared sense of calling to work for "the renewal and deepening of religion," and the common recognition that Judaism would play its proper role in this momentous process once it was reimplanted in the soil of Jerusalem, inspired by its sacred geography and memories.[22]

Magnes himself was in Jerusalem more than five years before he gave, aside from his activities on behalf of the Hebrew University, public expression to his commitment to the renewal of Judaism and its universal significance. Characteristically, this first public indication of his views reflected his conviction that religion and politics were conterminous, that one's political commitments should flow naturally and ineluctably from one's fundamental religious sensibilities. Prompted by the tensions in Arab-Jewish relations that became manifest in late 1928, Magnes resolved to found a religious association that would confront the *interlocking* social political, and religious problems facing the Jewish people, particularly in Zion. "When I talk of peace with Arabs," he wrote explaining his conception of the projected association, "it is not just a tactical . . . move in realpolitik: it is a result of a *Lebensanschauung* . . . " that is, of a given view of life, its meaning and purpose. Initially, the proposed association would be a discussion group, evolving hopefully into a wider "platform," with its seat in

Jerusalem and "later other places," where 'these questions of life and ethics, of work and doctrine may find deep and sincere expression." Magnes adds tellingly, "this platform would and could not unfortunately be a Synagogue."[24]

Magnes endeavored to solicit support for his project from several Jerusalem intellectuals. Enthusiastic interest was evinced by Hugo Bergman and Hans Kohn, both formerly of Prague, who regarded themselves as disciples of Buber. At the behest of Magnes, they sent the five-page program he had drafted for the proposed association to Buber, then still residing in Germany.[25] In his reply, dated January 29, 1929, Buber found the third point of Magnes's draft to be a most felicitious formulation, which reads in part:

> [The members of the Association] are social radicals in the sense that they want to realize here and now the social ideals of justice and righteousness of the Hebrew Prophets. They see in the present structure of society but little approximation of these ideals and they therefore, each in his own way, desire to cast in their lot with the 'masses,' or with 'labour,' with the submerged and the oppressed . . . [26]

Buber, however, took exception with the first part of the proposal, which he deemed too vague and fragmentary (*zu partiell*). In this part, which essentially served as the preamble to the program, Magnes states:[27]

> [The members of the Association] are united in seeking the intellectual basis of faith and in their endeavor to live in accordance with the mandate of the "God within" each. This does not necessarily mean a confession of faith in a Supreme Being. It means an abiding interest in the problems of religion and a vital and honest quest of answers to these problems. They regard social values such as family, nation, people, state, church, class as of but secondary importance over against the Absolute — absolute ethical or metaphysical values which must be the real forces determining and directing life.

Buber offers an alternative formulation of the same sentiment:[28]

> [The members of the Association[are united in the conviction that faith, not any particular faith but the believing sensibility or attitude (*die gläubige Gesinnung*), is the genuine ground of human life. By the believing attitude they mean that man strives to obtain an immediate relation to the truth of existence (*Sein*) *not* merely through intellect or feeling, but through his entire being (*Wesen*). Such a sensibility can not only be constituted by the inwardness of one's soul: it must manifest

itself (*sich auswirken*) in the entire fullness of personal and communal life, in which the individual participates . . . .

Buber does not intend to register disagreement with the substance and spirit of Magnes's proposal; he merely wishes to add nuance and especially to draw out the implications of Magnes's assertion that faith is grounded in the conviction that the Absolute — which Magnes, Buber seems to suggest, somewhat facilely equates with "absolute or metaphysical values" — should be the ultimate principle guiding our lives.

Buber's formulation is consistent with the theology of Religious Socialism, which evolved in the 1920s in Germany and Switzerland.[29] Together with such luminaries as the young Karl Barth, Leonard Ragaz, and Paul Tillich, Buber was one of the leaders of this small but intellectually influential movement. In the wake of World War I, they contended that the anguish and disunion of modern society was due primarily to the radical polarization of the spiritual and the secular. Religion has, alas, confined itself to the ecclesiastical precincts of confessional and ritual piety, relinquishing all claim on the "secular" world. But the division between the holy and the profane is not ontological; all of creation is potentially sacred. The sacralization of all existence required that faith in God the Creator and Redeemer be extended to our public and political activity — provinces of life hitherto abandoned to instrumental aims and cynicism. The tenets of Religious Socialism, Buber taught, are in consonance with the spirit of primal Judaism (*Urjudentum*), with what he also called Hebrew humanism.

Buber's Religious Socialism, which was shared by his disciples who settled in Jerusalem, was not far in spirit from the theology of the Social Gospel from which Magnes drew his inspiration.[30] Indeed, although Religious Socialism bore the distinctive intellectual inflections of Post-World War I Europe, and the Social Gospel was an American product, the two movements had their roots in the moral theology of nineteenth century liberal Protestantism which held that morality — labor for the Kingdom of God on earth — is an inseparable, and indeed, central component of religion.

Both Buber's Religious Socialism and Magnes' Social Gospel were joined in the founding of a religious society in Jerusalem in 1939, *Ha-'Ol* (the Yoke).[31] This society, which included Yitzhak Baer, Bergman, Buber, Scholem, and Ernst Simon, may be viewed as the realization of Magnes's 1929 proposal. Preceded by at least two other stillborn efforts by Magnes — one called somewhat cumbersomely 'A Community of Hebrew Religious Morality," the other more lyrically,

"Those Who Seek Thy Face" (*Mevakshei Panecha*)[32] — *Ha-'Ol* was founded together with Buber, in the spring of 1939, shortly after the philosopher of dialogue's long delayed *aliyah*.[33] The binding principle of this circle was formulated in a rhetorical question:[34]

> Are we Jews merely a persecuted people asking for mercy, or have we a message which we want both to proclaim and to carry out? Are we conscious of the Yoke which our Father has placed upon us?

The image of the Yoke is an allusion to a rabbinic midrash: "Take upon yourselves the Yoke of the Kingdom of Heaven, and judge one another in the fear of God, and act toward one another in loving kindness" (*Sifre Deuteronomy* 32:29).[35] The ideology of the circle is expressed in less ethereal terms in a programmatic statement, written in Magnes's hand, found in the archive of *Ha-'Ol*:

> We are united in the feeling of responsibility toward society in general, and the life of Israel in its land and in the Dispersion in particular. This sense of responsibility stems from a faith in eternal values whose source is God. We believe in a life of faith which carries a commitment to social action and practical political work, and we reject any attempt to separate the dominions, which are one in theory and practice.[36]

The first two sentences of this statement reflect Magnes's Jewish version of the Social Gospel; the last two sentences seem to bear the imprint of Buber's religious socialism.

Despite the activism pledged in these statements, the public activity of *Ha-'Ol* was confined to the publication of a brochure in English containing two open letters to Gandhi, one by Magnes, the other by Buber.[37] These letters, dated February 1939, were prompted by the Indian sage's refusal to give his blessings to Zionism as a movement of national liberation, as a movement of the spiritual, moral, and political rehabilitation of the Jewish people.[38] Writing with manifestly sincere reverence for the Mahatma, Magnes and Buber urge him to acknowledge the plight of the Jewish people in Nazi Europe, and the unique effort of Zionism to ground the political solution to that plight in the spiritual and moral rehabilitation of Jewry. As passionate advocates of Arab-Jewish reconciliation, each sought to assure Gandhi that the renewal of Jewish patrimony in the land of Israel need not be at the expense of the native Palestinian Arab population. Accordingly, they appealed to the great proponent of *satyagraha* or soul-force as a mode of nonviolent political struggle, to lend his awesome prestige to gain the Arabs' understanding of the pristine humanitarian and spiritual goals of Zionism, and thus immeasurably aid those Zionists such as Buber and Magnes who not only wish to spare the Holy Land of needless conflict and bloodshed but deeply appreciate the Mahatma's teaching that the recourse to violence ultimately vitiates all spiritual and moral values it may purport to serve.

Ha-'Ol also had a study circle in which abstract theological questions were discussed. In the protocol of one such meeting from July 1939, the discussion began with an exchange between Buber and Yitzhak Baer on the notion of "Messianic politics." Both were emphatic in their rejection of the proposition that politics *per se* could effect the Redemption. The most we can do, they concurred, is to *prepare* the world for Redemption. Buber quickly adds that even here we are never sure which of our deeds may *have* Messianic significance; we only know that Redemption by God's gracious design also depends on us. Magnes and Scholem then focus the discussion on another theme altogether: the authority of Torah, which neither accept. Magnes seems to view the resulting "anarchism," as Scholem put it, as a source of deep spiritual perplexity. Scholem on the other hand, is less troubled by this position. He states:

> Our anarchism is a transition . . . . We are the living example that this [anarchism] does not remove one from Judaism. We are not a generation without commandments (*mitzvot*), but our commandments are bereft of authority. But I don't have an inferiority complex vis-a-vis the Orthodox. We are no less legitimate than our forefathers, they simply had a clearer text. We are perhaps anarchists, but we are opposed to anarchy.

The already renowned scholar of Jewish mysticism adds, "I believe in God. This is the basis of my life and faith. All the rest [of Judaism] is subject to doubt and debate."[39]

This religious anarchism, which was basically shared by all the members of *Ha-'Ol*, is perhaps better understood as a secular religiosity.[40] Secular in the sense of being open to the public realm of worldly life, particularly politics, and secular also in a more fundamental sense of an estrangement from the authority of tradition and its sacred principles. Secularity in this sense need be neither atheistic nor antagonistic to religious concern and quest. Indeed, one can be jealous of one's intellectual and experiential autonomy, yet profoundly religious in sensibility and existential commitment. Buber's metanomian conception of Judaism, with its unequivocal rejection of the authority of the Rabbinic tradition and his concomitant emphasis on the individual's dialogue with the Eternal Thou, may be viewed as secular religiosity. A secular religiosity was also the animating idea of Magnes's proposed society, *Mevakshei Panecha*. In the program of this society, which he apparently hoped *Ha-'Ol* would eventually adopt, Magnes states that the society will be comprised of people who seek to know God, most of whom "have not found the path . . . and who knows if they ever will find it. Nonetheless, the most burning and deepest aspiration of their lives is the search for this path."[41] And they will be guided in their quest by "faith, theology, but not," Magnes emphasizes, "religion." This affirmation of faith in contradistinction to religion was central to the teachings of Buber, who was fond of quoting Rosenzweig that "God created the world and not religion."[42] As Magnes put it, "when one says religion one means one has already found the path [*to God*] and is bound to officially prescribed articles of faith . . . ."[43] Magnes may have also quoted Rosenzweig here: "Faith based on authority is not genuine faith."[44]

Ha-'Ol was short-lived; its intellectual, deliberative concerns were superseded by the urgent political issues facing the Jewish people at that fateful hour, the start of World War II and the heightened resolve of the Zionist leadership to seek Jewish sovereignty in Palestine despite Arab and British opposition. *Ha-'Ol's* celebration of pacifism now seemed utterly irrelevant and, indeed, absurd. The commanding necessity of an armed struggle against Hitler and his demonic schemes even obliged Magnes himself to reassess his lifelong commitment to pacifism.[45] Further, the passions and imagination of the members of *Ha-'Ol* were now engaged by political activities that had a more direct, immediate approach to the exigent, political issues facing the Jewish community of Palestine. Virtually all the members of *Ha-'Ol* were drawn to The League for Jewish-Arab Rapprochement and Cooperation.[46] Founded in April 1939, the League had become a rallying point for all those who sought to counter what was deemed to be the mistaken and perilous policy of the Yishuv's leadership to pursue Zionist priorities while ignoring Arab susceptibilities and political rights. For Buber and Magnes especially, their involvement in the League and allied activities still had a religious significance. Indeed, the Ihud, which was founded through the initiative of Magnes and Buber in August 1942 as an independent political association affiliated with the League, may be viewed as continuous with Magnes's earlier efforts to establish a religious society that would be politically engaged.[47] Although the official platform of the Ihud, which sponsored a binational solution to the problem of Palestine, was formulated in strictly political terms, both Magnes and Buber saw its activities in a religious perspective.

In a disarmingly candid and sentimental open letter addressed to Magnes on the occasion of his seventieth birthday,[48] Buber notes that the Ihud, especially as embodied in the person of Magnes, "has been a great gift of life to me." After some bitter disappointments, Buber confided, he had for years never truly believed that truth and politics, especially party politics, could be reconciled. But Magnes and the Ihud, Buber continues, "have made it possible for me to work politically once more within the context, and in the name of, a political group without sacrificing truth." Buber explained to Magnes:

> I am not concerned with the purity and salvation of my soul; if ever it should be the case — which in the nature of things is impossible — that I had to choose between the saving of my soul and the salvation of my people, I know I would not hesitate. It is a question of not violating the truth, since I have come to know that truth is 'the seal of God' (Babylonian Talmud, *Shabbat*, 55a), whilst we are the wax in which this seal seeks to be stamped. The older I grow, the clearer this becomes . . . .

And Buber significantly adds, "I feel that in this we are brothers. To you too, it becomes clearer every day. But from where we stand, there has for a long time been no longer any choice. There is no opposition between the truth of God and the salvation of Israel."[49]

For both Buber and Magnes — as well as, of course, their tight band of followers — genuine politics, that is, the politics of peace and reconciliation between peoples, is rooted in a religious faith that human beings are God's coworkers in the establishment of the rule of justice and love in the world. Such a faith led them to believe that a shared humanity in God ultimately binds the diverse communities of humankind, even those locked in conflict. This does not mean that they sought to trivialize differences and the conflicts of interests. On the contrary, they recognized the power and frequent authenticity of these differences, but they affirmed that by focusing on shared spiritual and moral sensibilities, mutual trust and reconciliation can be attained. Both Buber and Magnes vigorously denied that this position betrays a naive optimism. It is rather, as Buber put it, "a more comprehending, a more penetrating realism, the realism of a greater reality."[50] Moreover, far from being inspired by a naive optimism, their vision and commitment arose from a deep pessimism.

As his journals indicate, Magnes especially was recurrently plagued by pessimism. In a journal entry from February 1937, for instance, he notes: "Below my placid surface I am racked by religious doubt, by pessimism as to the world and Palestine; by the skepticism as to the efficacy of the pacifist point of view . . . ."[51] Such troubled musings — which harken to his youth and which seem to have grown more intense after his 1922 departure from America — Magnes confided mostly to his journals.[52] With the outbreak of the war against Hitler, and especially with the first reports of the tragedy we now call the Holocaust, Magnes expressed his anguish and Jobian doubt publicly and uninhibitedly.

For Magnes, Hitler and his death camps represented radical evil; the spectre of that evil has a firm and unyielding grip on the world. In an address to the student body of the Hebrew University in the fall of 1944, in what may very well be the first theological meditation by a Jewish thinker on the Holocaust, Magnes asked some unsettling questions:

> Is it possible that this can happen under God's heaven? . . . Is there a living God for whom all this has meaning? Is there design and purpose? Or, is the universe ruled by a blind, unmoral force, by some *deus absconditus*, who created the world and is no longer interested in its fate — withdrawn, asleep, or gloating over the writhing of his creatures upon the earth? I try to evade this question, and cannot.[53]

Magnes, however, refused to allow his doubt to lead him to despair. By a sheer decision of faith he resisted the howling conclusions beckoned by Hitler's wanton murder of millions. Although it be Sisyphian, the quest for meaning — for the presence of God in history — must continue. For he who seeks God, Magnes told the students of the Hebrew University, "can do no other than to persist in his quest to the last, to keep on inquiring, struggling, challenging. He will not be granted tranquility of soul. But if it be given him to renew the forces of his being day by day and constantly to be among the seekers, the rebellious — that is the crown of his life and the height of his desire."[54] This quest is to be guided by an existential affirmation of morality, of what the Hebrew prophets called righteousness and "the demand of justice and mercy, equity and liberty."[55] In another university address in which he considered the emergence of a moral nihilism and terrorism among the Jews of the Yishuv, Magnes cautioned: "Moral claims still find a listening ear. If you despair completely of all the other peoples of the world and you feel there is no longer any morality in the world, then all is indeed lost for you."[56] Hence, for Magnes morality — and politics grounded in the considerations of morality — is ultimately an act of faith; indeed, it is the only sure path by which we — at least we ordinary men not graced with special divine knowledge — could possibly "draw near to the supreme reality, the God of Israel."[57] Human history, and Israel's destiny, Magnes affirmed, could only have meaning in the struggle to secure the rule of goodness and justice.

Magnes delivered his message with edifying eloquence and consummate oratorial skill, but its power lay in the existential authenticity of his faith, in the depth of his anguish and the profundity of his commitment to serving God through what he called the politics of goodness. The significance that Magnes's exemplary faith had, at least for his circle of friends, is given cogent testimony by Shmuel Hugo Bergman, one of the founding members of the faculty of the Hebrew University and one of Magnes's intimate associates in his various political and religious endeavors in Jerusalem. In his volume, *Faith and Reason,* a series of portraits of individuals whom he considered to be the most seminal in modern Jewish religious thought, Bergman included Magnes in this esteemed pantheon. Following separate chapters on Hermann Cohen, Franz Rosenzweig, Martin Buber, A. D. Gordon, and Rav Kook respectively, Bergman concludes his precious little volume, in itself one of the masterpieces of modern Jewish thought, with a chapter devoted to Magnes. The chapter is befittingly entitled: "The Conquest of Pessimism by Faith." Although Magnes "was not a systematic thinker," Bergman explains, he nonetheless "was one of the crucial figures in the development of Jewish religious thought and life in our time, especially in Israel."[58] For Bergman, Magnes's religious significance lies precisely in his "breakthrough to God from the very depths of despair."[59] Magnes taught his contemporaries that "every act of faith is invariably a risk," and that faith must be rooted in the tragic character of life — a "tragic faith" that Magnes lived and suffered.[60]

I have suggested that an appreciation of Magnes's religious thought cannot be properly confined to his writings, but must also consider how this thought — and especially life — touched others. It is thus perhaps appropriate that we conclude with a quote within a quote. On the occasion of Magnes's seventieth birthday, Ernst Simon — again, one of the small but devoted circle of Central European intellectuals who gathered around Magnes in Jerusalem — extended the following greetings:

> Many admire and respect you, but we who follow your path are few. Today we recall the words of your beloved poet Bialik about your beloved teacher Ahad Ha-Am. With an elegant pun on the various meanings of the Hebrew word, 'rav' — many, rabbi, teacher, leader — Bialik affectionately declared to Ahad Ha-Am:

$$\text{אך רב לנו, אדון, אך מעט אנחנו}$$

'Your army is not great, O'Master, but we have a leader.'[61]

Figure 12. S.Y. Agnon, Israeli Nobel laureate in literature, c. 1950. *(Courtesy of Arnold Band)*

11

Gown and Town

ARNOLD J. BAND

Given the historical circumstances, Judah Magnes's stewardship as Chancellor, then President, of the Hebrew University, was one of the most paradoxical chapters both of his life and of modern Jewish intellectual history. His background, his history of brilliant failures in New York, his spiritual and psychological distance from the temper of the Yishuv from 1921 through 1948, all mitigated against success; yet, when one has to assess the enduring contributions of Magnes's intensely active community life, one is forced to concede that his most enduring achievement was the Hebrew University. The history of this stormy period has yet to be written. One thing is certain: neither Bentwich's hagiographic treatment in *For Zion's Sake* nor Goren's pages on the period in his Introduction to *Dissenter in Zion* are adequate assessments of his tale. While both report his struggles with Weizmann and other members of The Board of Governors, they slight the constant internal political struggle and the fascinating ideological and temperamental chasm which separated Magnes from most of his colleagues.

Magnes, after all, was not a scholar in the academic sense, certainly not in the Germanic-philologic tradition of many of his leading professors; he had no real experience in university administration; and he was by no means in tune with the burgeoning extra-academic intellectual community, mostly of Eastern European background. Magnes, it is true, had a vision of what a Hebrew University should be, but no vision could carry a man through such perilous times and formidable adversaries unless it was accompanied by meaningful that is, financially backed, political connections and the cunning for bureaucratic infighting. Magnes, fortunately, had both. The support

155

of wealthy Jews in America and England has been well documented; as yet, however, no description of the internal battles at the Hebrew University during Magnes's reign has been written. While this history is beyond the scope of this paper, we cannot approach our topic without noting the absence of any serious study of Magnes's administration of the Hebrew University.

To gain some perspective on Magnes's achievement at the Hebrew University, it would be helpful to study the image Magnes projected in modern Hebrew literature, specifically in the works of two of the key writers of the period. S. Y. Agnon and Uri Zvi Greenberg, both probably much better known today in Israeli intellectual circles than Magnes himself. Both, consequently, have contributed — and still do contribute — much to the formation of the historical image of the man and his activities. Before approaching Agnon or Greenberg, however, I conjure up, by way of introduction, the oracular figure of Berl Katznelson, the cultural Nestor of the Labor Movement during most of Magnes's tenure at the Hebrew University.[1] It was Berl who set the cultural tone of the Labor intelligentsia — which included most of the influential figures in the Yishuv — through his articles, his seminars, his editorial control of *Davar* and his launching of its literary supplement in the 1930's. If there was any other postsecondary institution of import in the Yishuv during the Magnes period at the Hebrew University, it was obviously the institutions of the Labor Party where all cultural paths — ideational, publications, organized seminars — led to and from Berl Katznelson. One cannot talk about the Hebrew University in this period without assessing the alternative postsecondary institution of culture.

Magnes and Berl first met when Berl came to New York in November 1921 to raise funds for a worker's bank in Palestine. Although he was in one of the most politically difficult periods of his life, Magnes extended himself to assist Berl and his delegation: he introduced him to Abe Cahan, the prestigious editor of the *Forverts*, a Bundist hence, anti-Zionist, newspaper, and even persuaded Cahan to publish a letter that Magnes wrote warmly endorsing the aims of the delegation while concealing their Zionist orientation. Magnes, in fact, became the Treasurer of the "Committee of American Workers for the Worker's Bank in Eretz Israel," Bank ha-Poalim, which throughout the years has developed into one of Israel's leading financial institutions. A year later in December, together with Einstein and Ahad Ha-Am,[2] Magnes attended the Third Conference of Berl's Ahdut ha-Avodah in Tel Aviv. A close friendship developed between them that endured even through the periods of great tension: 1929, the Hebron massacres, and 1939, the White Paper, which found Magnes and Katznelson on opposite sides of the political debate.

Despite this friendship, Berl closed the pages of *Davar* to open letters from members of Brit Shalom, many of whom he knew personally, and labelled the group as the *Telushim* (The Uprooted Ones; the Déracinés), implying that their Western European orientation blinded them to the true needs of the Jewish people. Their positions were polarized over educational issues. The Hebrew University, Berl felt, had no right to claim absolute independence from "the national will," while Magnes insisted upon complete academic freedom, as he saw it. When the Academic Senate passed a June 1941 resolution calling upon every unmarried student between the ages of twenty and thirty to enlist in the British army, Magnes objected to this decision as an unauthorized violation of academic freedom. Berl, of course, considered the vote as an expression of the national will and service as the duty of the student. If one is to seek the attitude of the enlightened segments of the Labor Movement toward Magnes and the Hebrew University, one would find it in the writings of Berl Katznelson. Berl Katznelson's position can be considered normative for the new Yishuv; the ideological postures of Uri Zvi Greenberg or S. Y. Agnon are extreme or idiosyncratic, but nonetheless illuminating.

Perhaps the most telling index of the varying ideological positions of Magnes, Katznelson (and the Labor Party), Greenberg, and Agnon is their varying attitudes toward the Balfour Declaration of 1917 in which His Majesty's government viewed with favor the creation of a Jewish homeland in Palestine. The official Zionist Organization, including the labor parties, welcomed it, on the whole, as a step forward towards their aspirations. Magnes objected to it as divisive between Jews and Arabs. Greenberg rejected it out of hand since he did not recognize the right of the British government to grant Jews rights or privileges in their own ancestral homeland. Agnon, though not an ideologue and ever-elusive in his fiction, intimates that reliance upon the good will of foreign governments is simply foolish.

Diametrically opposed to Magnes stood Uri Zvi Greenberg (1896–1981), now universally recognized as one of the most moving and accomplished Hebrew poets of the twentieth century.[3] Although nominally a member of the Labor Movement from 1923 until his break with it over the Hebron massacres in 1929, Greenberg was always independent, and increasingly radical in his opinions. In both his own journal, *Sadan*, and in the two volumes of poetry that he published privately, he castigated the establishment for its conciliatory attitudes towards the mandatory government. Striking the pose of the Biblical

prophet, Greenberg fulminated against those who would even concede that the mandatory government had any moral or political right
to determine the destiny of the Yishuv. Not coincidentally, Greenberg
broke with *Davar*, the Labor Movement's daily, precisely when *Davar*
would no longer publish open letters by Magnes's friends in Brit
Shalom: in 1929 after the Hebron massacres of August. Greenberg's
shift to the political right was precipitous and by 1931 he was in the
Revisionist camp, second on the electoral list after Jabotinsky, and
with him, withdrew from the World Zionist Movement at the Seven-
teenth Congress in August 1931. In newspaper articles, pamphlets,
and in his 1936 volume of poetry, *Sefer ha-Kitrug ve-ha-Emunah* (*The
Book of Accusation and Belief*), he branded the entire establishment as
traitors and referred to them metaphorically as *Sanbalatim*, the
Samaritan traitors in the days of Ezra and Nehemiah. Among these
traitors he included Weizmann and Magnes whom he never forgave
even in his dotage in 1980. When a small group of professors came to
the old age home in Raananah to present him with a fine edition of
his Collected Yiddish poems, in two volumes, Greenberg fulminated
uncontrollably when his failing eyes caught sight of the publishing
house imprint on the title page: the Magnes Press of the Hebrew
University.

The Greenberg-Magnes contrast has another dimension of
perhaps even greater import. Both men were obsessed by prophetic
Judaism; for each it was the touchstone of all behavior and ideologies.
But each interpreted prophetic Judaism in his own way. For Magnes
it was the zenith of universal humanism, of ethical monotheism, of
justice, compassion, academic freedom, pacifism — and Zionism. For
Greenberg, prophecy was the election of Israel, the promise of the
land, a mystical morality which viewed all history as a battle between
God's chosen and the Gentiles, their oppressors, ultimately an
apocalyptic summons to violent action. As early as his expressionistic
period, in the early 1920s, Greenberg writes, both in Yiddish and in
Hebrew, as God's prophet, elected to convey a message to His people.
The claim is clear, even blatant and relentless. The identification with
the prophet Jeremiah is a case in point. For Greenberg, who actually
identifies with Jeremiah literally and openly, this prophet is attractive
for his fiery temperament, for the agony he suffered as part of the prophetic charge, for his compulsion to utter the words of the Lord even
against his own will. Magnes, on the other hand, was fond of showing
visitors the village of Anata on the east slope of Mount Scopus, which
he could see from his study, for there the prophet Jeremiah is said to
have been born and Magnes saw himself as a modern Jeremiah, not

the frantic prophet of Greenberg's poems, but the lone dissenter from official norms. Zion, after all, is the seed-bed of prophets, but each man used his favorite prophet for his own purposes: for Greenberg Zion was the focus of messianism and apocalypse; for Magnes, it was a home where one could be the prophetic dissenter.

If the Hebrew University as a personification of the ideals of Judah Magnes assumes a significant role in any Hebrew literary work produced to date, it is in Agnon's posthumously published novel, *Shirah*, which, for all its incompleteness, still looms as one of the great Hebrew literary events of the second half of the twentieth century. Though published in 1971, most of the book was written in the late 1940s and parts were first published in the early 1950s. The novel, some 535 pages long, actually takes place in the late 1930s in Jerusalem precisely in the circle of Hebrew University professors and their students. In his characteristic dissembling narrative technique, Agnon presents us with what seems to be a roman à clef, which has indeed succeeded in misleading many readers to seek the key to the novel in the personalities of a variety of professors, all really composite caricatures of Hebrew University professors of the period. For years readers and critics have attempted to identify the main character, Dr. Manfred Herbst, a lecturer in Byzantine history and his paramour, the nurse Shirah who actually disappears about half way through the novel, let alone such obviously fictional figures (with grotesque names) such as Professor Bachlam, Professor Lamnar (both really acronyms designating Hebrew phonetic classes), or the two cousins, Professor Ernst Weltfremd and the unappointed Dr. Julian Weltfremd, both alienated from their surroundings as their names would indicate.

Reading or listening to the various hypotheses contemporaries of Agnon or Magnes often suggest for the character, I am repeatedly struck by the willingness to indulge in the trivia of gossip to the avoidance of the main issue Agnon raises, that is, the moral status and claims of the Hebrew University establishment and all it represents in a world which was literally disintegrating. As the novel progresses and the background becomes foreground, as Herbst's aimless flirtations are integrated into the fabric of the novel, the tension rises. We cannot escape the desperate anxiety of the period between 1936 and 1939. Daily Jews were being killed by Arab marauders throughout Mandatory Palestine, thus endangering the very existence of the Yishuv, while news of the expansion of Hitler's power was a staple item in the daily newspaper. Ironically, the Hebrew University, many of whose professors were refugees from Nazi Germany, is totally divorced from the real concerns of the Yishuv and the Jewish people.

Agnon portrays his hero as a scholar of Byzantine history, who dreams of writing a tragedy about the intrigues of the royal court of Byzantium while occasionally working at his card file in preparation for a book which he will never write on the burial customs of the paupers of Byzantium. Manfred Herbst is a member of Brit Shalom and cannot seem to square his concern for the welfare of the Arabs with the simple fact that his own home and family are threatened by Arab snipers. He had volunteered enthusiastically for the Kaiser's army in World War I, but would not join any of the Jewish defense organizations in Mandatory Palestine.

Herbst's wife, Henrietta, on the other hand, is deeply involved in the concerns of the family, the Yishuv, and her relatives in Germany. She expends much effort in a futile attempt to secure immigration certificates for her relatives in Germany; though already in her late thirties or her early forties, she bears Herbst two more children during the period of the novel, in addition to her two older daughters, one, Zohorah, a member of a Kibbutz who has her own son, and the other, Tamara, a member of the Irgun (right-wing militia) who constantly needles Manfred Herbst for his supine politics. Henrietta, Agnon tells us, "observes how the land is being rebuilt and who are its builders, and how certain people are threatening to destroy it and who are its destroyers."[4] In brief, Henrietta, without her university education — she detests Herbst's colleagues — has a proper grasp of reality, unlike her husband who wanders impotently about Jerusalem, unable to write the tragedy of which he dreams, collate his research cards, or find the nurse Shirah with whom he had a fleeting, unsatisfying affair. As in all Agnon's fiction, these ideological or ideational tensions are concretized in situations, characterization, and language. While Henrietta bustles about Jerusalem trying to secure certificates for immigration (aliyah) for her relatives fleeing Nazism, the only aliyah (ascension) Herbst can think of is his advancement, aliyah, to the rank of Associate Professor which would finally give him the public title of Professor rather than Doctor.

Ruling and symbolizing this academic world so removed from the real exigencies of life is the Nagid (President, at that time), in Agnon's words, whose name is never mentioned, giving it a mock-mystical quality in a novel where all persons have very specific, meaningful, often grotesque names. The reader cannot escape the reference to Magnes in the hilarious satiric passage describing the annual convocation opening the academic year:

> On the 15th of Heshvan [1938] Herbst went up to Mount Scopus
> to the celebration of the opening of the academic year at the university

. . . . The central hall of the Rosenbloom Building was full. Apart from the professors, lecturers, instructors, and students, and some of the university staff, visitors came from Jerusalem and Tel Aviv and Haifa and the other cities and settlements of the country. There were invited guests for whom a seat was designated in the invitation and uninvited guests who pushed their way into every public place and took the seats of the invitees . . . .

On the platform and close by it sat the great personages of the Yishuv who arrived before the opening of the ceremony and thus relinquished the practice of tribunes who usually come late so that they may enjoy watching everyone rise in their honor. Suddenly all conversation ceased and the hall fell silent and the guests turned towards the President of the university who began to speak. The President of the university was, in his youth, a Reform Rabbi who was forced to leave the Rabbinate because of his Zionism, and still had some of the mannerisms of Reform Rabbis which make one chuckle in Eretz Israel, but his stature, his carriage, and his virtues induced even the cynics in the hall to listen to what he had to say.

As was his custom every year, he began a discourse on the role of the Hebrew University, saying it was the university not only for Eretz Israel but for all of Israel (the Jewish people), wherever they are, and is destined to break through the boundaries which had been established for Judaic scholarship and to create a synthesis between Judaic scholarship and the other branches of the Humanities and the Sciences until all branches of science shall be one, because everything human is Jewish and everything Jewish is human.

After he described in detail the future of the University, he began to tell what had transpired in the university in the past academic year and what would take place in the coming academic year. Who was appointed Lecturer, who Senior Lecturer, who Associate Professor, who Full Professor, etc. After he finished detailing the activities of the university, he began to talk about the obligations of the instructors and the students, who have a double role: they come for the sake of knowledge and are therefore also obligated to strengthen the Torah of Israel and the ethics of Judaism without which there is no revival for the people or status for society.

After he mentioned the lofty and sublime hopes which people had pinned upon the university and the building of the land, he lowered his voice and spoke about the dangers rushing upon us together with (or because of) the building of the land, great and evil dangers which we have not imagined, and which are capable of undermining all the great and sublime hopes which brought us to this country.[5]

The description of the annual convocation is a satiric tour de force. The narrator anchors the situation in a recognizable milieu, the central hall of the Rosenbloom Building, and a recognizable, though shrewdly unnamed figure, Judah Magnes, who, we are told, was a Reform rabbi yet an impressive figure. The summary of the address is a string of all the clichés one finds in Magnes's Hebrew speeches regarding the Hebrew University, clichés which might sound impressive when isolated and cleverly couched in a speech, but are patently empty and even absurd when laid bare and strung together. The chain of clichés rises to a climax in the phrase, "because everything human is Jewish and everything Jewish is human," a phrase one finds often in Magnes's speeches and letters. The incongruity of the statement is highlighted by the background of violence in the novel which has broader ramifications given the unavoidable fact that most of the novel was written in the late 1940s, after the news of the extermination of Jews had reached Jerusalem. What could such a statement mean to a reasonable person in 1939 or 1943 or 1948? How could one reconcile the humanistic idealism and the model of Heidelberg with the relentless inhumanity Jews were experiencing both in Palestine and in Europe?

The final statement of the *Nagid* is kept a bit ambiguous and could be attributed to Magnes's sympathy with Brit Shalom and his leadership of Ihud, both pacifist groups which sought a peaceful accommodation with the Arabs who had shown little interest in accommodation: "He spoke about the dangers rushing upon us together with (or because of) the building of the land . . . " implying that the building of the land might actually lead to its destruction by invoking the wrath of the Arabs. The author totally abandons the orator at that point and shifts his narration to the thoughts of the audience as conveyed by the narrator. The President's hesitation and fears inspire in the audience thoughts, not of the university, but of the Zionist enterprise, its perils and successes, an enterprise that is contrasted with the university which the lengthy passage of audience ruminations assesses at its finale:

> You might say what importance could there be to a university in our days when books are available for everyone and whoever wants to learn opens a book and learns and certainly doesn't need the Torah of the professors; nevertheless, as long as all countries support universities, it is fitting that we, too, make ourselves a university.

The total negation of the value of the university was not, to be sure, Agnon's position either in this novel or in several other major works he wrote dealing with the world of academic learning. Agnon could be equally devastating in describing the world of the Yeshiva. Sensitive as he was, to the great moments in Jewish history of the past few centuries, he raised in his fiction questions which had to be raised about many of the phenomena of the Jewish world of his times — including the Hebrew University where many of his closest friends were professors.

The novel *Shirah*[6] stands as the most impressive literary statement on the Hebrew University in the Magnes years and is mostly a condemnation. There is, however, a significant mitigating factor which any literary historian must take into consideration in assessing the book: The novel is incomplete. Though he tried time and again, Agnon could not finish this work. While many have speculated about this failure, it seems to me that the reason is both obvious and simple. In the 1950s and 1960s when Agnon tried to finish the novel, the situation which had engendered it had changed radically. Israel was a sovereign state; Magnes had died; talk of binationalism was a matter of history; and the rebuilt Hebrew University was an educational institution of major national and international importance. To complete a novel in the original spirit of *Shirah* would have been foolish and Agnon was no fool. He realized that in this one area, at least, Magnes had succeeded.

This point is affirmed in the moving, last scene of the novel. As Herbst wanders aimlessly through Rehaviah, right near the small square called Kikar Magnes, he meets an unnamed professor of subtropical diseases who had just recovered from a near fatal illness incurred when he tried a dangerous virus on himself as a part of a scientific experiment. When Herbst sees the man, he says to himself: "Would I have endangered my life for my discipline?" As his tears well up, Herbst bows to the professor, and kisses his hand in reverence. This is actually the one positive conscious act of affirmation which Agnon has his hero make and although it is the last, fragmentary scene of the novel, it is obviously his tribute to what Judah Magnes had wrought.

V
Arabs and Jews

Figure 13. Magnes with Hebrew University faculty and students, 1929. Those who could be identified are: (1) Prof. Shmuel Klein, archeologist; (2) Magnes; (3) Louis Ginzberg; (4) Shlomo Ginsberg (Ginossar), son of Ahad Ha-Am, registrar; (5) Max Schloesinger; (6) Ari Ibn-Zahav, academic secretary; and (7) Yosef Or, translator. (*Courtesy of Hava Magnes*)

12

The School of Oriental Studies: A Memoir

S. D. GOITEIN

I believe that Judah Magnes was misunderstood by many of his contemporaries and often misjudged after his death. Every opportunity, therefore, ought to be taken to set the record straight. Magnes was misunderstood by his contemporaries because in many respects he was so different from them, and misjudged as well by a later generation possessing the wisdom of hindsight.

When Magnes emigrated with his family to Palestine in 1922, the world of the Middle East was so different from what it is currently, that visualizing how it looked at that time is almost impossible. The prestige of Great Britain was unimpaired. It had put an end to the Ottoman empire and freed the Arabs from the yoke of the Turks. Western Europe and the United States of America were still regarded as the torchbearers of civilization, progress, and liberty. The small Arabic intelligentsia was still under the spell of liberalism. When a man like Magnes, coming from a land of plenty settled in poverty-stricken Palestine lacking all the amenities of culture, he was regarded as one who had come not to take, but one who was able and willing to give. And so Magnes regarded himself. As long as I knew him, I was overawed by the spirit of mission which pervaded him. "For Zion's sake I shall not be silent," did mean for him not only the realization of modern Zionism, but dedication to Zion in the sense of Isaiah, Chapter 2: "Nation shall not lift up sword against nation, neither shall they learn war any more."

True religion was, for him, identical with pacifism. I remember one evening when he and I walked down together from Mount Scopus, we entered the newly consecrated British war cemetery of World War I. We had barely gone a few yards, when he suddenly stood still while his face became purple-red with indignation. I noticed what aroused his anger: the huge cross in the midst of the cemetery on which an almost equally large sword was fixed. "What a desecration!" he exclaimed, "the emblem of bloodshed covering the sign of peace!" At first, I was a little bit taken aback that the cross of the *ecclesia militans* should be regarded as a symbol of peace. Slowly I understood: the very nature of religion, of any religion, consisted of the Torah from Zion, of which Isaiah spoke in Chapter 2: the message of disarmament.

Once Magnes asked me to bring to him a Muslim intellectual with whom he could discuss the nature of Islam. In those early days, it was difficult to find a person suitable for this purpose. Finally, I introduced to him an acquaintance of mine, a Muslim of Iranian origin, who had studied at European universities. The man understood the situation and pleased Magnes with a plethora of Muslim quotations preaching peace. When, after the interview, Magnes asked me about my opinion, I said to him: "You know of course, that Islam also contains quite different teachings. But if a modern Muslim wishes sincerely to emphasize this aspect of his religion, we can only be happy about it."

In the early and middle 1920s, Jerusalem was a small and peaceful place. The intellectuals of all races and religions met with one another frequently and amiably. The country was secure; one could go to the most remote places without fearing anything. Magnes himself took domicile in an Arab neighborhood, the most prestigious one in the town. I believe that his outlook on Arab-Jewish symbiosis was formed by the experience he had in the years immediately following his settlement in Palestine. It became apparent that one could live side by side, even closely. This was not self-deception, but a task, a mission. To accuse the Zionist leaders of those days of neglecting what then was called "the Arab question" is unjust. I remember Chaim Weizmann warning the Zionist Congress in Karlsbad in 1921: "Keep well in mind that we are only a drop in the Arab ocean."

For Magnes, the Jewish-Arab symbiosis was not only a practical consideration, but a possible reality on the one hand, and a moral and religious obligation on the other. Nor was this a pious dream. Anyone who had experienced the events leading to, and through, the massacres of 1929, realized that these happenings were not inevitable. They were due to the miscalculations and blunders of certain Arabs and the British, as well as of some Jews. The Irgun and Mr. Begin did not invent terrorism, as it is so often said today. It was done by the so-called Mufti of Jerusalem[1] and his cohorts, on a small scale in 1920, and in ever larger dimensions in 1929, 1936, and 1947. What was the result? A Jewish state was created; the Mufti, then as notorious as Yasser Arafat is today, died in oblivion in exile, and the Arabs of Palestine were exposed to endless sufferings from 1936 to this day. I was present when Ben-Gurion was granted the Bublick Prize by the Hebrew University for exceptional service to the Jewish people, culminating in the creation of the Jewish state. In his very short acceptance speech, during which those present were standing, Ben-Gurion said: "The prize belongs really not to me, but to the Mufti. Had it not been for him, a Jewish state would never have come into being. In the Zionist program of Basel (Bâle), nothing was said of a Jewish state. The ideal was a Jewish homeland and secured by international agreements." No one can say, of course, how things would have developed had the moderate Arabs, who were inclined to accept the idea of a Jewish homecoming under certain conditions, gotten the upper hand. I mention all these things only to explain Magnes's pleading against the partition of Palestine and for a binational Jewish-Arab state. At that time, I no longer believed in such a possibility; violence had gone too far; but I refrained, like other members of the School of Oriental Studies of the Hebrew University, from taking a stand on the matter publicly. Magnes was deeply hurt and worried. I see him standing at the gate of his garden a few days before his journey to the United States in 1948, from which he did not return, explaining, with a raised voice, why the decision of the United Nations was wrong. He concluded by saying: "Now there will never be peace between Jews and Arabs," and without saying "Shalom," he went a few paces towards the door of his home. Then, he turned back to the gate of the garden, and raising his hand, he exclaimed: "Not even after two hundred years." And disappeared, again, without taking leave. May I add that I learned later from American friends that during the last days of his life he became reconciled to the idea of a Jewish state and found even that it was beneficial.

Indeed, Magnes tried with all his might to translate his ideas about Jewish-Arabic and Islamic studies at the Hebrew University into reality. In this respect, too, attention must be drawn to the change of times. Today, a western Arabist is often slandered as subservient to Imperialism and Colonialism and as detracting from the glory of the Arabs and their unique place in history. During the first half of the century, an Orientalist from Europe or America who had made a substantial contribution to Islamic and Arabic studies, was received in the East as a friend, treated with respect and, in some cases, even with reverence. This was the ultimate hope Magnes entertained for the students of Islamic and Arabic history at the Hebrew University. He was fortunate to find a mind of the highest qualifications, and entirely to his taste, in Leo Ary Mayer,[2] who had come to Palestine in 1921 and served in the Archaeological Department of the Government during the first eleven years of his stay in the country. Mayer was a student of Islamic art in all its manifestations. He published annual bibliographies on Islamic Art and Archaeology, a Bibliography of Islamic Numismatics, and in 1933 a magnificent volume on Islamic Heraldry,[3] thus enriching Islamic studies with a new field of study. These activities brought Mayer into direct contact with practically each and every person and institution in the world related somehow to Islamic art and history. He travelled constantly in the countries of Islam and Europe, and also visited America repeatedly. He was possessed of an urbane and winning personality. His Arabic, French, German, and, of course, his English and Hebrew were impeccable — and so was his comportment. Without intending it, he was a roving ambassador for the Hebrew University, as Magnes wished it to be presented to the world: a luminous center of rigorous research on the one hand and an avenue to universal contacts on the other.

As early as 1924, that is, a year before the official opening of the Hebrew University, I received a letter from Mayer asking me to join him and two others as fellows of the future Institute of Oriental Studies of the Hebrew University. I was then a teacher at the Reali School in Haifa, but Mayer knew me well, because together we had studied Ancient Near Eastern and Islamic art with Ernst Herzfeld[4] in Berlin and attended the lectures of the great interpreter of Islam, Carl Heinrich Becker,[5] who at that time, however, already functioned as a most brilliant Minister of Education and Culture in Prussia. When we studied with him in 1920 and 1921, we could not know that this man would have a special impact on the destinies of the School of Oriental Studies of the Hebrew University. The story is this: When the creation of an Institute of Arabic studies was placed at the Hebrew University, we thought also about an impressive scientific project which should be carried out by it. In a memorandum sent to Magnes, I suggested an edition of all the Arabic writings of Moses Maimonides to be published in 1935 on the 800th anniversary of his birth. This is not what he had in mind. He wished to have something addressed to the Arab world. Here C. H. Becker came into the picture. Shortly before World War I, he had discovered in Istanbul the manuscript of a huge and most important ancient history of the Arabs, arranged in genealogical order, called *Ansāb al-Ashrāf,* "The Genealogies of the Nobility," the edition of which would require ten volumes, or more, depending on how extensive a commentary accompanied the edition. Becker intended to organize an international body of editors for this vast undertaking. But the war intervened, and after the war, Becker went into politics. When Josef Horovitz,[6] the professor of the newly created chair of Islamic studies at the University of Frankfurt, who was a friend of Magnes, discussed with Becker the plans for the School of Oriental Studies of the Hebrew University, Becker suggested the *Ansāb al-Ashrāf* as the major scientific publication to be untertaken. This was agreed, but the difficulties were great. At that time, only one complete manuscript, the one discovered by Becker, was known. Editing an Arabic text from the ninth century, which contained much poetry — poetry was the journalism of the time — on the basis of one single manuscript was a hazardous undertaking. But there was a remedy. Ancient Arabic literature consists mainly of short, mostly very short, so-called traditions, which found their way into many different books.

What an editor of the *Ansāb* had to do first was to screen the entire manuscript (about 1,220 folios) looking for parallels and, second, to do the same with relevant ancient Arabic works in general. Naturally, this was a very prolonged process. Another difficulty was that no suitable Arabic type was available at that time in Jerusalem. Needless to say, Magnes was very involved with each step in the project's development. The type was provided and the first volume, edited by me, appeared in 1936.[7] It was well received and, by the way, later reprinted in Baghdad, where, however, the title page lists only my name and the place of publication — Jerusalem; there is no mention of the Hebrew University. Another half volume appeared in 1938, prepared by Max Schloessinger, an intimate friend of Magnes since the beginning of the century when both had studied Arabic and Rabbinics in Berlin.[8] He settled in Jerusalem after a very successful business career, serving occasionally as Magnes's deputy and reviving his Arabic in meetings with me. Because of his premature death, the other half volume prepared by him appeared much later and was readied for publication by Professor M. J. Kister of the Hebrew University,[9] today perhaps the most knowledgeable expert in the world on Arab antiquities. Kister himself had prepared a very comprehensive volume in the series in his Ph.D. thesis, and a prominent non-Jewish Italian Orientalist, Francesco Gabrieli,[10] another, part of which we had already printed when World War II broke out. The war, combined with other circumstances, interrupted the work and later the League of Arab States declared that they would carry out that huge undertaking. In the course of ten years or so, however, they brought out only one volume. Finally, the German Oriental Society, together with its Oriental Institute in Beirut, took over the project, and two volumes appeared recently,[11] albeit without the commentary our edition had provided.

Another field of Oriental studies with which Magnes was deeply concerned was the history and life of Jews in Muslim countries, for it was the symbiosis of the adherents of the two religions which was to be tested in Palestine. Each and every step of my prolonged study of the languages, life, and history of the Jews of Yemen enjoyed the support, or at least interest, of Dr. Magnes. Of one of my books, *Travels in Yemen*,[12] he even read partial proofs. Here it is appropriate to mention the name of Walter Joseph Fischel,[13] who had studied not only Arabic, but also economics, and, as the scion of an ancient family of merchants, also possessed a practical mind. Magnes recognized this, and asked him to travel to Iraq, Iran, India, and Hong Kong, and to arouse there the interest of wealthy Jews in the Hebrew University of Jerusalem. Fischel used his firsthand knowledge of the life of wealthy Jews in those countries for the study of the Jewish past in those regions. A number of his publications in this field appeared already during Magnes's lifetime and many more afterward. Magnes was particularly intrigued by Fischel's book, *Jews in the Economic and Political Life of Medieval Islam*, published by the Royal Asiatic Society of Great Britain in 1937,[14] where Jews of stature playing leading roles were described. The end of the most prominent of these Jews was tragic and cruel, but in 1937 one still believed that the Middle Ages were a matter of the past.

Dr. Magnes was much pleased when one of our professors, Dr. Joseph Joel Rivlin,[15] translated the Koran, the holy book of Islam, into modern Hebrew. Once when a group of Midwestern clergymen from the United States visited the University, Magnes proudly showed them Rivlin's book. "What," exclaimed one of the visitors, "translating the work of the Devil into God's own language!?" This exclamation shows precisely the spirit which Magnes wished to keep away from the pursuit of Oriental studies at the University.

Thirty-four years have passed since Magnes's death. Much has changed during this time. The School of Oriental Studies of the Hebrew University has much expanded and is now called the Institute for Asian and African Studies, but it has retained the good name it had at the time of Leo Ary Mayer. This is due, of course, to the excellence of the young scholars who ornament the Institute today, all, with two or three exceptions, members of the third generation trained at the University. By chance, four of the most prominent scholars who had studied in the School in Magnes's time, Eliyahu Ashtor,[16] David Ayalon,[17] Meir J. Kister,[18] and Pessah Shinar,[19] retired in 1982 and to our great sorrow, Gabriel Baer,[20] died unexpectedly.

I believe that a good spirit still guides research and teaching at the Institute, painstaking scholarship untainted by contempt or hatred for an inimical environment, so common at Arab universities, but also unfalsified by a well-meaning romanticism, not absent today from Western schools. It seems to me that the foundations laid there fifty years ago and more were sound, and they owed much to the guidance of Dr. Magnes. I personally regard it as a special privilege that I could pass the first twenty years of my academic life in a University to whose leader I could look to with respect and affection.

Figure 14. Magnes with two Arab visitors at Kibbutz Ein Gev on the shores of the Sea of Galilee c. 1940. *(Courtesy of the Jewish National and University Library)*

13

He Looked Out on Zion from Atop Mount Scopus and Dreamt of Peace: A Memoir

GABRIEL STERN*

Not long ago, I made a pilgrimage to the study of Dr. Judah Leib Magnes, the first president of the Hebrew University. To be precise, I should say that I made an ascent, for the room is in the lofty dome of the building which, in the early days of the University, was the loftiest of them all — the National and University Library, now the Law School — at the highest elevation in the Judean hills surrounding the city of Jerusalem: Mount Scopus. Narrow iron steps lead up to the well-aired room. As in the days when Magnes sat there, it is simply furnished. Today, one can still find the old leather armchairs which I would sit in occasionally (but only very occasionally, for he did not encourage people to climb up to his domed retreat) in those days long ago, generally to get some advice about peaceful alternatives, "In the Perplexity of the Times," as Magnes called a volume of his collected speeches, and even once or twice in the company of Arab friends.

Our first meeting occurred in November 1938. A new academic year was about to begin, and a problem arose. The Hebrew University was atop Mount Scopus, which was then outside the municipal boundaries of Jerusalem. The British mandatory power had issued orders requiring everyone who crossed the municipal borders to have a special blue permit in addition to an identity card. There were quite a few students at the university, so-called illegal immigrants, who could not get these permits, as well as individuals in the underground movements such as the Irgun. Magnes was very much opposed to these movements politically. They already had committed acts of terrorism against Arabs — setting bombs in market places and committing indiscriminate killings in retaliation for attacks on Jews. Innocent Jews and Arabs were killed, and Magnes was certainly one of the most extreme opponents of violence.

I was a member of the Students' Committee, which requested and succeeded in obtaining Magnes's intervention in combatting the taking of emergency measures against members "suspected" of participating in blockade-running or terrorist Irgun activities. I asserted that the emergency regulations were against human rights and that students should have the opportunity to come and go, stroll about at will, and enjoy academic freedom. Magnes listened very quietly and then said: "Why didn't you say these things a year ago when those emergency regulations were issued and used against the Arabs?" It is difficult to reconstruct his tone, for he addressed the matter solely in human terms, if you understand what I mean.

Three chemistry students who belonged to right wing militant groups were arrested under suspicion that they had made bombs at the chemistry laboratories. Magnes looked into the matter. The upshot was that the regulation requiring blue cards was suspended by the British for Bus #9 which went to the Hebrew University.

We went by Bus #9, but sometimes we also went by foot. During the Arab disturbances, it was dangerous to walk. One day, I saw Magnes walking from his home in the Arab Quarter. He wore a white linen suit and a yellow straw hat. The bus stopped to see if he was coming but he very solemnly and courteously declined and continued on his way. Apparently this was a daily event, a kind of ritual practiced by a man who was, I think, without guile and devoid of physical or moral fear. When activity at the Hebrew University on Mount Scopus was suspended in 1948 and the city was divided between Jordan and Israel, the bus company did not run Bus #9 again until 1967 when the connection with Mount Scopus was resumed.

When I was once again in that same room, I felt that it symbolically embodied and revealed the hidden dimensions of the personality of this man of great vision who was concerned with the fate of the world yet who was driven into extreme isolation. I looked out in all directions, for it is not by chance that it is called Mount Scopus, (Har ha-Tsofim). No view in the world equals it. The holy city of Jerusalem, with its churches, mosques, and synagogues — that unique blend of Zion and Jerusalem — is all spread out before your eyes. Even San Francisco — one of the most beautiful cities in the world, where Magnes was born more than one hundred years ago — cannot compare to it. Just as in San Francisco, whose citizens lament the destruction of its views even while tourists marvel at what remains, here also, as I look out from Magnes's dome, some changes are apparent, for the university is no longer "800 meters above the town," as the phrase used to go. Now Mount Scopus has taken its place alongside the three other university campuses — Givat Ram, the Medical Center in Ein Karem, and the Agricultural School in Rehovot.

Between the cupolas of the Dome of the Rock and Al-Aqsa Mosque on one side, and those of the Churches of the Holy Sepulchre on the other, the domes of the Hurvah and Nisan Bak Synagogues, — so dear to Magnes's heart, are no more to be seen. Near the end of his life, he made an abortive attempt to save them. At the same time, he did succeed in rescuing Mount Scopus from total destruction by making a dramatic plea to King Abdullah of Trans-Jordan.

Yet all in all, although monstrous hotels and luxury apartment buildings stand alongside the holy towers, Jerusalem remains the Jerusalem of gold, especially at sunset. To the east I gaze out at the Judean Desert, the Jordan Valley, and the Dead Sea. In the background loom the Mountains of Ammon and Moab, and in the distance, one can see the ancient village of Anatot or Anata, the site of the birthplace of the prophet Jeremiah. They appear just as the late Magnes himself must have seen them for this view, which man cannot alter, is primeval and imperishable, whereas below us are to be seen at every hand evidences of destruction, whose extent is hard to assess.

Not long ago, I went walking with friends in the Mount Scopus district. It has changed beyond recognition. The mountain summit has become a virtual crater, with new buildings erected daily. It is far removed from that day in 1912 when, on his second visit to Eretz Israel, Magnes instantly fell in love with the spot where the house of Sir John Gray-Hill stood solitary and alone atop the Mount of Olives and exclaimed to his wife, Beatrice, at his side, "It is here, on this very spot, that our university must stand!" It is, of course, impossible to know if Magnes would have approved of the new fortress-style architecture, not to mention the image of the institution as it has developed over the years. He saw in the "Hebrewness" of the institution no contradiction to its panhumanistic principles or to its openness to Arabs and to their religious and national values, and he proudly adhered to this claim in 1946 before the Anglo American Inquiry Committee. Nonetheless, even in his lifetime there was no lack of sharp disagreements as to the character and direction of the university between him and those who wanted to give the natural sciences priority, most notably Chaim Weizmann, who, along with Magnes, was awarded the university's first honorary Doctoral degree on the latter's seventieth birthday, exactly thirty years ago.

Also opposed to Magnes in this matter was Albert Einstein, whose severe censure of Magnes was mentioned in a symposium on intellectuals in politics last week held at the Van Leer Institute.[2] Yet, coincidentally, an exhibition of great interest that opened a week later at the National Library in celebration of the one hundreth anniversary of Magnes's birth, featured a letter from Einstein to Magnes on his sixtieth birthday which extolled him. "Although we have had our quarrels," wrote Einstein,

> today I assure you of my sympathy and esteem, for in your life you have heeded not the call of convenience but the call of conscience. You especially merit praise because you have attempted, with every means at your disposal, to have our fellow Jews pursue a sagacious and conciliatory policy with the Arabs. Now, the vindictive will understand how right you have been.[3]

Some weeks later Magnes also received an enthusiastic birthday greeting from Musa Husayni, an Arab student, who informed him of the favorable reaction of Arabs to his aspirations for peace.

I assume that Husayni is Ishaq Musa al-Husayni,[4] later a professor in Cairo, who aroused the ire of his extremist relatives by calling for nonviolence in his allegorical book *Memoirs of a Hen*,[5] which, in the mid-1940s, predicted with alarming accuracy the fate of the Palestinian Arab refugees. It is important to remember that during most of the years that Magnes lived in Palestine, from 1922 to 1938, he lived in the Arab Husayni quarter adjacent to the American Colony, until the tragic murder of a cab driver just outside his front door forced him to move to the square in the Rehavia area which still bears his name, Kikar Magnes.

One day in February 1948, two Jews came to see the late Rabbi Benyamin.[6] They were natives of Hebron and still retained contacts in that town (whose Arabic name, al-Khalil, the good friend, commemorates Abraham, father of the two peoples and often referred to in Moslem tradition as the good friend of God) with former neighbors who had rescued them in the riots of 1929, when Hebron's Jews were slaughtered. The elderly Rabbi Benyamin, personally connected with the orthodox kibbutz of Kfar Etzion,[7] near Hebron, was then very anxious about the fate of the kibbutz and the other three collective religious settlements nearby, which constituted an isolated Jewish enclave. A number of lives had already been lost in the defense of this bloc of settlements and in attempts to reinforce it (such as the dispatch of the famous thirty-five young men who died a heroic death on their way there from Jerusalem). Rabbi Benyamin was attempting to seek out ways of rescuing it.

His two visitors, with whom he had engaged in exploring possible avenues of endeavor in this direction, came to him that day with a message that had been related to them through their Arab contacts with some of Hebron's leading notables, proposing a sort of truce between Hebron and the Etzion settlements. It was decided to hold a preliminary meeting for the discussion of the terms of the truce. The Arab representative was to be one of the Hebron notables who held no official post but who exercised a good deal of influence behind the scenes and does so to this day, which is why his name cannot be mentioned. The Jewish spokesman was to be Judah L. Magnes, President of the Hebrew University, who also represented no one in an official capacity but whom Arabs far and wide respected for his integrity and will for peace.

The meeting had to be held as soon as possible, but the main difficulty was setting a time and a place. After many vicissitudes, the date was set for February 22, and the spot — a stroke of genius in divided Jerusalem — the building of the Anglo-Palestine Bank in Jaffa Road, next to the entrance to what was then known as "Bevingrad," the fortified British military and police compound between the Arab and the Jewish parts of the city. The Bank building was a forward outpost on the Jewish side and as such had undergone a number of searches, but it had the advantage of two separate entrances, both covered and protected: one at the front, facing "Bevingrad" and the Arab area, the other in the back, in a dark, narrow alley.

It was decided that Magnes would enter the building from the back, while the Arab notable would call at British police headquarters in "Bevingrad" on some pretext, then slip through its gates for the short distance separating them from the front entrance to the bank. To prevent any possible mishap, the Hagana and volunteer Jewish militiamen posted in the area were given careful instructions. The operation was thoroughly planned, but its objective was peace, not war.

The few of us who were in on the plan awaited the appointed date tensely and with a great deal of anxiety; and indeed, one day before the scheduled meeting Magnes, already in poor health then, six months before his death, took to bed with what was feared might turn out to be pneumonia. The weather was cold and wet. Would he be able to go? He insisted on going; this was a rescue operation as well as an opportunity for advancing the cause of peace. He would take a cab to the very door of the bank building; it could not possibly do him any harm. Of course, we were not certain that the other side would be ready and able to keep the appointment, and some questioned the reliability of the good and simple Jews who had been the intermediaries.

Morning came, and with it a terrible disaster: the blowing up with three truckloads of explosives, of half a dozen houses on both sides of Ben Yehuda Street, a thoroughfare in Jerusalem's new Jewish quarter. Only later was it discovered that the job had been done by Englishmen in police uniforms. Magnes was profoundly shaken. Would there be any point to a meeting under such circumstances? "I have to go there no matter what!" was his decision by the time I had reached his house.

By the way, if my memory serves correctly, it was on the same occasion that I met Dr. Sukenik,[8] authenticator of the Dead Sea Scrolls, in the hallway of Dr. Magnes's home. I did not pay much attention to it then, and it was not until some time later that I discovered that plans had been woven at that meeting for purchasing the first Scrolls. Magnes had been instrumental in the decision to carry out the transaction, for he was one of the first to believe in the historic importance of the Dead Sea find.

To return to the "truce meeting" — the question was how to get there. All the streets around Ben Yehuda had been sealed off, so going by taxi was impossible. The sick, elderly man had to go on foot, over the uneven alleyways alongside the Mamilla Moslem cemetery, then an unsafe, desolate area.

We arrived at the bank building with very little hope that the meeting would materialize. Indeed, the Hebron notable did not come, and after a long hour of forlorn waiting we had to retrace our steps.

We found later that the notable had risen early that morning, donned his cloak and *Kefiya* (headcloth), taken up his heavy walking stick, and set off by bus for Jerusalem together with his son. When they got to the bus station at Bab al-Khalil, the Jaffa Gate, they saw columns of smoke going up in the Jewish city. All was chaos and panic, and all sorts of rumors spread like wildfire, but the old man stood by his determination to go. "I have something to take care of," he kept insisting to his astounded friends, who began to wonder what was the reason for this forceful stand. Off he went firmly in the direction of "Bevingrad," paying no heed to the panic all around.

At the compound, however, the British guards turned him back roughly. "No entry!" shouted the police, pushing him back bodily. He had to retrace his steps, the meeting did not take place, and the attempt at rescue failed.

No one can tell, of course, what the real prospects of a truce were in those dazed, chaotic days; but something symbolic may be found in the fact that the British policemen who carried out the wanton attack on the heart of Jewish Jerusalem incidentally ruined this opportunity for a chance at a limited and modest Arab-Jewish agreement. Historically, the explosion in Ben Yehuda Street was a link in the chain of events that deepened the enmity between the two peoples and thwarted the implementation of the plan to set up two states, a Jewish one and an Arab one, in peaceful collaboration with each other. This series of events reached its inexorable climax in the two massacres of Deir-Yassin and the Mount Scopus convoy.

These were also the days when the fate of the Etzion settlements was sealed. They were conquered and destroyed, after a stand of supreme heroism, by the "Arab" Legion of Sir John Glubb Pasha[9] — who did not savour the fruits of his victory for long either.

The mission of the old man of Hebron had been in vain. But he was not alone in his stand. (Gabriel Stern, "How Dr. Magnes and Rabbi Benyamin Tried to Rescue Kfar Etzion," *Ner* (May–June, 1958) *Monthly for Political and Social Problems and for Jewish-Arab Rapprochement*, 44–46.)

I have heard from the University spokesman that there is a plan afoot to convert Magnes's solitary study, with its fabulous views, into a Magnes memorial, but I understand that there are difficulties in carrying out such a plan, partly because of the steep, narrow iron staircase. If tourists find no difficulty in climbing up to see the antiquities of Masada, perhaps they will find a way to overcome this obstacle too; otherwise, perhaps a technical solution can be found.[10] In any case, it would be appropriate for a Magnes Museum to exist not only in Berkeley, near his native San Francisco (under the devoted direction of Seymour Fromer), with its emphasis on the Jews of the "Wild West," but also in Jerusalem, where, wrote Magnes, a week before his death in New York, "I never realized before how deeply my roots were planted."[11] Such a museum would be a proper place to house at least a portion of the immense collection of materials which have been gathered with such care for the current exhibition, for it would be a shame if they were kept together for only a few weeks. Appropriately, the site is not too far from Martin Buber's restored study, in the Center for Mass Education, which is named after him.

More important, perhaps, this lofty dome will serve as a vantage point from which to monitor the expanding campus in the hope that it may increase not only in size but also in depth, in the spirit of one of Magnes's last letters from America shortly before his death. Wrote Magnes on the eve of the new State of Israel's first academic year and the Jewish New Year, to the new Rector of the Hebrew University, Professor Simcha Assaf:

To my deep regret, it will not be possible for me to be present at the opening of the new academic term. I have had the rare privilege of standing before the university community almost every year since the university's establishment. This year, during which so many radical changes have taken place in the life of the Land, I am compelled to send from afar my heartfelt good wishes for a year of blessing in the life of the university.

In the war, from which the Land suffered during the past year, members of the university, both teachers and students, have played a most honorable part. Many of them fell on the field of battle. Doubtless the university will take the first fitting opportunity to tell of them and to perpetuate their memory. The field of battle included the very buildings of the university and those of our former sister institution, Hadassah, and also the perilous road to Mount Scopus where so many of the dearest of human beings and so many distinguished scientists were swept away. For a long time to come we shall be missing them in developing the university, in deepening its foundations and enlarging its borders. May God comfort their families in the midst of the other mourners of Zion and Jerusalem.

Permit me a remark or two as to the new and basic problems with which the new situation confronts us. Why have our people and our land suffered destruction time and again? The answer of the prophets and sages of Israel has been: Idolatry, the worship of idols, our prostrating ourselves before the works of our own hands and before the hosts of the heavens. In the course of the generations, the idols change their forms. Among the more important tasks before each generation is to point to the idols which pretend to be God almighty, and before which mankind are expected to bend the knee and to sacrifice their most precious offerings, their sons and daughters. Today the world stands trembling and fearful on the brink of Gehennah, the new world war — Heaven protect us. Among the idols of our own day, we find militarism and totalitarianism, that is, the exalting of the army above everything else, and the exalting of the state above every other social form. Of course, my words are not intended to lessen the great value of the army and the State of Israel. I refer to every army and to every state. There are spiritual values such as the House of Learning, *bet-hamidrash*, or the University and the House of religious Assembly, *bet ha-knesset*, or the Synagogue which must be independent of army and state. And there are ethical qualities such as justice and mercy which are *autonomous* and not subservient to army and state. The people of Israel now confront such problems as subjects and not merely as objects. In the eyes of many among us, the chief value of an independent state is that we ourselves bear the responsibility for our own decisions and that we do not just have to accept the consequences of decisions made for us by others. It is as well that history places us face to face with grave and fateful human problems such as these. Perhaps it may be possible for us as the bearers of direct responsibility to answer some of these questions not only for our own sake but also for the sake of humanity.[12]

I said that Magnes was many-sided and complex, and yet on second thought, I wonder if this was quite as true of him as it was of his friend and colleague Martin Buber. Certainly Magnes had many talents and was active in many fields. The son of immigrants from Russia and Poland, he was the first Reform rabbi to be born in the American West and one of Herzl's first followers in the United States. His Zionism brought him into conflict with the Reform establishment, which was at that time extremely anti-Zionist. In 1902, in Berlin, he was summoned to a disciplinary sitting by his professors for his outspokenness, along with five other student Zionists, among them Dr. Biram, later the founder of the Reali School in Haifa. The Tel Aviv architect Hadassah Cohen, then a little girl, recalls how Magnes protested before the judges: "I thought this was a free institution of higher learning, but I now see that it is no more than a *heder*, where the *yeshivah-bochers* are fed leftover salted fish. The day will come when we will found in Jerusalem a university which is truly free."

Did Magnes remember his prophecy in 1930 when the Organization of Students at the Hebrew University rejected the demand to fire him because of his active role in promoting Arab-Jewish understanding, and when he got off with "only" a severe reprimand? (As reported in *Do'ar ha-yom*, which is on display at the exhibition.) It is interesting to note that the extreme Revisionist, Professor Joseph Klausner, present at that stormy meeting, was then a relative moderate.

This is, of course, not the only paradox in Magnes's life. He was from the outset an enthusiastic supporter of the Jewish Labor and Zionist movements, the organizer of mass demonstrations to protest the 1905 massacres in Russia and subsequently an unpopular friend of the early Soviet regimes. He was the initiator of the first democratically inspired Jewish Community, the New York *Kehillah*, a sworn supporter of the Haganah and of Hashomer Hatzair, and most especially of Mania Shochat,[13] whom he got out of prison in 1924 by personally interceding for her with the High Commissioner; during the riots of 1948, she ascended Mount Scopus in a symbolic peace gesture, passing safely through hostile Arab lines.

After he made *aliyah*, he became ever more disillusioned with the Histadrut, finding allies in such people as Moshe Smilansky and Pinhas Rutenberg, until the 1940s, when he reached a renewed and mutually reserved rapprochement with Ha-Shomer Ha-Tzair. An extreme pacifist during World War I in the United States, in World War

II he unreservedly supported the British war effort against Hitler, even while defending the rights of conscientious objectors. Although bitterly opposed to the pro-British policies of most American Zionists and skeptical about the Balfour Declaration ("Be wary of generosity!"), he acquired a deep, although not uncritical, familiarity with the Mandatory Authorities in Palestine.

This gives us only a partial image of him as a representative of those groups and their allies in Palestine. He had a strong contempt for terrorism, yet he was untiring in his efforts to free, or at least to mitigate the condition of those suspected of belonging to dissident organizations and to the Communist Party. Magnes was not naive. He helped people even when he was not quite convinced that they were innocent for, above all else, he was interested in due process of law which did not prevail in Palestine. There was the death sentence, of course. Many times Magnes and his friends angered Jews by intervening for Arabs who were sentenced to death. But later it enabled us to intervene in good conscience for Jewish prisoners who were on death row. In the exhibit we find, for example, letters to the authorities regarding (1) Shmuel Katznelson (now Knesset member S. Tamir), a member of Irgun, and (2) Hitler, in whom he saw the Devil. As a representative of the Joint Distribution Committee, he was committed to desperate rescue efforts. It was from Magnes, who spent that fateful period (July 1944) in Istanbul, that I first heard cryptically about Rudolf Kastner (1906–1957), who sought to carry out the exchange of Jews for trucks.[14]

However, these paradoxes are only seeming contradictions. They resulted from circumstances of time and place, rather than from a dual or irresolute character. Basically, he was a sincere and honest man, and it must be said, as far as his Zionist policies were concerned, even one-sided. I do not deny that he devised many different plans to solve the Palestine problem, but their main thrust was always the guaranteed existence of a Jewish national home based on a strong moral, political, cultural, and social foundation. He saw peaceful coexistence with the neighboring Arab countries as a prerequisite for this. His final trip to America was devoted to this objective, leading to the appointment of Count Folke Bernadotte as mediator and to the ceasefire which saved Jerusalem. Magnes's version of this effort — as opposed to the tendentious version given in other sources — is to be seen in the exhibition.

On that last trip, Magnes spoke of financial sanctions, insisting on their application to Arab and Jew alike, but only if all else failed, as a last resort, to put an end to the fighting. In his talk at the opening of the exhibition, Aryeh Goren quoted an alarming passage from

Magnes's diary, testifying to the bewilderment of those days, which drove him to do everything in his power to prevent the outbreak of war: "If we are victorious over the Arabs, there will never be peace, yet if we should lose the war, the Zionist enterprise will be crushed, and for generations to come, we will have no revival in Palestine."[15]

I will not conceal the fact that Magnes's bitter objection to partitioning the land also came out of his passion for maintaining the integrity of the Holy Land. I can still hear his words of explanation on July 14, 1947, before the special United Nations committee, which sent a ripple of amazement through the audience in the crowded YMCA auditorium: "I have the feeling that every point in this country, every square foot of it, is something that I am in touch with, through my history, through my tradition. I cannot exclude Jenin, which was at one time in the Bible called Ein Ganim, which is going to be, by all calculations, in the Arab State."[16]

It is interesting to note that even then Judge Ivan C. Rand, a committee member from Canada, brought up the question whether it would necessarily follow that without a binational state, Magnes would not be allowed to set foot in Jenin. If I may hazard a guess, in light of the experience of the last few decades, if Magnes were alive today, given the alternatives of a "whole land of Israel" championed by our Nationalist and Religious right wing, and a "secular and democratic" Palestine, supported by extreme elements in the PLO, even he would opt for a territorial compromise between Israel and her Arab neighbor within open borders.

Alas, the great dream Dr. Magnes envisioned from atop Mount Scopus remains a dream. In the aforementioned symposium on "Intellectuals in Politics," the Finnish statesman Max Jakobsen, concluded his talk on the tragic death of United Nations Secretary General Dag Hammarskjold,

> The paradox of our era is that technology and science have made borders obsolete, yet at the same time, the nationalist aspirations of many peoples have multiplied greatly, and it seems that only after every single one of them, even the smallest among them, has attained full self-determination, is there a chance that Hammarskjold's supranational dream may be realized.[17]

The issue of self-determination seems to apply to us as well, Israelis and Palestinians alike. It is a rung on the narrow iron ladder leading to the realization of the vision Magnes had from atop Mount Scopus.

Figure 15. The Magnes residence, second floor, Husayni House, Arab East Jerusalem c. 1925–1938. (*Courtesy of Hava Magnes*)

14

The Arab-Jewish Dilemma

BERNARD WASSERSTEIN

The last person to have favored an uncritical celebration of the life and legacy of Judah Magnes would have been Magnes himself. The diary notes and other writings recently published by Professor Arthur Goren[1] reveal a deeply self-critical, self-questioning spirit — perhaps the essential private aspect of a public figure whose primary role was as radical critic and asker of awkward questions. In any assessment of his work in Arab-Jewish relations, on which he expended such passionate efforts in the last two decades of his life, we therefore owe it to his shade to paint the portrait, warts and all, to follow this man's own example in seeking the unvarnished, unadorned, and sometimes unpalatable truth.

There is a poignant irony in the fact that Magnes today is chiefly remembered less for his great constructive and in some respects enduring achievements in the social and educational spheres in America and Palestine than for his activities in an area that he would have been the first to acknowledge candidly as one in which he failed almost utterly. The political arena into which he flung himself with such energy and zeal was almost completely barren of success and it might be thought a matter for wonder that he is recalled today not so much as the creator of the New York *Kehillah*, nor as first head of the Hebrew University of Jerusalem, but rather as the chief inspiring force of a small band of intellectuals on the political fringe of Zionism, a group which had negligible support among the *Yishuv* and one whose binationalist political objectives were trampled into the dust by the onward rush of competing nationalist forces.

The reasons for this failure belong in the main to the larger macrocosmic level beyond the capacity of any individual or group to influence. But since we are concerned here with the microcosmic level of human biography, we may pose the question which Magnes would surely have expected to be raised: how far was the failure to realize Magnes's political ideas the result of intellectual, emotional, or other failings in Magnes himself?

Magnes was a complex man, intellectually as well as emotionally. He did not belong to that breed of prophet whose moral force derives from a pure simplicity of character and outlook: whatever political views he shared with them he was in this respect quite distinct from Albert Einstein and Mahatma Gandhi. Magnes's critique of mainstream Zionism, his doubts, his questions were rather the product of a process of internal fermentation, spiritual conflict, and perhaps of the self-doubts and self-contradictions with which he was afflicted. Writing in his journal on Rosh Ha-shana, the Jewish New Year, 1923, Magnes confessed:

> I am a deeply "religious" man, but Divinity is hazy and vague to me, not always active in me. I may be a religious man, but I am not a religious leader. An understanding of God is what is lacking within me. I doubt Him and question Him — His ways, His aloofness, the sufferings He causes man, the uncertainty of life, the blackness of death.[2]

The core of spiritual uncertainty, which can occasionally be glimpsed in such private reflections, was transmuted in his public persona into a strange failure of communication: this master of the spoken and written word, when faced in the final act of his life with a supreme task of political propagandising and proselytising, found again and again that while he could carry conviction he could not convince, while he could impress he could not persuade.

Although he settled in Palestine in 1922, Magnes initially abstained from public involvement in political issues. When the binationalist Brit Shalom (Covenant of Peace), society was formed in 1925 he did not become a member, even though he was in general agreement with its objectives.

The outbreak of fierce Arab-Jewish violence in 1929, however, shocked Magnes deeply and he felt compelled to speak out. In a speech on the occasion of the opening of the new academic year at the Hebrew University of Jerusalem, Magnes set forth his credo. The Jewish National Home, he declared, could not be established on "the bayonets of some empire"; Zionism could not be achieved through the conquests of some latter-day Joshua but only by peaceful means.[3] In a letter written to Chaim Weizmann about the same time, Magnes set out for the Zionist leader the essence of his view:

A Jewish Home in Palestine built up on bayonets and oppression [is] not worth having, even though it succeed, whereas the very attempt to build it up peacefully, cooperatively, with understanding, education, and good will, [is] worth a great deal, even though the attempt should fail.[4]

If Magnes had limited himself to the private expression of these views, possibly even if he had restricted his political activity to the realm of propaganda on the platform and in the press, he might have maintained cordial relations with the Zionist leadership. But what aroused their ire was Magnes's decision to go beyond this and to undertake political initiatives, which the official heads of the Zionist Organization pointed out were unauthorized and in some cases (so they argued) damaging to the Zionist cause. In spite of repeated clashes with the Zionist leaders, Magnes insisted on his right to continue to work to try to improve Arab-Jewish relations. "You do not expect of course," he wrote to Felix Warburg in August 1930, "that once having felt it to be my duty, after much hesitation, to enter the political fray, I can, because of possible misunderstanding, refrain from continuing to say and do what I think necessary."[5]

From 1929 onwards, Magnes engaged in a sequence of efforts at private diplomacy in an attempt to arrive at an agreed basis for Arab-Jewish coexistence in Palestine. All were unsuccessful, and most tended to follow a pattern wherein Magnes would persuade himself (or allow himself to be persuaded) that he had discovered the essential ingredients of such a formula and that he had found worthwhile Arab interlocutors who were inclined at least to discuss his ideas. Inevitably it would be found that the supposed basis for agreement was a *fata morgana* that evaporated whenever approached. In spite of his capacity for private self-criticism, Magnes tended to lay the blame for these successive failures at the door of the Zionist leaders whom he increasingly blamed for their alleged lack of seriousness in the matter of relations with the Arabs.

Undoubtedly, one cause of these repeated setbacks was Magnes's tendency towards credulousness and his poor judgment of the characters of some of those who presented themselves to him as mediators. An early example of what was to become a recurring pattern was the attempt, immediately after the 1929 riots, to arrive at an agreement with Arab leaders through the mediation of H. St. John Philby, a former British official in Trans-Jordan. An unreliable adventurer who was not taken seriously by the British government who had found him a severe embarrassment during his period in Trans-Jordan, Philby found that his letters to the Colonial Secretary, Lord Passfield, pressing his scheme for Arab-Jewish rapprochement, evoked no interest in Whitehall. Magnes, on the other hand, took up Philby's proposals with enthusiasm, only to discover that Philby spoke for himself alone, that not only was Arab agreement not forthcoming, but that the British and the Zionists refused to take Philby seriously either.

Magnes could inspire admiration even among his enemies; yet even his friends had to admit that internal contradictions and inconsistencies in his thought tended to weaken its persuasive impact. These were apparent in the evidence he gave to the Anglo-American Committee of Inquiry on Palestine in March 1946. Magnes appeared together with Martin Buber and Moshe Smilansky as representatives of the Ihud which had been established at Magnes's initiative in 1942 on a binationalist platform. Their very appearance represented a breach of Zionist discipline since the Zionist Executive had decreed that no independent submissions were to be made by Zionist groups. Magnes's testimony greatly impressed the members of the committee whose chairman, Judge Joseph Hutcheson, told him: "You are not denominated a Christian, Dr. Magnes, but you talk as I should like Christians to act. I am not ready to assess your proposals, but I am a fairly old man and I recognize moral power when I see it."[6]

The compliment was obviously genuine, but a diary entry by one of the British members of the committee shows that the political as distinct from the moral effectiveness of Magnes's testimony was limited, particularly in the light of his answer to one question about his own university — whether he would be prepared to change the name to the University of Palestine. Magnes replied that the name Hebrew University of Jerusalem had been chosen quite deliberately since it was to be the university of all the Jewish people, established to fructify and revive Judaism. He went on to say that the conception of Judaism is that the truly just society has to be established by the Jews among the Jews, and that through establishing it first of all among the Jews perhaps it would be possible to establish the really just society in other parts of the world. Such a view might have been calculated to appeal to a British socialist sympathetic to the moderate wing of Zionism; but in fact the British committee member in question, Richard Crossman, was not persuaded and commented in his diary: "What this came to was a complete contradiction with regard to his own university of the binational politics he had been talking throughout his speech."[7]

In a sense, Crossman's was both an unfair question and an unfair conclusion by a master of the art of unfair questions. Magnes, after all, had always made a clear distinction between the cultural and the political: he did not argue that Jewish culture should be subsumed with Arab in a cosmopolitan hodgepodge, but rather that the two cultures should live side by side within a binational political framework. On this occasion as on many others Magnes was misunderstood and misrepresented.

A similar incident had occurred nine years earlier in 1937 when Magnes addressed the Council of the Jewish Agency, urging rejection of the Palestine Royal Commission's proposal for the partition of Palestine into separate Arab and Jewish states. In his opposition to partition, Magnes enjoyed the company of many prominent Zionists from various points on the political spectrum. Magnes's reasons for opposing partition were, however, principled rather than tactical. Charging that the advocates of a Jewish state were guilty of a false messianism, Magnes eloquently opposed what he presented as their lack of realism. Stressing the dangers to a Jewish state of a large Arab minority, he said: "If you can get the consent of the Arabs, it would be different. But you do not even think of asking them for their consent." Magnes was interrupted by David Ben-Gurion who inquired whether Magnes himself had immigrated to Palestine with Arab consent. Magnes replied:

> His question is a legitimate one. He asks, did I go to Palestine with Arab consent. No, I did not, but I did not have a Jewish state there in the first instance, and I was not trying to get a Jewish state in the second place, and everything I have said and done in my life, as far as Palestine is concerned, from the beginning up to this day, has been based upon the fundamental thought that in what we do and what we plan, we should endeavor to get Arab consent. And that is the purport of this resolution that we are presenting. This resolution provides for a binational state, if it can be secured with the consent of the Arabs and the Jews and of the British government.[8]

Here was, in Magnes's own view, the nub of the matter; and yet here too was the essential weakness of Magnes's entire position. The ultimate test, as he insisted, was the consent of all parties concerned. But as his Zionist critics often pointed out, with a certain measure of self-righteous *Schadenfreude*, Magnes's own program failed his own test, for it never secured the support of politically significant or representative Palestinian Arabs.

A typical Arab reaction to Magnes's ideas was that of Awni Abd al-Hadi, member of a notable Nablus family, one of the earliest Arab nationalist activists in Palestine and among the most prominent nationalist leaders in the interwar period, who wrote in reply to an approach by Magnes in 1931 that while the Arabs were prepared to accord the Jews "the same rights as the Arabs" in Palestine, the political problem could be solved only by Jews, "accepting the Arab national political aims." If the Zionists would only "give up altogether the idea of creating a Jewish National Home with political aspects," he concluded, "there will remain nothing which will prevent an agreement between both parties."[9] As Professor Neil Caplan writes in his penetrating analysis of Arab-Zionist contacts in this period: "Only outside of leadership circles did a few individuals dare to depart from the official 'line,' but their willingness to compromise on basic goals was not enough to produce an agreement which could command support in either camp."[10]

There were, it is true, some Arabs, Palestinian and non-Palestinian, who formulated tentative outlines of agreement with Magnes, and, indeed, at certain points in the 1930s, Magnes played a minor political role in arranging meetings between Ben-Gurion (also Moshe Shertok) and one of his Arab interlocutors, Musa Alami.

Of all the Palestinian Arabs with whom Magnes spoke, Alami was probably the one with whom he came closest to finding common ground. Yet, even Alami fell into the common mold of admiring Magnes while remaining unpersuaded by his message. On the one hand, Alami could write of Magnes to their mutual friend, Norman Bentwich: "I can't tell you how much I admire and respect him."[11] On the other hand, looking back over the passage of years, Alami told his biographer, Sir Geoffrey Furlonge, of the successive changes of attitude he discerned in Magnes:

> At first, Musa Alami recalls, he [Magnes] would have been prepared to settle for a Palestine composed of two-thirds Arabs and one-third Jews; then he thought that the proportions should be 60:40; then parity; and at last he was driven back to advocating that, whatever the actual numbers of the two communities they should always enjoy political equality.[12]

There is a certain pathos in this failure of understanding between Magnes and Alami for in some respects Alami occupied in relation to the Palestinian Arabs a position analogous to that of Magnes among the Jews. Both were deracinated European-educated liberals without any broad power base within their own communities. Both found the most welcoming audience for their ideas not among their own people but among liberal-minded Englishmen and Americans. If a man like Alami could not be won over to Magnes's binationalist program, what hope was there of persuading the mainstream Arab nationalist leadership in Palestine?[13] As one of the more moderate Palestinian Arab politicians, Anwar Nusseibeh, was to put it later: "Of course, the ordinary man in the street could not understand even the idea of a single nationalism let alone the idea of a dual nationalism."[14]

Magnes's failure to secure the consent on which he insisted as a *sine qua non* for a political program in Palestine was hardly less marked among his own people. It is true that he commanded respect and influence among important sections of American Jewry and that he had allies in Henrietta Szold, leader of the Hadassah women's Zionist organization, the *New York Times* (an important platform for Magnes's ideas, particularly in the last phase of the Palestine mandate), and some of the old-style notables of the American Jewish leadership. The binationalist idea was also embraced by the Ha-Shomer Ha-Tzair socialist-Zionist movement in Palestine and by many of the middle-class liberal immigrants to Palestine from central Europe. Yet what remains striking is Magnes's signal failure to build a really effective political coalition to seek to give effect to his ideas. It was a failure all the more remarkable in a man who had been the great artificer of unity among the warring factions of Jewry in New York, and who had evinced such sympathy for, and at times solidarity with, the Jewish working-class in the United States. Here, again, was perhaps a failing which was both intellectual and personal.

The intellectual aspect may be seen when comparing his political evolution with that of Ben-Gurion and Weizmann. There were periods when these men expressed views somewhat similar to those of Magnes, Ben-Gurion particularly in the mid-1920s, Weizmann in the early 1930s. But they arrived at these conclusions by radically different routes. For Magnes, Arab-Zionist agreement was a necessary condition of Zionist development, certainly of any Zionist political development, in Palestine. For Ben-Gurion, Weizmann, and the mainstream Zionist leadership, such agreement was desirable, and even worth making some sacrifices to achieve; but they could never regard it as a condition failing which the entire political content of Zionism might be jettisoned.

Moreover, unlike Magnes, they did not delude themselves as to the likelihood of success in reaching an Arab-Zionist accord. As early as 1919, Ben-Gurion declared:

> Everybody sees a difficulty in the question of relations between Arabs and Jews. But not everybody sees that there is no solution to this question. No solution! There is a gulf and nothing can fill this gulf. It is possible to resolve the conflict between Arab and Jewish interests only by sophistry . . . . We must recognize this situation.[15]

Ben-Gurion did not hold consistently to this view, as his contacts with Magnes and much else in his career indicate, but this outburst did express an essential pessimistic strain in his attitude. Above all, he remained totally consistent in his rejection of Magnes's suggestion that political Zionism could proceed only on the basis of Arab consent.

As for Weizmann, he was capable of writing, in words which Magnes himself might have used: "For us the State is not an end in itself and is not surrounded by the halo with which other peoples nowadays adorn the 'State,' turning it into an idol or a Moloch." But in the same letter to Albert Einstein in April 1938, Weizmann condemned what he termed Magnes's "holier-than-thou manner," adding:

> The Jewish people is not returning to Palestine to become 'Arab citizens of the Mosaic faith' in their ancient homeland. Anybody who from his own observation has any idea how the Arab states are being administered today, what minority status signifies altogether in the world nowadays — let alone what it would mean for us in an Arab state — can visualize what would be in store for us if we were to accept these so-called peace plans. After all, the one and only basis for all our work, all our suffering for Palestine has been the consciousness that here at last we shall find liberation from the curse of ghetto status. Would it not be a monstrous deception of the last hope of a desperate people, if here in the very land where they had been promised national freedom, they were to be subjected to the rule of Levantine gangster politicians?[16]

Magnes's response to such objections took time to evolve and took the form of a painful ideological contortion. In the 1920s and 1930s he continued to believe, against all the accumulating evidence to the contrary, that an Arab-Zionist agreement was attainable. In April 1936, he wrote a vehement letter of rebuke to Arthur Ruppin, who until then had shared his faith, insisting that faith in such a rapprochement must be an essential qualification for Jewish leadership in Palestine:

> Someone like you who has lost the belief in an agreement with the Arabs, at least for the next ten years, and therefore has also lost the desire to search for it, should in my opinion leave the political leadership. The least he can do is to hurry out to where the shooting and fighting is and man the front line. After all, it is not possible to present the Agreement with the Arabs as an eternal topic of discussion and quietly come to a negative conclusion. As long as there is no agreement, there will be many dead and wounded. The leaders who are not able to bring about such an agreement should leave the task to others who believe more firmly in it.[17]

But to insist that consent was the *conditio sine qua non*, while palpably failing over nearly two decades of political activity to achieve it, was a position of which time itself was an increasingly ferocious critic.

Magnes himself seemed to recognize this by 1942 when he wrote in his journal: "America must come in and help impose a compromise."[18] This was an idea which he presented in a more worked-out form in an article in *Foreign Affairs* magazine in January 1943 when he called for a binational form of government which should, if necessary, be imposed by joint action of Great Britain and the United States.

Here was a sad intellectual gyration whereby the principle of consent, hitherto sacrosanct in his thought, was transmuted into its very antithesis, an imposed solution, precisely what Magnes had been arguing against on moral grounds throughout the previous decade or more. One is inevitably reminded of the late Jacob Talmon's discussion of Rousseau's inversion of the principle of liberty, what Talmon termed "the paradox of freedom in totalitarian democracy . . . If the people does not will it, it must be made to will it."[19]

Magnes maintained this belief in an imposed compromise, or what might be called consent by coercion, until the end of the British mandate in Palestine. Hence, his welcoming of the brief hiccup in American policy in March 1948 when the chief American delegate to the United Nations announced a retreat from American support for partition and advocated for a United Nations trusteeship over Palestine, an event of which Magnes wrote to Thomas Mann:

> You think the reversal of the United States' support of partition 'the most humiliating and revolting political event since the treachery against Czechoslovakia in 1938.' I, on the other hand, think it the most humane and wisest decision which American statesmanship could have taken. It is humane because it calls for a cessation of this 'warfare,' for a stop to this bloodletting. It is wise because it is an attempt — long since overdue — to meet the problem through conciliation, compromise, understanding, cooperation between Arabs and Jews.[20]

At this time of supreme crisis in the mid-1940s, Magnes's political construct, founded on the principle of voluntary consent and cooperation between Arabs and Jews, thus proved as fragile to the assaults of an unconsenting majority as did Robespierre's unilateral interpretation and attempted imposition of the general will in 1793–1794.

That Magnes himself was uncomfortable with this inversion of the principle of consent is suggested by one of his last political statements, quoted by Arthur Goren, a message Magnes sent to the opening of the academic year of the Hebrew University of Jerusalem in September 1948, in which he sought to come to terms with the new reality of the Jewish state against the foundation of which he had struggled for so long:

> The people of Israel [he wrote] now confronts such problems as sub-
> jects and not merely as objects. In the eyes of many among us the chief
> value of an independent state is that we ourselves bear the responsibil-
> ity for our own decisions and that we do not just have to accept the
> consequences of decisions made for us by others.[21]

With this statement, a little more than a month before his death,
Magnes had come full circle. The idea of an imposed settlement was
forgotten and the principle of consent, of the collective exercise of free
will, was elevated once again to the highest political ideal.

It might be argued that the weakness of Magnes's intellectual position in relation to the Arab-Jewish conflict was that it lacked a solid
ideological basis. His outlook was that of a radical liberal who sought
to view things as they were and without ideological blinkers — but
also without the familiar reference points of the socialist or nationalist
ideologues by whom he was surrounded. His primary concerns in
politics were the traditional Anglo-Saxon liberal ones with the form
rather than the content of politics — with freedom of speech, press,
and assembly; due legal process; responsibile government; and so on.
These reference points provided him with little help in his confronta-
tion with the harsh realities of Palestinian politics.

In this regard, it is instructive to compare Magnes with his binationalist allies of the Ha-Shomer Ha-Tzair movement. Unlike him they
arrived at binationalism by way of an analysis of the economic and
social structure of the Arab and the Jewish communities in Palestine.
It was an analysis which turned out to be based on several mistaken
premises (most notably that of the supposed alignment of interests of
the Jewish and Arab working classes in Palestine); but these mistakes
did not invalidate their whole approach which was to seek to construct a political movement and a political reality on the basis not
merely of an intellectual superstructure but on real social foundations.
Magnes's writings leave one with the impression that he never really
grasped that an effective political movement could not be formed out
of a handful of unorganized intellectuals. It was, perhaps, a strange
failure in a man whose most notable success had been to draw
together uptown and downtown New York. Maybe Magnes did not
want to build a political movement, but merely wanted to state a moral
position. But that, too, was a strange failure in a man who did, after
all, want passionately to help change the direction of history.

We come back, therefore, to the personal aspect. The animus
Magnes inspired among certain sections of the Zionist movement can
be explained largely in political terms. In particular, the venomous
hostility of the Revisionist Zionists can be traced to their resentment

of Magnes's influence among American Jewry and his readiness to challenge their hysteria-mongering in the United States. The mainstream Zionists, particularly Ben-Gurion and Shertok, increasingly regarded Magnes as a dupe in the hands of non-Zionist or anti-Zionist forces. But, beyond the political was a personal aspect. Magnes, at any rate in his later years, was something of a cold fish. Abba Eban, in his *Autobiography*, writes that he conceived with Magnes "as much of a friendship as our gap in years and his own frigid temperament would allow."[22] Magnes held himself rather aloof even from his colleagues at the Hebrew University. Indeed, in one of the documents published by Goren, he makes a virtue of such aloofness.[23] To this was added, particularly in his final years, a hectoring tendency which can be detected even in his letters to close associates. Magnes's correspondence over four decades with Chaim Weizmann shows a sad progression in their relationship, from an easy intimacy around 1905 through periods of hostile silence, renewed cooperation, and fierce conflict, culminating in a meeting of reconciliation, apparently arranged by Henrietta Szold, in December 1944. Magnes's personality did not generate enthusiastic support at either the mass or even, save in a few cases, the individual level.

The indisputable failure of Magnes's work for Arab-Jewish cooperation in Palestine should not, however, blind us to his enduring legacy. He, perhaps more than anybody else, founded the tradition of vigorous intellectual dissent which is such a crucial ingredient of Israeli political culture. His insistence that the Hebrew University must be a center of open and free inquiry rather than a Zionist university acting as academic handmaiden to the state was of vital importance in enabling the university to resist the inevitable pressures of the early years of statehood that have destroyed the academic independence and integrity of so many universities in newly decolonized countries. It is no accident that the Hebrew University remains, by and large, an oasis of civilised values in regard to Arab-Jewish relations.

It has also been of supreme importance for American Jewry, and perhaps never more so than now, to have established a firmly rooted tradition of vigilance and criticism of Israel among her supporters in the Diaspora, a vigilance which can draw on the principles of liberal-minded Zionism enunciated by Magnes, a criticism which, as in the case of Magnes himself, can be justified on the ground that the most sincere friend is not the one who agrees automatically but, rather, the one who asks the most awkward, disturbing, or disquieting questions.

Abbreviations
of Document Sources

MP	Judah Leib Magnes Papers, Central Archives for the History of the Jewish People, Jerusalem, Israel
MPWJHC	Judah L. Magnes Papers, Western Jewish History Center, Berkeley, California
NGP	Nelson Glueck Papers, American Jewish Archives, Cincinnati, Ohio
IFP	Israel Friedlaender Papers, Jewish Theological Seminary, New York, New York
WEWOHL	William E. Wiener Oral History Library, American Jewish Committee, New York, New York
CZA	Central Zionist Archives, Jerusalem, Israel
CAHJP	Central Archives for the History of the Jewish People, Jerusalem, Israel
AHP	Ahad Ha-Am Papers, Archives Division, The Jewish National and University Library, Jerusalem, Israel
WA	Chaim Weizmann Archives, Rehovot, Israel
LDBP	Louis D. Brandeis Papers, University of Louisville Law School Library, Louisville, Kentucky
SSWP	Stephen S. Wise Papers, American Jewish Historical Society, Waltham, Massachusetts
HMOA	Hadassah Medical Organization Archives, New York, New York
MB	Martin Buber Archive, The Jewish National and University Library, Jerusalem, Israel

Notes

Introduction: Like All the Nations?

1. Horace M. Kallen, *Utopians at Bay* (New York, 1958), 123.

2. See *A Land of Two Peoples: Martin Buber on Jews and Arabs* ed. with commentary by Paul R. Mendes-Flohr (New York, 1983).

3. Quoted in Joan Dash, *Summoned to Jerusalem* (New York, 1979), 319.

4. Melvin I. Urofsky, *We Are One: American Jewry and Israel* (New York, 1978), 149 and Barnet Litvinoff, ed., *The Essential Chaim Weizmann* (London, 1982), 24–5; for Weizmann's ideological background, see Ben Halpern, "The Disciple, Chaim Weizmann" in *At the Crossroads: Essays on Ahad Ha-Am*, ed. Jacques Kornberg (Albany, 1983), 156f; Arthur Goren, ed., *Dissenter in Zion: From the Writings of Judah L. Magnes* (Cambridge, 1982), 38.

5. *New York Times*, 10 October 1982, Ey 17.

6. Peter Grose, *Israel in the Mind of America* (New York, 1983), 338.

7. Norman Bentwich, *For Zion's Sake: A Biography of Judah L. Magnes* (Philadelphia, 1954), vii.

8. Abba Eban, *Address at Magnes Symposium* (14 October 1982), 2. (Typescript — MPWJHC.) Also see Abba Eban, "The Unending Conflict: The Middle East" in *The New Diplomacy: International Affairs in the Modern Age* (New York, 1983), 189–233.

9. Isaiah Berlin, *Chaim Weizmann* (New York, 1958), 60; Goren, *Dissenter in Zion*, 7.

10. See Bentwich, *For Zion's Sake*.

11. Goren, *Dissenter in Zion*, 61; Arthur Goren, "Judah L. Magnes's Trip to Przedborz," in *Studies in Contemporary Jewry*, ed. Jonathan Frankel (Bloomington, 1984), I, 164.

12. "The *Kehillah* Idea and Jewish Community Development," an unpublished paper available in MPWJHC, prepared for the symposium by the late

201

Sidney Vincent, addressed the question in schematic form. See also Samuel C. Kohs, "The Kehillah Experiment: A Learning Experience (An Essay Review)," *Journal of Jewish Communal Service* 48 (Fall 1971), 113–19, a many-sided analysis of Goren's *New York Jews and the Quest for Community* by one of the nation's most scholarly communal workers.

13. See especially, "Reformed Judaism: Plans for Reconstruction" in Goren, *Dissenter*, 107–15 and 193–5; Mordecai M. Kaplan, *Judaism as a Civilization: Toward a Reconstruction of American Jewish Life* (New York, 1934); Sefton D. Temkin, *The Life and Times of a Centenarian: Mordecai Kaplan and the Development of American Judaism* (New York, 1982), 9f; Charles Liebman *Aspects of the Religious Behavior of American Jews* (New York, 1974), 189f; Arnold M. Eisen, *The Chosen People in America* (Bloomington, 1983), 127–48.

14. Barbara W. Tuchman, *Practising History* (New York, 1981), 214; Melvin I. Urofsky, "Review of *Dissenter in Zion: From the Writings of Judah L. Magnes.* Edited by Arthur A. Goren," in *American Jewish History* 73 (March 1984), 339.

15. P. E. Lapide, *A Century of U. S. Aliya.* (Jerusalem, 1961), 27–8, 65–6, 137f; Kevin Avruch, *American Immigrants in Israel: Social Identities and Change* (Chicago, 1981) by an ethnographer, based on field work conducted in Israel between December 1975 and March 1977, is the most ambitious effort to study *olim* of recent years. There is nothing comparable for the Mandate period. Also see Harold R. Isaacs, *American Jews in Israel* (New York, 1966) and Aaron Antonovsky and Abraham Katz, *From the Golden to the Promised Land* (Darby, PA, 1979).

16. Cited in Norman Bentwich, ed., *Hebrew University Garland* (London, 1952), 12.

17. Herbert Parzen, *The Hebrew University, 1925–1935* (New York, 1974), is a brief monograph.

18. Samuel Hugo Bergman, *Faith and Reason: An Introduction to Modern Jewish Thought* (New York, 1961), 143, 149–51.

19. Gershom Scholem to Moses Rischin, 25 October 1981, MPWJHC.

20. Also see S. D. Goitein, "Oriental Studies in Israel (Hebrew and Ancient East Excluded)," in Bentwich, *Hebrew University Garland*, 96f.

21. Goren, *Dissenter*, 455. Also see Shabtai Teveth, *Ben-Gurion and the Palestinian Arabs from Peace to War* (New York, 1985), 87–92.

22. Bentwich, *For Zion's Sake*, 38.

23. George Santayana, *Character and Opinion in the United States* (New York, 1920), 118.

24. Josiah Royce, *The Hope of the Great Community* (New York, 1916), 129; Ralph H. Gabriel, *The Course of American Democratic Thought*, 2nd ed. (New York, 1956), 303f; John Clendenning, *The Life and Thought of Josiah Royce* (Madison, 1985), 366–75, 391–4.

1. San Francisco-Oakland: The Native Son

1. Goren, *Dissenter*, 3–57.

2. Bentwich, *For Zion's Sake*, 25.

3. Fred Rosenbaum, *Free to Choose: The Making of a Jewish Community in the American West* (Berkeley, 1976), 4.

4. Joan London, *Jack London and his Times: An Unconventional Biography* (Seattle, 1968).

5. Remarks by Isaac Magnes, April 1964, Box 68/30, Folder 141, MPWJHC.

6. Rosenbaum, *Free to Choose*, 15–20.

7. Earl Raab, "There's No City Like San Francisco," *Commentary* 10 (October 1950), 371.

8. Rosenbaum, *Free to Choose*, 6–7; Fred Rosenbaum, *Architects of Reform: Congregational and Community Leadership, Emanu-El of San Francisco, 1849–1980* (San Francisco, 1981), 17–9.

9. Rosenbaum, *Free to Choose*, 20–4; Simon Litman, *Ray Frank Litman: A Memoir* (New York, 1957).

10. David Magnes to his children regarding their mother (1902), Box 68/30, Folder 21 MPWJHC. Also see Bentwich, *For Zion's Sake*, 12–4.

11. *Ibid.*

12. Rosenbaum, *Free to Choose*, 44–5.

13. *Ibid.*

14. *Oakland Tribune*, 6 July 1890.

15. Rosenbaum, *Architects of Reform*, 45–65.

16. *Ibid.*, 48–54.

17. Jacob Voorsanger to Magnes, 10 November 1895, Box 68/30, Folder 8, MPWJHC.

18. *Emanu-El* (San Francisco), 11 August 1900; Kenneth C. Zwerin and Norton B. Stern, "Jacob Voorsanger: From Cantor to Rabbi" *Western States Jewish Historical Quarterly* 15 (April 1983), 200–1.

19. Rosenbaum, *Architects of Reform*, 58.

20. *Emanu-El*, 10 January 1896, 12–3.

21. See the *Aegis* (Oakland High School), 15 December 1983; 26 January; 8 February; 9, 26 March; 4, 18 May; 11 June; 7 September 1894 MPWJHC.

22. Bentwich, *For Zion's Sake*, 16.

23. Goren, *Dissenter in Zion*, 7.

24. Remarks by Isaac Magnes, April 1964, Box 68/30, Folder 141 MPWJHC.

25. Oscar Lewis, *The Big Four* (New York, 1971), 253.

26. *Arthur McEwen's Letter*, 17 February 1894–15 June 1895.

27. *Aegis*, 4 May 1894.

28. Goren, *Dissenter in Zion*, 431.

29. See Gunther Barth, *Instant Cities: Urbanization and the Rise of San Francisco and Denver* (New York, 1975).

30. See Moses Rischin, "The Jews and Pluralism: Toward an American Freedom Symphony," in Gladys Rosen, ed., *Jewish Life in America* (New York, 1978), 61–91.

31. Goren, *Dissenter in Zion*, 106.

2. Cincinnati: The Earlier and Later Years

1. Goren, *Dissenter in Zion*, 8.

2. *Cincinnatian 1897*, 55.

3. *Cincinnatian 1898*, Letters, Magnes to family 15 December 1897 and 23 January 1898. MP.

4. Reginald C. McGrane, *The University of Cincinnati: A Success Story in Urban Higher Education* (New York, 1963), 158; *Cincinnatian 1898*, 49; *McMicken Review* 12:1 (October 1897)1; Letters, Magnes to his family, 23 December 1897; 26, 30 January 1898, MP.

5. Max Raisin, *Great Jews I Have Known: A Gallery of Portraits* (New York, 1952), 212.

6. *Ibid.*, 213.

7. Goren, *Dissenter in Zion*, 8; *Emanu-El* (San Francisco) 6 January 1896, 13. On Zionism and the Hebrew Union College, See Herbert Parzen, "The Purge of the Dissidents: Hebrew Union College (HUC) and Zionism, 1903–1907," *Jewish Social Studies* 37 (1975), 291–322, and Michael A. Meyer, "A Centennial History," in *Hebrew Union College-Jewish Institute of Religion at One Hundred Years*, ed. Samuel E. Karff (Cincinnati, 1976), 49–78. On Voorsanger, see Marc Lee Raphael, "Rabbi Jacob Voorsanger of San Francisco on Jews and Judaism: The Implications of the Pittsburgh Platform," *American Jewish*

Historical Quarterly 63:2 (December 1973) 185-203. This remarkable 1896 essay contradicts the statement by Max Raisin, a contemporary of Magnes at Hebrew Union College, that "It was from Europe that he brought back with him his interest in Zionism . . . ." *Great Jews,* 211.

8. Letter, Magnes to family, 11 February 1903.

9. Letters, Magnes to family, 1 April; 10, 22 October 1903; 15 January, 10 February 1904, MP; Goren, *Dissenter in Zion,* 77; Letter, Leon M. Nelson to Magnes, 10 February 1904, MP.

10. Judah L. Magnes, "Some Poems of H. N. Bialik," *HUC Annual* 1 (1904) 177-8; *Hebrew Union College Journal* 3 (1907) 233; Letter, Magnes to family, 5 May 1904. On Magnes's Zionist activities in Germany between 1900 and 1902, see Yohai Goell, "Aliya in the Zionism of an American Oleh: Judah L. Magnes," *American Jewish Historical Quarterly,* 65:2 (December 1975) 101-4.

11. *Hebrew Union College Journal* 7 (1907) 230-5; Circular, 11 October 1903, American Jewish Archives; Letters, Magnes to family, 7, 16, 23 January; 11 February 1903; and 6 April 1904, MP.

12. Letters, Morgenstern to Magnes, 30 January 1936 and 9 June 1937; Letters, Magnes to Morgenstern, 15, 22 May 1936, in ms. Collection #5, A-18/1, Judah L. Magnes, 1922-1936, Box 516, NGP.

13. *The Hebrew University: Its History and Development* (Jerusalem, 1939), 3; Letters, Morgenstern to Magnes, 13 May 1925; 7 January, 16 September 1926; 23 December 1929; Letters Magnes to Morgenstern, 3 April 1922; 14 May, 3 December 1925; 2 February, 13 April, 8 June 1926; 29 March 1927, NGP.

14. Oral interview with Helen Glueck, 28 July 1982, by Marc Lee Raphael, in WJHC; Letters, Morgenstern to Glueck, 13 April 1927; Letters, Glueck to Morgenstern, 7 March, 13 May, 24 July, 18 September 1927, NGP.

15. Letters, Glueck to Magnes, 18 July 1927; 19 May 1947; 2 January, 10 February, 8 May 1948; Letters, Glueck to Beatrice Magnes, 2 November 1948; Letters, Magnes to Glueck (month and day torn off), and 1, 8 December 1947; 23 January, 11 May 1948, NGP See also Nelson Glueck, *Dateline: Jerusalem* (Cincinnati, 1968), 17.

3. A New American Judaism

1. For a good portrait of the political activity of New York Jews in these years see Moses Rischin, *The Promised City: New York's Jews, 1870-1914* (Cambridge, 1962), ch. 11 and appendix, 270, on immigration statistics. Irving Howe and Kenneth Libo also provide a sense of the impact of the pogroms on New York Jews in *World of Our Fathers* (New York, 1976), 125-7.

2. *The Publications of the American Jewish Historical Society* 14 (1906) contains a good sampling of addresses delivered on the occasion.

3. Bernard Pucker in an unpublished paper cited in Herbert Rosenbloom, "The Shaping of an Institution," *Conservative Judaism* 27 (Winter 1973) 40, argues that wealthy Reform Jews supported the fledgling Jewish Theological Seminary as part of their efforts to shift the center of Jewish organizational life from the midwest to New York City. Also see Ben Halpern, "The Americanization of Zionism, 1880–1930," *American Jewish History* 59 (September 1979) 20–1.

4. Leo N. Levi, "Address Delivered at the National Conference of Jewish Charities Held at Detroit, Michigan, March 1902," in *Memorial Volume* (Chicago, n.d.), 54–5.

5. *Ibid.*, 59.

6. For a lucid discussion of the new philosophy of American Judaism see Baila Round Shargel, *Practical Dreamer: Israel Friedlaender and the Shaping of American Judaism* (New York, 1985), ch. 9.

7. Israel Friedlaender, "Ahad Ha-Am," *Past and Present* (Cincinnati, 1919), 397.

8. Yonathan Shapiro, *Leadership of the American Zionist Organization, 1897–1930* (Urbana, 1971), 37–9.

9. For a concise biography of Judah Magnes see Goren, "Introduction: The Road to Jerusalem," *Dissenter in Zion.* Also see Bentwich, *For Zion's Sake.*

10. Evyatar Friesel, "The Age of Optimism in American Judaism, 1900–1920," *A Bicentennial Festschrift for Jacob Rader Marcus*, ed. Bertram W. Korn (New York, 1976), 138.

11. Israel Friedlaender, "The Organization of Religious Education in New York," *The American Hebrew*, 21 July 1911.

12. Goren, *Dissenter in Zion*, 75–6.

13. *Ibid.*, 76.

14. Friedlaender, "Dubnov's Theory of Jewish Nationalism," *Past and Prsent*, 376.

15. Emphasis in the original. Letter, Judah L. Magnes to Solomon Lowenstein, 9 November 1912, p. 3, file 85, MP.

16. Friedlaender, "The Problem of Judaism in America," *Past and Present*, 273–4.

17. On Kraus and the B'nai B'rith, see Deborah Dash Moore, *B'nai B'rith and the Challenge of Ethnic Leadership* (Albany, 1981), ch. 4. On Kohler and Hebrew Union College, see Michael Meyer, "A Centennial History," *Hebrew*

Union College-Jewish Institute of Religion at One Hundred Years, ed. Samuel E. Karff (Cincinnati, 1976).

18. Myer Solis-Cohen to Israel Friedlaender, 2 April 1908, Box 1, Correspondence, IF.

19. Judah L. Magnes, "Zionism and Jewish Religion," Address Delivered before the Philadelphia Section Council of Jewish Women, 12 April 1910, n.p.

20. Judah L. Magnes, "Discourse" (17 March 1907), 12-3, 3442, MP.

21. Goren, *Dissenter in Zion*, 61-2.

22. Solomon Schechter, "Zionism: A Statement," *Seminary Addresses* (Cincinnati, 1915), 102.

23. Israel Friedlaender to Harry Friedenwald, 29 November 1907, Box 1, Correspondence, IF.

24. Moshe Davis, "Israel Friedlaender's Minute Book of the Achavah Club (1909-1912)," *Mordecai M. Kaplan Jubilee Volume* (New York, 1953), 162.

25. Quoted from Evyatar Friesel, "Ahad-Ha-Amism in American Zionist Thought," in Jacques Kornberg, ed., *At the Crossroads: Essays on Ahad Ha-Am* (Albany, 1983), 136.

26. *Ibid.*, 139.

27. Israel Friedlaender to Clarence DeSola, 22 December 1910, Box 2, Correspondence, IF.

28. As Ben Halpern suggests in his paper on ideology presented at the conference on "The Impact of Israel on the American Jewish Community," in *Jewish Social Studies* 21 (January 1959), the desire of the wealthy New York Jews to be leaders of American Jewry overshadowed their ideological commitments. See also Herbert Parzen, "Conservative Judaism and Zionism (1896-1922)," *Jewish Social Studies* 23 (October 1961) 252-3.

29. Israel Friedlaender to Harry Friedenwald, 4 December 1907, Box 1, Correspondence, Israel Friedlaender Papers, Jewish Theological Seminary.

30. Jacob Schiff to Israel Friedlaender, 11 April 1911, Box 2, Correspondence, IF.

31. Louis Lipsky, "Community or Nation," *The Maccabean*, 16 (April 1909), 130.

32. Hayim Zhitlowsky, "The Future of the Nationalities in America," 1:14-5, 2:17, 31, #2022, Hayim Zhitlowsky mss, YIVO Institute of Jewish Research.

33. Abraham Karp, "Ideology and Identity in Jewish Group Survival in America," *American Jewish Historical Quarterly* 65 (June 1976) 325.

34. Judah L. Magnes, "A Republic of Nationalities," *The Emanu-El Pulpit* 2 (1909) 8.

35. Friedlaender, "The Problem of Judaism in America," *Past and Present*, 274, 276.

36. Quoted in Davis, "Israel Friedlaender's Minute Book of the Achavah Club (1909–1912)," *Mordecai M. Kaplan Jubilee Volume* (New York, 1953), 205, 210–1.

37. "Secretary Magnes's Report to the Eleventh Convention," *The Maccabean* 15 (August 1908) 69.

38. Judah L. Magnes, *What Zionism Has Given the Jews*, pamphlet published by the Federation of American Zionists (October 1911), 8.

39. Eugene Kohn, "The Nationalism of the Prophets," *The Maccabean* 16 (March 1908) 108–9.

40. Magnes, "Zionism and Jewish Religion," Address Delivered before the Philadelphia Section of the Council of Jewish Women, 12 April 1910, n.p.

41. Mordecai M. Kaplan, "Judaism and Nationality," *The Maccabean* 16 (August 1909) 171.

42. Mordecai M. Kaplan, "The Future of Judaism," *The Menorah Journal* 2 (June 1916) 171.

43. Friedlaender, "Dubnov's Theory of Jewish Nationalism," *Past and Present*, 396.

44. Israel Friedlaender, "Speech to Canadian Zionists," in letter to Clarence DeSola, 22 December 1910, Box 2, Correspondence IF.

45. Israel Friedlaender to Jacob Schiff, 10 April 1911, Box 2, Correspondence, IF.

46. Friedlaender, "The International Zionist Congress," *Past and Present*, 453.

47. Israel Friedlaender to Jacob Schiff, 10 April 1911, Box 2, Correspondence, IF.

48. Friedlaender, "Palestine and the Diaspora," *Past and Present*, 472.

49. Arthur A. Goren, *New York Jews and the Quest for Community* (New York, 1970), ch. 10–11.

50. Naomi Cohen, *Not Free to Desist* (Philadelphia, 1972), ch. 4; Jeffrey Gurock, "The 1913 New York State Civil Rights Act," *Association of Jewish Studies Review* 1 (1976), 93–115.

51. Oscar Handlin, *Race and Nationality in American Life* (Garden City, NY, 1957), ch. 5.

52. Herbert Parzen, "Conservative Judaism and Zionism (1896–1922," *Jewish Social Studies* 23 (October 1961) 246–8; Herbert Rosenbloom, "Ideology and Compromise: The Evolution of the United Synagogue Constitutional Preamble," *Jewish Social Studies* 35 (January 1973) 18–31.

53. See Israel Friedlaender to Solomon Schecter, 15 September 1911, Box 2, Correspondence, IF.

54. Halpern, "The Americanization of Zionism, 1880–1930," *American Jewish History* 59 (September 1979) 22–3.

55. Jack Wertheimer, "The Founding of the ADL," unpublished paper in possession of author.

56. Jonathan Frankel, "The Jewish Socialists and the American Jewish Congress Movement," *YIVO Annual of Jewish Social Science* 16 (1976) 202–341.

57. Deborah Dash Moore, "From *Kchillah* to Federation: The Communal Functions of Federated Philanthropy in New York City," *American Jewish History* 65 (December 1978).

58. Friedlaender, "The Present Crisis in American Jewry," *Past and Present*, 345, 348, 350.

59. *Ibid.*, 349.

4. Between "Priest and Prophet"

1. For a brief biographical essay see Goren, *Dissenter in Zion*, 3–57.

2. Zosa Szajkowski, "The Impact of the Russian Revolution of 1905 on American Jewish Life," *YIVO Annual of Jewish Social Science* 17 (1978) 64–9, 87–95; Moshe Davis, "Israel Friedlaender's Minute Book of the Achavah Club, 1909–1912," *Mordecai M. Kaplan Jubilee Volume* (New York, 1953), 157–213; Goren, *Dissenter*, 131–134; Magnes to Jacob Schiff, October 31, 1916, MP.

3. Goren, *Dissenter in Zion*, 80–2, 107–17, 123–5; Herbert Parzen, "Conservative Judaism and Zionism, 1896–1922," *Jewish Social Studies* 23 (October 1961) 235–64; Evyatar Friesel, *Ha'tnua ha'zionit b'artsot ha'brit, 1897–1914* (Tel Aviv, 1970), 77–89; Yonathan Shapiro, *Leadership of the American Zionist Organization, 1879–1930* (Urbana, 1971), 176; Bernard G. Richards, Interview, WEWOHP.

4. Zosa Szajkowski, "The Pacifism of Judah L. Magnes," *Conservative Judaism* 22 (Spring 1968) 36–55; Norman Bentwich, *For the Sake of Zion: A Biography of Judah L. Magnes* (Philadelphia, 1954), 102–10; Goren, *Dissenter in Zion*, 22–8, 33–6, 162–8, 276–87.

5. Bentwich, *For Zion's Sake*, 14–20; Michael A. Meyer, "A Centennial History," in *Hebrew Union College-Jewish Institute of Religion at One Hundred Years*, ed. Samuel E. Karff (Cincinatti, 1976), 25–7.

6. "Isaac Mayer Wise," *Encyclopedia Judaica*, 16, 564–5; "Emil Gustave Hirsch," *ibid.*, 8, 503–4; "Jacob Voorsanger," *ibid.*, 16, 223.

7. Bentwich, *For Zion's Sake*, 24–31.

8. Goren, *Dissenter in Zion*, 12–3; Judah L. Magnes, "Isaac M. Wise," in *American Hebrew*, 18 March 1907; Judah L. Magnes, "Zionism and Jewish Religion," Address Delivered before the Philadelphia Section of the Council of Jewish Women, 12 April 1910, 5.

9. Arthur A. Goren, *New York Jews and the Quest for Community* (New York, 1970), 37–8; Bentwich, *For Zion's Sake*, 36–41.

9. Goren, *Dissenter in Zion*, 13.

10. Goren, *New York Jews*, 37–8; Bentwich, *For Zion's Sake*, 36–41.

11. *New York Times*, 31 January 1912, 1; Mordecai M. Kaplan, *Journals*, 6 August 1915.

12. Goren, *New York Jews*, 81–82; David Stein, "East Side Chronicle," *Jewish Life* 23 (January–February 1966) 31–32.

13. Goren, *Dissenter in Zion*, 25–6; Norman Thomas, Interview, 12 July 1966; Norman Thomas to Judah Magnes, 28 July 1919 and 26 November 1920, MP.

14. Judd L. Teller, "America's Two Zionist Traditions," *Commentary* 20 (October 1955) 343–52; Melvin I. Urofsky, *A Voice That Spoke for Justice: The Life and Times of Stephen S. Wise* (Albany, 1981), 91–107.

15. Evyatar Friesel, "Ahad Ha-Am in American Zionist Thought," mss. in possession of author.

16. Leon Simon, ed., *Selected Essays by Ahad Ha-Am* (Philadelphia, 1912), 133, 135.

17. *Ibid.*, 311–2.

18. Goren, *Dissenter in Zion*, 261–2, 292–4.

19. Judah L. Magnes, "The Harmonious Jew," *American Hebrew*, 25 January 1907, 311; Goren, *Dissenter in Zion*, 149–52, 183–90; Bentwich, *For Zion's Sake*, 35, 72.

20. Judah Magnes to Mayer Sulzberger, 10 October 1917, MPWJHC.

21. Mordecai M. Kaplan, *Journals*, 10 May 1922.

22. Goren, *Dissenter in Zion*, 50–3; Bentwich, *For Zion's Sake*, 210, 252.

23. Bentwich, *For Zion's Sake*, 315–7.

5. Magnes: Zionism in Judaism

It is my pleasure to thank my friends Arthur A. Goren and Stanley F. Chyet for their suggestions and corrections.

1. "Palestine — or Death," *Emanu-El* (San Francisco), cited in Goren, *Dissenter in Zion*, 7–8.

2. Magnes's Berlin period is described in detail in his letters to his family, MP. Also see the memoirs of Gotthold Weil, "Errinnerungen an die Zeit des Aufenthaltes von Magnes in Berlin," P3/383. CAHJP.

3. Letter to family, 9 October 1901; Goren, *Dissenter in Zion*, 65.

4. Letter to family, 26 December 1901, in Goren, *Dissenter in Zion*, 64–67. Two articles Magnes wrote in 1904 still belong to that first period of his Zionist development: "Some Poems by H. N. Bialik," *Hebrew Union College Annual*, 1 (1904) 177–86; "Herzl's Influence Upon Jewish Students in German Universities," *The Maccabean* 6 (August 1904) 103–5.

5. Letters to family, from 1903–1904, 10/C. MP.

6. Letter to family, 10 February 1904, 10/D, MP; *Journal*, 14 January 1904, in Goren, *Dissenter in Zion*, 77.

7. Judah L. Magnes to David Wolffsohn, 21 May 1906; Wolffsohn to Tannersville Convention of the Federation of American Zionists, 6 June 1906, CZA.

8. Goren, *Dissenter in Zion* (19 June 1906) 82.

9. *Ibid.*

10. Evyatar Friesel, *Ha'tnua ha'zionit b'artsot ha'brit* 1897–1914 (Tel Aviv, 1970), 126–31.

11. Apart from some general messages, there is only one full-length letter by Magnes to Ahad Ha-Am, 5 September 1910 4° 791-1360, AHP. In it, Magnes asked for Ahad Ha-Am's opinion about his plan to establish in New York and in other American cities "synagogues and seminaries" aiming to disseminate the "national religion" or "religious nationalism" among the Jews. Ahad Ha-Am, answering on 18 September 1910, wrote that Magnes's plan was unclear. Among other things, he stressed the difference between "national religion," with which he agreed, and "religious nationalism," with which he disagreed, a difference that Magnes had overlooked; *Iggrot Ahad Ha-Am* 4° (Tel Aviv, 1958) 283–5. Magnes published an article on Ahad Ha-Am, "The Harmonious Jew," *American Hebrew* (25 January 1907) 311.

12. Eliyahu A. Lubarsky to Ahad Ha-Am, 7 April 1907, 4° 791/522, AHP.

13. By "heathen," Lubarsky was referring ironically to the Cincinnati leaders of the Reform movement. He was describing the signatories of a congratulatory letter sent to Ahad Ha-Am by some of the participants at the 1906 Convention of the Federation of American Zionists, among them Magnes. 4° 791/596.AHP.

14. The fact is well-shown in the composition of the *Ahva* Club, a discussion group established in 1909 in New York City, where outstanding Jewish intellectuals met, and where Magnes was one of the important figures. Among the participants were most of the people of the "Schechter circle," and also Mordecai M. Kaplan, Morris D. Waldman, Senior Abel, Solomon Bloomgarden (Yehoash), David Pinski, and even Haim Zhitlovsky — activists in the Zionist Federation, people from the *Kehillah*, teachers from the Seminary, writers and poets — taken together a most select group. On the Achavah Club, see M. Davis, "Israel Friedlaender's Minute Book of the Achavah Club (1909–1912)," *Mordecai M. Kaplan Jubilee Volume* (New York, 1953), 157–213.

15. See his famous sermon "Reform Judaism — Plans for Reconstruction," delivered at Temple Emanu-El, 14 April 1910; Goren, *Dissenter in Zion*, 107–15. Also see his sermon about the 1909 convention of the CCAR, *American Hebrew* (26 November 1909), 107. Then as later, his religious approach and his Zionist ideas were closely integrated.

16. "What Zionism Has Given the Jews," the most complete exposition of his Zionist ideas, in *American Hebrew* (11 August 1911) 412–3, was also published as a brochure in 1911. Other articles by Magnes dealing with Zionism and Jewish nationalism were "Evidences of Jewish Nationality," *The Emanu-El Pulpit*, 1 (New York, 1908); "A Republic of Nationalities," *The Emanu-El Pulpit*, 3 (New York, 1909); "The Melting Pot," (1909), Goren, *Dissenter in Zion*, 101–6; *Zionism and Jewish Religion* (New York, 1910); "Eretz Israel and the Galut," (1923); Goren, *Dissenter in Zion*, 208–14. There are also some references in Magnes's private correspondence which are quoted later.

17. 8 June 1914, WA. The letter was written in German. See also Yohai Goell, "Aliya in the Zionism of an American *Oleh*: Judah L. Magnes," *American Jewish Historical Quarterly* 65 (1975) 99–120. The German word "Kultur" has a broader meaning than "culture" in English. The same ideas were expressed also in "The Melting Pot" (1909).

18. "What Zionism Has Given the Jews."

19. "Evidences of Jewish Nationality," 2.

20. *Ibid.*

21. *Ibid.*

22. "The Melting Pot" (1909).

23. "What Zionism Has Given the Jews."

24. "A Republic of Nationalities," 6–7.

25. See Allon Gal, *Brandeis of Boston* (Cambridge, 1980), 147–58. Magnes's argument about the necessary attachment to the original immigrant cultures was also to be integral to Brandeis's Zionism. See Louis D. Brandeis, "The Jewish Problem — And How to Solve it," in *Brandeis on Zionism* (Washington, 1942), 30–1.

26. See Endnote #15 herein. The central role of Jewish religion in Jewish life is mentioned in most of the addresses quoted thus far.

27. "A Republic of Nationalities," 8–9.

28. "What Zionism Has Given the Jews."

29. *Ibid.*

30. Magnes Papers, American Jewish Archives, Cincinnati.

31. For a fuller explanation, see Friesel, "Ahad Ha-Am in American Zionist Thought," in Jacques Kornberg, ed. *At the Crossroads: Essays on Ahad Ha-Am* (Albany, 1983), 133–41.

32. Solomon Schechter, "Zionism — A Statement" (1906), *Seminary Addresses* (New York, 1959), 2nd ed., 91–104. Bernard Mandelbaum, ed., *The Wisdom of Solomon Schechter* (New York, 1963), 98.

33. The position is most clearly explained in a lecture given in Jerusalem, 1923. Goren, *Dissenter in Zion*, 208–14.

34. Preface, *Past and Present* 2nd ed. (New York, 1961), xxxiii.

35. Israel Friedlaender, who knew Dubnow and his work, was the exception.

36. In his 1923 lecture in Jerusalem. Goren, *Dissenter in Zion*, 210.

37. Proceedings of the Tenth Convention of the Federation of American Zionists, Atlantic City, July 10–4, 1908, *The Maccabean* (August 1908) 68–9.

38. Mordecai M. Kaplan, *The Future of the American Jew* (New York, 1948), 66; *A New Zionism* (New York, 1959), 12.

39. See his letter of May 1920; his address of 22 May 1923, delivered in Jerusalem on the theme, "*Eretz Israel* and the Galut," *Journal*; "The Arab Question," 4 July 1928 in Goren, *Dissenter in Zion*, 183–90, 208–14, 271–2. Goren brought to my attention a most interesting document: the minutes of a discussion by a commission of the Jewish Agency, for the study of the Arab problem, which met on 14 May 1942, in which Magnes took part, S25/8987. CZA. Magnes formulated his position in terms that were precisely the ideas formulated thirty years earlier. He explained, among other matters, that the three important things in his eyes were the Torah of Israel, the people of Israel, and the land of Israel — the land of Israel being the least important among the three.

6. Two Paths to Zion: Magnes and Stephen S. Wise

1. Melvin I. Urofsky, *American Zionism from Herzl to the Holocaust* (New York, 1975), ch. 3.

2. The *Kehillah* is discussed in Goren, *New York Jews and the Quest for Community* (New York, 1970). Magnes's Zionism is explored in Yohai Goell, "Aliyah in the Zionism of an American *Oleh*: Judah L. Magnes," *American Jewish Historical Quarterly* 65 (December 1975) 99–120.

3. For Wise, see his autobiography, *Challenging Years* (New York, 1949); Carl Hermann Voss, *Rabbi and Minister: The Friendship of Stephen S. Wise and John Haynes Holmes* (Cleveland, 1964); and Melvin I. Urofsky, *A Voice that Spoke for Justice: The Life and Times of Stephen S. Wise* (Albany, 1982).

4. Magnes to Felix Warburg, 10 February 1937, in Goren, *Dissenter in Zion*, 321.

5. Wise, "I Am an American," *Opinion*, 12 (July 1942) 5.

6. Magnes to family, 19 October 1902, quoted in Aryeh Goren, "Judah L. Magnes: The Wider Pulpit." I am indebted to Professor Goren for a copy of his paper, which he presented 1 April 1982 at a session of the Organization of American Historians in Philadelphia, entitled "The Twentieth Century Rabbi."

7. *Ibid.*, 8.

8. Voss, *Rabbi and Minister*, 17.

9. Wise, *Challenging Years*, 96–100.

10. Magnes to family, 7 November 1901, quoted in Goell, "Aliyah," 103.

11. Wise to Louise Waterman Wise in Justine Wise Polier and James Waterman Wise, eds., *The Personal Letters of Stephen S. Wise* (Boston, 1956), 56.

12. Goren, *Dissenter in Zion*, 7–8.

13. Magnes to family, 9 October 1901, *ibid.*, 65.

14. Magnes to David Wolffsohn, 19 June 1906, *ibid.*, 82.

15. Magnes to family, 26 December 1901, *ibid.*, 69.

16. Magnes to Chaim Weizmann, 25 May 1913, *ibid.*, 137.

17. Urofsky, *A Voice That Spoke for Justice*, 10.

18. *New York Herald*, 31 August 1897, quoted in Marnin Feinstein, *American Zionism, 1844–1904* (New York, 1965), 114–5.

19. For the Federation of American Zionists in its early years see Urofsky, *American Zionism*, 85–92.

20. Wise, "The Beginnings of American Zionism," *Jewish Frontier* 14 (August 1947) 7.

21. Louis Lipsky, *A Gallery of Zionist Profiles* (New York, 1956), 147.

22. Wise to Richard Gottheil, 21 April 1904, Richard J. H. Gottheil Papers, Record Group A138, CZA.

23. Goren, *New York Jews and the Quest for Community*, 54.

24. Urofsky, *A Voice that Spoke for Justice*, 116–8.

25. Urofsky, *American Zionism*, ch. 4.

26. For the Committee, see Naomi W. Cohen, *Not Free to Desist: A History of the American Jewish Committee, 1906–1966* (Philadelphia, 1972).

27. Horace M. Kallen, *Zionism and World Politics* (Garden City, 1921), 143–4.

28. Urofsky, *American Zionism*, ch. 5.

29. Urofsky, *A Voice that Spoke for Justice*, ch. 4.

30. Wise to Louis D. Brandeis, 18 November 1914, LDB.

31. Magnes to Editor, *Yiddishes Tageblatt*, 24 September 1909, in Goren, *Dissenter in Zion*, 95.

32. Goren, *New York Jews*, 45–6.

33. Jacob H. Schiff to Bernard G. Richards, 31 January 1916, LDB, Nathan Schachner, *The Price of Liberty* (New York, 1948), 65.

34. Wise to Henry Morgenthau, 23 August 1915, SSW.

35. Urofsky, *American Zionism*, 150–5, 168–71.

36. Magnes, Memorandum for President and Members of Executive Committee of American Jewish Committee, 9 May 1915, Goren, *Dissenter in Zion*, 139–43.

37. See, for example, the near replication of the Congress fight in the Committee's opposition to the American Jewish Conference during World War II, in Melvin I. Urofsky, *We Are One! American Jewry and Israel* (New York, 1978), ch. 1.

38. Magnes to Brandeis, 30 June 1915, Goren, *Dissenter in Zion*, 144–45; for Brandeis's response, see his letters of 18 July 1915, Brandeis mss, and of 8 September 1915, MP.

39. Magnes to [Norman Bentwich], May 1920, Goren, *Dissenter in Zion*, 183–9.

7. Doing Good in Palestine: Magnes and Henrietta Szold

1. 13 January 1933, CZA. At the CZA, Szold's letters are kept in the Henrietta Szold archive; her correspondence with her family is in chronological order, therefore, when these letters are referred to, they are designated by date only. All other CZA references include folder number or other identification.

2. Rose Zeitlin, *Henrietta Szold: Record of a Life* (New York, 1952), 35.

3. *American Jewish Yearbook, 1946–47*, article by Lotte Levensohn.

4. For diary of her trip, consult American Jewish Archives 363G, obtainable on microfilm.

5. Marvin Lowenthal, *Henrietta Szold: Life and Letters* (New York, 1942), 76.

6. Richard Gottheil, 13 May 1917, CZA.

7. Margaret Doniger, "Remembering Jessie Sampter," *Hadassah Newsletter*, January 1939.

8. A125/26N, 16 September 1917, CZA.

9. A125/26N, 21 September 1917, CZA.

10. For minutes of the meeting see A125/18N, 23 September 1917, CZA.

11. A125/18N, 13 October 1917, CZA.

12. For an account of the rescue ship, see "American Zionist Medical Unit," Zionist Organization of America, 1919.

13. Lowenthal, *Henrietta Szold*, 117.

14. HMO folder, Rubinow to Szold, 29 November 1919, HMOA.

15. Lowenthal, *Henrietta Szold*, 114.

16. Zeitlin, *Henrietta Szold*, 98.

17. Margaret Doniger, "Remembering Jessie Sampter," *Hadassah Newsletter*, January 1939.

18. To Harriet Leven, 2 July 1922, CZA.

19. Telephone conversation with Benedict Magnes, January 1983.

20. National Board folder, 23 September 1929, HMOA.

21. Szold to Alice Seligsberg, 16 May 1928, HMOA.

22. Interview with Hanoch Rinott, Jerusalem 1975.

23. Marian Greenberg, "Youth *Aliyah* Under Henrietta Szold" (unpublished, mimeographed pamphlet, August 1961).

24. A125/55, 24 June 1934, CZA.

25. A125/30, CZA.

26. A125/30, 10 October 1937, CZA.

27. Zeitlin, *Henrietta Szold*, 200.

28. For the history of Ihud see: Susan Lee Hattis, *"The Binational Idea in Palestine During Mandatory Times* (Haifa, 1970).

29. Szold to Rose Jacobs, 125/35, 7 June 1943, CZA.

30. A125/151, CZA.

31. A125/151, CZA.

32. A125/152, CZA.

33. Zeitlin, *Henrietta Szold*, 140.

34. Hadassah. Judah Magnes, "Last Days" a mimeographed pamphlet of the diary he kept during this period. HMOA.

8. Golda Meir and Other Americans

1. See "Noah, Ararat, USA," in M. Syrkin, *The State of the Jews* (Washington, 1980), 215–21; Jonathan Sarna, *Jacksonian Jew: The Two Worlds of Mordecai Noah* (New York, 1981), 61–75, 163.

2. Emma Lazarus, "The Jewish Problem," *The Century Magazine*, 25:4 (February 1883) 610.

3. Frank E. Manuel, *The Realities of American-Palestine Relations* (Washington, 1949), 114.

4. *Ibid.*, 93.

5. *Ibid.*, 94.

6. Funds for the support of the Jewish inhabitants of Palestine from contributions of Jews in the Diaspora organized especially after the end of the eighteenth century but begun in the sixteenth century. See "Halukah" in *Encyclopedia Judaica*, vol. 7, 1207–15.

7. Manuel, *The Realities of American-Palestine Relations*, 44–6.

8. See Alex Bein, *The Return to the Soil* (Jerusalem, 1952), 223.

9. M. Syrkin, *Golda Meir: Israel's Leader* (New York, 1969) new rev. ed., 64.

10. The Merhavia Period is briefly portrayed in M. Syrkin, ed., *Golda Meir Speaks Out* (London, 1973), 38–42.

11. Syrkin, *Golda Meir: Israel's Leader*, 85.

12. Syrkin, ed., *Golda Meir Speaks Out*, 240–1.

13. *New York Times*, 14 January 1976, "Golda Meir, on the Palestinians," 35.

14. *Ibid.*

15. Syrkin, ed., *Golda Meir Speaks Out*, 141–3.

16. *Ibid.*, 139–40.

17. David Ben-Gurion, *My Talks with Arab Leaders* (New York, 1973), 22–3.

18. *Ibid.*, 162–82.

19. Syrkin, *Golda Meir: Israel's Leader*, 156–7.

20. *Ibid.*, 343.

21. Syrkin, ed., *Golda Meir Speaks Out*, 242.

22. Ben Zion Ilan (Applebaum), *An American Soldier/Pioneer in Israel* with an introduction by Golda Meir (New York, 1979).

9. The Idea of a Jewish University

1. For a brief history of the university, see "Hebrew University of Jerusalem," *Encyclopedia Judaica*, vol. 8, 219–26. Also see Norman Bentwich, *Hebrew University of Jerusalem, 1918–1960* (New York, 1961) and the very useful article by Joseph Klausner in *Ha-Universita ha-Ivrit be-Yerushalayim* (Jerusalem, 1950), 41–7, a volume that contains a number of other good historical essays.

2. The pamphlet has been reprinted with a Hebrew translation by Shaul Ash, with an introduction by S. H. Bergman, (Jerusalem, 1968).

3. In Magnes's "Notes on the Meeting of the Board of Governors of the Hebrew University," (Munich, September 23–24, 1925) in Goren, *Dissenter in Zion*, 251.

4. For a detailed account of the university project during the prewar years and especially of Chaim Weizmann's key role in it, see Jehuda Reinharz, *Chaim Weizmann: The Making of a Zionist Leader* (New York, 1985), esp. 375–401.

5. *Kol Kitvei Chaim Nachman Bialik* (Tel Aviv, 1938), 232–4.

6. For Bialik's attitude toward the role of Hebrew in rejuvenating the Science of Judaism, see his "Open Letter" to the editors of *Devir* 1 (1923).

7. "Der Lehrstuhl," *Der Jude* 2 (1917). The essay was reprinted in Shazar's *Ore Dorot* (Jerusalem, 1971), 385–9.

8. The essay was originally published in *Luah Ha-Aretz* (1944–45), and reprinted in Gershom Scholem, *Devarim Be-Go-Explications and Implications:*

Writings on Jewish Heritage and Renaissance (Tel Aviv, 1976), where the quotation can be found, 396.

9. "The Science of Judaism — Then and Now," in *The Messianic Idea of Judaism and Other Essays on Jewish Spirituality* (New York, 1971), 310.

10. Evidence of Weizmann's view of Magnes is found in his letters to Albert Einstein of 19 May, 19 July, and 13 May 1928, published in Pinhas Ofer, ed., *The Letters and Papers of Chaim Weizmann*, vol. 13, (New Brunswick, 1978), 16–7, 67, 399–400.

11. Scholem has recounted this episode in Harry Zohn, trans., *Walter Benjamin, The Story of a Friendship* (Philadelphia, 1981), 137ff; see also *Walter Benjamin — Gershom Scholem Briefwechsel* (Frankfurt, 1980), especially letters from 1928–29.

12. The controversy has been documented in Herbert Parzen, *The Hebrew University, 1925–1935*, (New York, 1974); see also Goren, *Dissenter in Zion*, 30f.

13. Goren, *Dissenter in Zion*, Journal entry, 13 February 1928, 265.

14. Goren, *Dissenter in Zion*, Journal entry, 28 April 1929, 274.

15. Goren, *Dissenter in Zion*, Journal entry, 22 March 1925, 231–3, and letter to Ahad Ha-Am of April 1925, 234–5.

16. Goren, *Dissenter in Zion*, Journal entry, 7 August 1927, 262–4.

17. Goren, *Dissenter in Zion*, Journal, March 1924, 227.

18. *Ibid*.

19. S. L. Hattis, *The Binational Idea in Palestine During Mandatory Times* (Haifa, 1970). For Magnes's role, see Goren, *Dissenter in Zion*, 38ff.

20. The best exponent of this view was the Hebrew writer, M. Y. Berdichevsky (1865–1921), but it became a virtual cliché by the late 1920s in Palestine.

21. Bentwich relates this incident in his *Mandate Memoirs*, (New York, 1960), 150.

22. The struggle over the chair in Yiddish is described in Joshua A. Fishman, ed., *Never Say Die* (The Hague, 1981). Scholem related his view of the controversy in a letter to Martin Buber in Buber Archive (National Library of the Jewish People), VIII/709.

23. Scholem, *Davarim*, 402.

10. The Appeal of the Incorrigible Idealist

*I wish to thank Professor Arthur Goren for encouraging me to undertake this essay, and for so generously sharing with me unpublished writings he found among the *Judah Leib Magnes Papers*, Central Archives for the History of the Jewish People, Jerusalem.

1. Undated letter which from the context was apparently written by Magnes on the eve of his departure for Europe and Palestine in May 1922. *Cited in Judah Leib Magnes: On the Centenary of His Birth. Exhibition.* Catalog prepared by Margot Cohen with the cooperation of the Department of Manuscripts and Archives of the Jewish National and University Library (Jerusalem, 1977), 64.

2. Hesse, *Das Glasperlenspiel* (Zurich, 1943). English translation by Richard and Clara Winston, *Magister Ludi* (New York, 1969).

3. Buber and Hesse maintained a warm and mutually respectful friendship for approximately sixty years. On September 16, 1945, Buber wrote Hesse apologizing for his epistolary silence during the war. After apologizing for his "paralysis," he gratefully declares to Hesse that "one cheerful tiding (*Botschaft*) during these awful days was your *Glasperlenspiel*. This book strikes me as a triumph of the spirit . . . ." Grete Schaeder, ed., *Martin Buber, Briefwechsel aus Sieben Jahrzehnten* (Heidelberg, 1975).

4. On this circle of intellectuals in Jerusalem of the 1920s, see the testimonies of Hans Kohn, *Living in a World Revolution. My Encounters With History*, The Credo Series, Ruth Nanda Anshen, ed. (New York, 1964), ch. 12, especially 136–44; and G. Scholem, *From Berlin to Jerusalem: Memories of My Youth*, Harry Zohn, trans. (New York, 1980), 161–74.

5. See *Jüdische Gesellschaft fuer Internationale Verstandigung.* Erstes Rundschreiben. London, 5. December 1921; Zweites Rundschreiben, London, 3. January 1922. MB, varia 350, Mappe vav 60. This document consists of two circular letters (*Rundschreiben*) signed by Hans Kohn; the first letter presents for consideration a statement outlining the *Gesellschaft's* purpose drawn up by Martin Buber. The letters were sent to the following individuals: H. Arlosoroff, Moses Beilinsohn, Hugo Bergman, Siegfried Bernfeld, H. N. Bialik, Adolf Boehm, Max Brod, S. Brodetzky, M. Buber, Z. Diesendruck, Nahum Goldmann, Eugen Hoefflich, Hugo Knorpfmacher, Jakov Klatzkin, Hans Kohn, Isidor Margulies, Ernst Mueller, Leon Simon, Abraham Sonne, Ludwig Strauss, Friedrich Thieberger, Felix Weltsch, Robert Weltsch, and J. Wilkansy. Prior to sending the *Rundschreiben*, Kohn (or Buber) had apparently discussed the *Gesellschaft* with each of these prospective members.

6. G. Scholem, "A Free Man. On J. L. Magnes," *Devarim Be-Go Explications and Implications: Writings on Jewish Heritage and Renaissance.* (Tel Aviv, 1976), 489. Essay originally appeared in *Be'ayot* 5 (July, 1947) 207–10.

7. *Ibid.*

8. *Ibid.*, 489–91.

9. *Ibid.*, 490.

10. Max Scheler, "Vorbilder und Führer," *Schriften aus dem Nachlass* (Bern), 1. Band, Maria Scheler, ed., 255–344.

11. MB, varia 350, Mappe chet 2/46, 467a (photo copy).

12. See Buber, "Man's Duty as Man," in "A Centenary Gathering for Henry David Thoreau." A symposium by John H. Hicks, *The Massachusetts Review* (Autumn 1962) 55. (Contains German and English translation.) Also see Buber's response to the question addressed to twenty-three philosophers, writers, and politicians concerning the principle of "civil disobedience" in light of the threat of nuclear war, Clara Urquhart, ed., *Matter of Life* (London, 1963) 51–2.

13. Response in *A Matter of Life*, 51.

14. "Man's Duty as Man," 55.

15. Goren, *Dissenter in Zion*, letter dated 16 March 1948, 472.

16. "Dr. Magnes, the confidant of the Great Philanthropist," Robert Weltsch to Buber, letter dated 23 June 1924, in Buber, *Briefwechsel*, II, 194. Although Weltsch does not mention it in his letter to Buber, Magnes was also known to share their commitment to cultural Zionism. Moreover, Magnes had, on several occasions, indicated that he viewed the future university in Jerusalem as the fulcrum of the spiritual and moral renaissance to be sponsored by cultural Zionism. On Magnes and cultural Zionism, see Goren's discussion in his introduction to *Dissenter in Zion*. Also see Magnes's letter to Ahad Ha-Am, dated 25 April 1924 on the role of the nascent Hebrew University in the cultural and spiritual life of the Yishuv, in Goren, *Dissenter in Zion*, 234–5. Cf. Magnes to Chaim Weizmann, letter dated 25 May 1923, expressing his support of the World Zionist Organization's decision to establish a university in Jerusalem: ". . . The university should serve as a spiritual center for the Jewish people and therefore, an institute for the humanities should be set up first, in which research would be carried out from a Jewish point of view." Cited in *Judah Leib Magnes: On the Centenary of His Birth*, 100f.

17. Magnes to Ahad Ha-Am, letter dated 7 July 1924 (Hebrew). Cited with English translation in *Judah Leib Magnes: On the Centenary of His Birth*, 104f.

18. Cf. Buber to Franz Rosenzweig, letter dated 15 August 1929: "Die Bombe ist geplatz: Magnes hat mir in aller Form den Antrag gemacht, als 'akademisches Oberhaupt' (auf deutsch: lebenslanger Rektor) der Universität nach Jerusalem zu kommen; er selber will Chancellor, auf deutsch: Kurator verbleiben. Was tun? . . . Ich habe Magnes mitgeteilt, dass es zwei Menschen gibt, die ich zu konsultieren habe: Paula [Buber's wife] and Dich . . . ." Buber, *Briefwechsel*, II, 338.

19. See M. Buber to Paula Buber, undated letter, Buber, *Briefwechsel*, II, 339.

20. In his repeated attempts to have Buber appointed to the faculty of the Hebrew University, Magnes encountered the determined opposition of faculty members who either objected to his unorthodox perception of Judaism or questioned his scholarship. Finally, in 1935, Magnes with the active assistance of G. Scholem successfully lobbied to have Buber appointed on a "personal basis," with the definition of his appointment temporarily left open. A bit later, the compromise formula, professor of social philosophy, was approved by the university's trustees and faculty. Buber assumed the position in the spring of 1938. Cf. Buber, *Briefwechsel*, II, letters nos. 297, 469, 472, 491, 495, 514, 530.

21. Juda [sic] L. Magnes, "Al Har Hazophim," *Der Jude*. Sonderheft zu Martin Buber fünfzigsten Geburtstag (Berlin, 1928), 50. The title is a transliteration of the Hebrew, "On Mount Scopus," *i.e.*, the site of the Hebrew University campus.

22. *Ibid*. In this disarmingly frank appreciation of Buber, Magnes admits that prior to their acquaintance, he regarded Buber with great suspicion because of his Germanophilic writings during the early years of World War I. *On Buber's Kriegsbegeisterung*, see Paul Mendes-Flohr, "The Road to *I and Thou*. An inquiry into Buber's Transition from Mysticism to Dialogue," *Texts and Responses: Studies Presented to Nahum N. Glatzer*, eds., M. Fishbane and P. R. Flohr (Leiden, 1975), 201–25.

23. From a fragment of a letter (first page is missing) Magnes apparently to Felix Warburg; from the context the letter seems to be from 1929. MP miscellany.

24. *Ibid*. Cf. " . . . Alas, I have no confidence that the official communities of the *galut* will seize this unparalleled opportunity to make Judaism a vital, decisive, spiritual force at this critical period of history . . . . Nevertheless, there are, happily, throughout the *galut* Jewish groups (*most of them strangely enough outside the synagogue*) who have been loyal and who will continue to prove their loyalty to this truly religious ideal." Magnes, "Eretz Israel and the *Galut*." Address Delivered in Jerusalem, 22 May 1923, Goren, *Dissenter in Zion*, 213. (Emphasis added.)

25. Hans Kohn sent the program, written in English, to Buber with an accompanying letter, dated 13 January 1929. The letter reads in part: " . . . Dr. Magnes wäre Ihnen sehr dankbar, wenn Sie dieser Text, den er bisher *nur* Hugo Bergmann und mir gezeigt hat, durchlesen und ihm Abänderungsvorschläge oder sonstige kritische Bemerkungen machen wollten, da er erst nach eingehender Prüfung dieser Erklärung durch Personen, von denen er glaubt, dass sie diesem Gedankengang im allgemeinen nahestehen und sich autoritäten dazu zu äussern vermögen, diese einem weiteren Kreise von in Betracht kommenden Personen zugänglich machen will . . . ." MB, varia 350, Mappe vav 371.

26. Buber to Hans Kohn, letter dated 26 January 1929. MB, varia 350, Mappe vav 376 I.

27. *Loc. cit.* In March 1928 — several months before he presumably penn-ed this statement — after having read an article about Karl Barth's Dialectical Theology in *Christian Century*, Magnes recorded the following observations in his journal: ". . . There is no way to God. But there is a way from God to us. Man needs God, seeks him but the search is futile . . . . But let a man open himself to receive God's influence upon him . . . . [Thus Barth's] ethical paradox: 'To seek God zealously, with the foregone conclusion that God's will cannot be found — to join the contemporary crusades for righteousness with the conviction that they will one day be proved, like the great crusades, to be ill-advised and wrong. This is not *discovering* God's will, but it is, after all, *acknowledging* it.' To whom, to what, our highest loyalties? The State, the fam-ily, the nation, the Land — all of this important but all of it imperfect. Loyalty to the spirit — if only we dared say 'God' — the only really worthy loyalty . . . . The war has shown the hollowness of Church, School, and State. Real loyalty can only be rendered the Spirit. But Spirit is vague. If one only had a real God!" Goren, *Dissenter in Zion*, 268.

28. Buber to Hans Kohn, letter dated 26 January 1929, *loc. cit.*

29. Renate Breipohl, ed., *Dokumente zum religiosen Sozialismus in Deutschland: Mit einer historische-systematischen Einführung* (Munich, 1972); also see Markus Mattmuller, *Leonard Ragaz und der religiöse Sozialismus, eine Biographie* (Zollikson, 1957); also see the proceedings of the conference on religious socialism which Buber helped organize: *Sozialismus aus dem Glauben. Verhandlungen der sozialistischen Tagung im Heppenheim, a.d.B., Pfingstwoche 1928* (Zurich/Leipzig, 1929). On Buber's Religious Socialism, see the aforemen-tioned proceedings, 90ff, 121, 217ff. Also see Richard Falk, *Martin Buber and Paul Tillich: Radical Politics and Religion* (New York, 1961), and my discussion in *A Land of Two Peoples. Martin Buber on Jews and Arabs*, ed. with commentary by Paul R. Mendes-Flohr (New York, 1983), 1–31.

30. On Magnes's relation to the American liberal Social Gospel move-ment, see Goren's introduction to *Dissenter in Zion*, 25. Both the American Social Gospel movement and the Central European movement of Religious Socialism have their roots in the moral theology of Albrecht Ritschl (1822–1889) who taught that religion is "labor for the Kingdom of God on earth." Following Ritschl, both Social Gospel and Religious Socialism, *mutatis mutandis, interpret redemption as a moral, social, and progressive process. On religious socialism in the Yishuv and later the State of Israel*, see Ernst Simon, *"Religiöser Sozialismus in Israel" (1954)*, in *Brücken. Gesammelte Aufsätze* (Heidelberg, 1965), 409–20. Simon specifically refers to Magnes as a represen-tative of Religious Socialism in the Yishuv. Cf. "[Magnes's] motive waren ebenso sehr religiös-moralisch wie politisch-soziale." *Ibid.*, 411. Simon also compares the Ihud — the association for Arab-Jewish reconciliation so singularly associated with the person of Magnes — and its fate with that of the Swiss Religious Socialist movement under the leadership of Leonard Ragaz (1868–1945): "Nach Magnes's Tod hat sich diese Arbeitsgemeinschaft [*i.e.*, the Ihud] aufgelöst eine Spaltung, die in manchem Persönlichem und Sachlichen an des Schicksal der religiös-sozialen Bewegung der Schweiz nach Leonard Ragaz' Tode denken Lasst." *Ibid.*, 412.

31. On *Ha-Ol*, see S. H. Bergman "J. L. Magnes Seeks His God. On the First Anniversary of His Death." *Ha-Aretz* (Tel Aviv Daily) 17 October 1949, 2. Also see *A Land of Two Peoples*, 111–2. Paul R. Mendes-Flohr, "Law and Sacrament. Ritual Observance in Twentieth Century Jewish Thought" in *Jewish Spirituality*, 2nd. ed. by Arthur Green (New York, 1987).

32. On "A Community of Hebrew Religious Morality," see *Judah Leib Magnes Papers*, Mappe 2436, document no. 143 (B of F) — Magnes's 5 page outline of the community's program (Hebrew). In a letter to S. Bergman, dated March 1932, Magnes requested he seek Hans Kohn's and G. Scholem's thoughts about the proposed community. In his reply, dated March 25, 1932, Bergman expressed his doubts whether there were sufficient numbers of individuals interested in such an endeavor: ". . . I do not see even half a *minyan*." Bergman suggested to Magnes that it would be more prudent to start with a journal, such as the *Zeitschrift fur judische Theologie*, edited by Sinai Ucko. See Mappe 2436, document no. 143 (LB of F), MP. For the proposed program of *Mevakshei Panecha*, drafted by Magnes, see Bergman, "J. L. Magnes Seeks His God," 2.

33. Buber left Germany for Palestine in May 1938. This relatively late date was due not only to his protracted negotiations with the Hebrew University (#20 above), but also and perhaps primarily to his central position in organizing "the spiritual resistance" of German Jewry to the Nazi regime, especially through the establishment of an elaborate network for Jewish adult education. See E. Simon, "Jewish Adult Education in Nazi Germany as Spiritual Resistance." *Leo Baeck Institute Year Book*, I, (1956), 68–104.

34. Cited on the inside cover of a pamphlet, containing letters by Magnes and Buber respectively to Mahatma Gandhi, published in English and Hebrew by *Ha-Ol*, which called itself in English "The Bond." *Two Letters to Gandhi*, (Jerusalem, 1939), pamphlet no. 1 of the "The Bond."

35. Cited on the front cover of the aforementioned pamphlet.

36. Mappe, 2273 (*Ha-Ol*), MP.

37. See #34 above. Buber's letter is reproduced in full in *A Land of Two Peoples*, 111–29.

38. See Mohandas K. Gandhi, "The Jews," *Harijan*, 26 November 1938, 352–3. Reprinted in *A Land of Two Peoples*, 106–113. On the extensive background to the exchange with Gandhi, see G. Shimoni, *Gandhi, Satyagraha and the Jews* (Jerusalem, 1977).

39. Mappe 2273 (Ha-Ol), MP.

40. This concept is developed in P. Mendes-Flohr, "Secular Religiosity. Reflections on Post-Traditional Jewish Spirituality and Community," in Marc Lee Raphael, ed., *Approaches to Judaism in Modern Times* (Chico, CA, 1983) 19–30. An abridged version of this article appeared in *Bulletin of the Center for the Study of World Religions*, Harvard University, Spring 1982, 5–16.

41. Cited in Bergman, "J. L. Magnes Seeks His God," 2.

42. F. Rosenzweig, "Das neue Denken," in Rosenzweig, *Kleinere Schriften* (Berlin, 1937), 389.

43. Cited in Bergman, "J. L. Magnes Seeks His God," 2.

44. Franz Rosenzweig to Eugen Rosenstock, undated letter, in Rosenzweig, *Briefe*, ed., Edith Rosenzweig (Berlin, 1935), 717.

45. Magnes's journal entry from 22 February 1937. See his opening address of the academic year 1939–40 of the Hebrew University in which he declared his reluctant support for the war against Hitler. "War and the Remnant of Israel," (29 October 1939), in Goren, *Dissenter*, 357–65.

46. On the League, founded on 16 April 1939, see Susan Lee Hattis, *The Binational Idea in Palestine During Mandatory Times* (Haifa, 1970), 134f, 137f., 148.

47. Buber, "Politics and Morality," (April 1945), in *A Land of Two Peoples*, 169–73. (Originally published in the Ihud's journal, *Be'ayot*.) Also see Magnes's address at the founding conference of the Ihud, summarized by Goren in his introduction to *Dissenter in Zion*, 51.

48. Buber, "Truth and Deliverance," *Be'ayot*, no. 506 (July 1947), 189 (Hebrew). Partial translation in *A Land of Two Peoples*, 65, n. 2.

49. *Ibid.*

50. Buber, "Hope for This Hour," (1952), in *Pointing the Way. Collected Essays*, ed. and trans. by M. Friedman (New York, 1974), 227.

51. Journal entry from 22 February 1937, Goren, *Dissenter*, 324. Magnes also discerned in Buber a similar pessimism, see Magnes, "He Who Sees Reality in Its Totality," for Professor Buber on his seventieth birthday (1948), *Ner*, Nos. 9–10 (1965) 20–1 (Hebrew).

52. See Goren's introduction to ch. 4 of *Dissenter in Zion*, 205.

53. Magnes, "For Thy Sake We Killed All the Day Long," (Psalm 44:23), Address at the opening of the academic year 1944–45 of the Hebrew University (1 November 1944), in Magnes, *In the Perplexity of the Times* (Jerusalem, 1946), 67. In this address Magnes also employs the term "holocaust" to describe the Nazi liquidation of European Jewry, *ibid.*, 69.

54. *Ibid.*, 77.

55. "The Source of Prophetic Morality," Opening address for the academic year 1943–44 of the Hebrew University (14 November 1943), in *In the Perplexity of the Times*, 59.

56. "Rebellion," Address at Degree Day, the Hebrew University, (6 December 1945), in *In the Perplexity of the Times*, 111.

57. "The Source of Prophetic Morality," *op. cit.*, 61.

58. S. H. Bergman, *Faith and Reason. An Introduction to Modern Jewish Thought* trans., A. Jospe (New York, 1961), 142.

59. *Ibid.*, 149.

60. *Ibid.*, 150.

61. Ernst Akiva Simon, "The Teacher," *Be'ayot*, 3rd year, vol. 5, nos. 5–6 (July 1947) 202f. Simon strenuously rejects the tendency of some of Magnes's admirers to refer to him as a "prophet"; he is rather, Simon insists, a "teacher" — and "a true teacher in Israel, to be sure, endeavors to learn from the prophets, to be among the pupils of the prophets." *Ibid.*, 195.

11. Gown and Town

1. Anita Shapira's biography in Hebrew of Berl Katznelson, *Berl*, (Tel Aviv, 1980), 2 vols., captures much of the achievement and stature of this central figure. For illustrations of Katznelson's friendship with Magnes, see his letters in *Berl Katznelson. Igrot* ed. Yehudah Erez (Tel Aviv, 1973), vol. 5.

2. Magnes had been an admirer of both Ahad Ha-Am and Bialik during his student years at Hebrew Union College when both of these Hebrew writers were at the peak of their popularity and influence. Both have left copies of letters written to Magnes. See *Igrot Ahad Ha'Am*, ed. Aryeh (Leon) Simon (Tel Aviv, 1960), vol. 6, 364, and *Igrot Hayyim Nahman Bialik* ed., F. Lachower, (Tel Aviv, 1939), vol. 5, 370.

3. For a bio-bibliography of the stormy career of U. Z. Greenberg, see Arnold J. Band's essay in *Prooftexts*, vol. 1, 316–31.

4. *Shirah* (Tel Aviv, 1971), 83.

5. *Shirah*, 104–107.

6. Although Agnon derides secular scholars throughout his fiction, there are, in addition to the passage from *Shirah*, two other passages where such scorn is also obvious. Both were written about the time of the composition of *Shirah*. See *Temol Shilshom (Only Yesterday)*, vol. 5, 471f, of the 2nd ed. of *Kol Sipurav shel Shai Agnon*. (Tel Aviv, 1953), no English translation, and "Ido ve' Enan," vol. 5, 343–95, of *Kol Sipurav Shel Shai Agnon* (Tel Aviv, 1953), English translation in S. J. Agnon, *Two Tales*, trans. Walter Lever (New York, 1966) 141–233.

12. The School of Oriental Studies: A Memoir

1. Hajj Muhammad Amīn al-Husaynī (1893–1974) was appointed Grand Mufti in 1921 and pursued an extremist anti-British and anti-Jewish policy.

Between 1941 and 1945, he lived in Germany and led the Arab forces which fought with the Nazis on the Russian front. Imprisoned by the French between 1945–1946, he spent the remainder of his life alternating between Beirut and Amman.

2. 1895–1959. The Islamic museum in Jerusalem is named for him. See also *Encyclopaedia Judaica*, vol. 2, 1144.

3. *Saracenic Heraldry: A Survey* (Oxford, 1933). Other important works are *Mamluk Costume: A Survey* (Geneva, 1952) and a series similar to *Islamic Architects and Their Works* (Geneva, 1956).

4. Ernst Emil Herzfeld, 1879–1948. Archaeologist whose writings included *Archaeological History of Iran* (1932) and *Zoroaster and His World*, 2 vols. (1947). *Encyclopaedia Judaica*, vol. 8, 406.

5. 1874–1933. Some of his works were *Beiträge zur Geschichte Ägyptens unter den Islam*, 2 vols. (Strassburg, 1902–1905) and *Vom Werden und Wesen der Islamischen Welt*, 2 vols. (Leipzig, 1924–1932).

6. 1874–1931. German orientalist, author of *Koran Studien*, (1926). See *Encyclopaedia Judaica*, vol. 8, 950–81.

7. *The Ansāb al-ashraf of al-Balādhurī*, vol. 5 (Jerusalem, 1936), S. D. F. Goitein, ed.

8. *Ibid.*, Max Schloessinger, ed. vol. 4b (1938), (1877–1944).

9. Vol. 4a appeared in 1971 in Schloessinger's edition, but with extensive revisions and annotations by Meir J. Kister.

10. 1904–?, Professor of Arabic, Institute of Islamic Studies, University of Rome.

11. Vols. 2–3, Muḥammad Bāqir Maḥmūdī, ed., (Beirut), 1974–1977.

12. S. D. Goitein, ed., *Travels in Yemen: An Account of Joseph Halevy's Journey . . . in the Year 1870 . . . written . . . by his guide, Hayyuim Habshuish* (Jerusalem, 1941).

13. 1902–1973. Author of *Ibn Khaldun and Tamerlane, Their Historic Meeting in Damascus, 1401 A.D.* (Berkeley, 1952).

14. Reprinted by Ktav Publishing House, New York, 1969.

15. 1889–1971. Scholar of Arabic language and literature, trans. *The Koran* and *A Thousand and One Nights* into Hebrew. *Encyclopaedia Judaica*, vol. 14, 201–02.

16. Eliyahu Ashtor, (Eli Strauss) 1914–84. Author of *The Jews of Moslem Spain* (Philadelphia, 1973), 2 vols. and *A Social and Economic History of the Near East in the Middle Ages* (Berkeley, 1976).

17. David Ayalon (Neustadt) 1914–. Author of *L'esclavage du Mamelouk* (Jerusalem, 1951), and *Gunpowder and Firearms in the Mamluk Kingdom* (London, 1956).

18. Meir J. Kister 1914–. Author of *Studies in Jahiliyya and Early Islam* (London, 1980). Leading scholar of early Muslim tradition.

19. Pessah Shinar (Schusser), 1914–. Orientalist specializing in Arabic language and in North African history.

20. Gabriel Baer, 1919–1982. Author of *A History of Landownership in Modern Egypt, 1800–1882* (London, 1962) and *Studies in the Social History of Modern Egypt* (Chicago, 1969).

13. He Looked Out On Zion From Atop Mount Scopus and Dreamt of Peace: A Memoir

*Gabriel Stern died a few months after the Magnes symposium in which he took such a spirited part. The editors, therefore, had to reconstruct his paper from his notes, a taped interview recorded at the Symposium by Eleanor Mandelson, and two of Stern's important but little known articles (one in English, one in Hebrew), which cast a special light on Magnes and on Stern's relations with him. The articles appeared originally in *Ner* (May–June 1958), and in *Al-Hamishmar* (July 1977). Michael Chyet is responsible for the translation of the second article from the Hebrew. The editors are indebted to Paul Mendes-Flohr and especially to Arthur Goren for their unfailing assistance in identifying Stern's writings.

1. The Hurvah is the popular name for the Rabbi Judah he-Hasid Synagogue begun by Judah he-Hasid, c. 1701. Nisan Bak is the popular name of the Tiferet Israel Synagogue built between 1864 and 1872 for the Ruzhin and Sadagura hasidim. Nisan Bak helped raise funds for the synagogue. Both synagogues were captured and destroyed by the Arab Legion on May 20, 1948.

2. Van Leer Institute, Conference Center in Jerusalem.

3. See *Judah Leib Magnes on the Centenary of His Birth — Exhibition* (Jerusalem, 1977), *passim.*; Albert Einstein to Judah L. Magnes, 21 June 1937, File 229, (The original is in German.) MP

4. Ishaq Musa al-Husayni (1903–). A Palestinian Semitic scholar, born in Jerusalem and educated in Cairo, he received his doctorate at the University of London. From 1937 to 1943, he served in the Mandatory Government's department of education and until 1946 as principal of the Rawdah School. From 1955 to 1967, he was professor of Arabic literature at the American University in Cairo.

5. *Mudhakkirāt dajāja* (Cairo, Dar al-Maaref, 1967), with an introduction by the leading Egyptian novelist, Taha Husayn (1889–1973), who was nominated for a Nobel prize.

6. Rav Benyamin, pseudonym for Benjamin Feldman-Radler, (1880–1958) immigrated to Palestine from Eastern Galicia in 1897. His eclectic ideology mixed socialism, religion, pan-Semitism, maximalist Zionism, and binationalism.

7. Kfar Etzion was founded as a religious kibbutz in 1943 by Polish Jews. Together with several other settlements, known as Gush Etzion, it was surrounded by the Arab Legion. It held out for a number of months until it fell on May 14, 1948. Many of its members were massacred and the rest were taken captive. It was reestablished in September 1967.

8. Eliezer Lipa Sukenik, (1889–1953).

9. John Bagot Glubb (1897–1986), a friend of the Arabs and British commander of the Arab Legion in Trans-Jordan.

10. Thus far, nothing has come of the plan to convert the office into a memorial to Magnes.

11. J. L. Magnes to Leon Simon, 19 October 1948, MP.

12. L. L. Magnes to Simcha Assaf, 7 September 1947 (Elul 3, 5708), MP. This is the first draft of the translation of the letter sent by Magnes for the opening of the academic year of the Hebrew University 17 November 1948 (Elul 3, 5708), MP. The letter was not read in the fall of 1948 because the Hebrew University did not open. The students were away defending their new nation.

13. Manya Shochat (1880–1961), a Socialist Zionist leader, was born in Byelo-Russia where she joined the Russian revolutionary movement. In 1903, she became a Socialist Zionist and in the following year immigrated to Palestine where she helped found the Hashomer self-defense organization and participated in efforts to promote Arab-Jewish relations.

14. See Yehuda Bauer, *The Holocaust in Historical Perspective* (Seattle, 1978) on the chimerical "trucks for blood" offer, a million Jewish lives for 10,000 trucks and an undeterminate amount of such goods as cocoa, coffee, and tea.

15. Judah Magnes, diary. MP.

16. See J. L. Magnes *et. al.*, *Palestine — Divided or United? The Case for a Binational Palestine Before the United Nations* (Jerusalem, 1947), 67.

17. Gabriel Stern, notes.

14. The Arab-Jewish Dilemma

1. Goren, *Dissenter in Zion.*

2. *Ibid.*, 221.

3. Quoted in Susan Lee Hattis, *The Binational Idea in Palestine in Mandatory Times* (Haifa, 1970), 66-7.

4. Quoted in Neil Caplan, *Futile Diplomacy, Volume One: Early Arab-Zionist Negotiation Attempts 1913-1931.* (London, 1978), 42.

5. Quoted in Hattis, *Binational Idea,* 69.

6. Quoted in Bartley C. Crum, *Behind the Silken Curtain* (London, 1947), 185.

7. Richard Crossman, *Palestine Mission: A Personal Record* (London, 1946), 143.

8. Goren, *Dissenter in Zion,* 333.

9. Quoted in Caplan, *Futile Diplomacy,* 123-4.

10. *Ibid.,* 124.

11. Alami to Bentwich, 10 February 1931, Central Zionist Archives, Jerusalem, A255/623.

12. Geoffrey Furlonge, *Palestine is My Country: The Story of Musa Alami* (London, 1969), 103.

13. For a fuller discussion of Alami's career see Bernard Wasserstein, *The British in Palestine: The Mandatory Government and the Arab Jewish Conflict 1917-1929* (London, 1978), 190-3.

14. Interview with the author, Jerusalem, 9 September 1969.

15. Quoted in Neil Caplan, *Palestine Jewry and the Arab Question 1917-1925* (London, 1978), 42.

16. Weizmann to Einstein, 28 April 1938, in Aaron Klieman, ed., *The Letters and Papers of Chaim Weizmann,* Series A.

17. Goren, *Dissenter in Zion,* 312.

18. *Ibid.,* 383.

19. Jacob Talmon, *The Origins of Totalitarian Democracy* (London, 1970), 57.

20. Goren, *Dissenter in Zion,* 480.

21. *Ibid.,* 57-8.

22. Abba Eban, *An Autobiography* (New York, 1977), 57.

23. Goren, *Dissenter in Zion,* 300.

Index